Ted Hughes, Sylvia Plath, and Writing Between Them

Ted Hughes, Sylvia Plath, and Writing Between Them

Turning the Table

Jennifer D. Ryan-Bryant

LEXINGTON BOOKS
Lanham • Boulder • New York • London

Published by Lexington Books

An imprint of The Rowman & Littlefield Publishing Group, Inc.

4501 Forbes Boulevard, Suite 200, Lanham, Maryland 20706

www.rowman.com

86-90 Paul Street, London EC2A 4NE

Copyright © 2022 by The Rowman & Littlefield Publishing Group, Inc.

All rights reserved. No part of this book may be reproduced in any form or by any electronic or mechanical means, including information storage and retrieval systems, without written permission from the publisher, except by a reviewer who may quote passages in a review.

British Library Cataloguing in Publication Information Available

Library of Congress Cataloging-in-Publication Data

Names: Ryan-Bryant, Jennifer D., author.
 Title: Ted Hughes, Sylvia Plath, and writing between them : turning the table / Jennifer D. Ryan-Bryant.
 Description: Lanham : Lexington Books, [2022] | Includes bibliographical references and index.
 Identifiers: LCCN 2021053817 (print) | LCCN 2021053818 (ebook) | ISBN 9781793614155 (cloth) | ISBN 9781793614179 (paper) | ISBN 9781793614162 (epub)
 Subjects: LCSH: Hughes, Ted, 1930-1998--Technique. | Plath, Sylvia--Technique. | Hughes, Ted, 1930-1998--Influence. | Plath, Sylvia--Influence. | Hughes, Ted, 1930-1998--Themes, motives. | Plath, Sylvia--Themes, motives. | LCGFT: Literary criticism.
 Classification: LCC PR6058.U37 Z86 2022 (print) | LCC PR6058.U37 (ebook) | DDC 821/.914--dc23/eng/20211214
 LC record available at https://lccn.loc.gov/2021053817
 LC ebook record available at https://lccn.loc.gov/2021053818

*To Miranda
my joy, my heart,
and the person who asked me if my book has a plot*

I know the bottom, she says. I know it with my great tap root:

It is what you fear.

I do not fear it: I have been there.

Sylvia Plath, "Elm"

I wanted to make you a solid writing-table

That would last a lifetime.

. . .

It did not take you long

To divine in the elm, following your pen,

The words that would open it.

Ted Hughes, "The Table"

Contents

List of Abbreviations	xi
Acknowledgments	xiii
Introduction	1
Chapter One: Revision and Transformation in Hughes's Early Work	31
Chapter Two: Figures and Flowers: Plath's Approaches to Draft and Revision	51
Chapter Three: Silent Partners: *Ariel* and *Crow*	87
Chapter Four: "This is the last": Words Between Them	123
Conclusion	165
Bibliography	171
Index of Names and Subjects	179
Index of Works	185
Permissions	191
About the Author	193

List of Abbreviations

CPH	*Collected Poems of Ted Hughes*
CPP	*Collected Poems of Sylvia Plath*
JP	*Johnny Panic and the Bible of Dreams*
LTH	*Letters of Ted Hughes*
LSP1	*Letters of Sylvia Plath, Volume I*
LSP2	*Letters of Sylvia Plath, Volume II*
UJ	*The Unabridged Journals of Sylvia Plath*
WP	*Winter Pollen*
BL	British Library
Emory	Manuscripts, Archives, and Rare Book Library, Emory University
Lilly	Lilly Library, Indiana University
Smith	Mortimer Rare Book Room, Smith College

Acknowledgments

I first began thinking about this project while preparing for the Sylvia Plath 75th-Year Symposium at the University of Oxford in October 2007. Both the paper that I gave and the scholars whom I met at this conference contributed to my book's research plan. I am grateful for the support of my institution, the State University of New York College at Buffalo, which granted me a sabbatical leave in the fall of 2013 so that I could work with the Ted Hughes and Sylvia Plath papers at Emory University and Indiana University. My dear friend Karen Sands-O'Connor co-led a graduate study-abroad program with me in the summer of 2017, during which I was able to study Ted Hughes's *Birthday Letters* manuscripts at the British Library. Karen cheered on my efforts throughout the seven years it took me to finish thinking through my argument and sustained my motivation through many walks, coffees, and conversations. She and my other colleagues in SUNY—Buffalo State's English Department, including David Ben-Merre, Lisa Berglund, and Lorna Perez, provided generous readings of my in-progress manuscript during the review of my application for promotion to full professor. I also thank my outside recommenders, Laura Hinton, Aldon Lynn Nielsen, and Malin Pereira, for the time that they dedicated to reading my work during this process. The students in my Ted Hughes and Sylvia Plath seminar—Anthony Aughtmon, Jillian Custodi, Connor Dry, Christina Housler, Brittani Mroz, and Daniel Sendker—introduced novel readings of the poetry and pursued our class investigations with unflagging enthusiasm as well.

    I could never have written this book without the assistance of several skilled and generous librarians. Thank you very much to Karen Kukil, Research Affiliate in English Language and Literature at Smith College, who took time out to send me scans of many of Plath's *Ariel* drafts from the Mortimer Rare Book Room; to Kathy Shoemaker, Reference Coordinator at

Emory's Manuscripts, Archives, and Rare Book Library, who arranged for me to view Hughes's manuscripts during my initial research visit in 2013 and then, during the 2020 quarantine, obtained permission from the Hughes estate to send me scans of several drafts from *The Hawk in the Rain*; and to David K. Frasier, Reference Librarian at the Lilly Library, who scheduled my visit and arranged for me to view their Plath and Hughes archives in 2013.

My family is my strongest and most consistent source of support. Thank you to my parents, Dennis Ryan and Linda Shubert Ryan, for encouraging me to study throughout my life and for supplying models of intellectual curiosity. Thank you to my brother, Joe Ryan, for staying in touch and for being a voice of reason. My biggest thanks of all go to my husband, Tim Bryant, and our daughter, Miranda, who were patient with my constant reading and writing, who kept me going every day with walks around the block and games and bouts of silliness, and who always reminded me how lucky we are. We are living through the most unusual and challenging year of our lives; there is no one with whom I would rather quarantine and protest and laugh. Your love and creativity inspire me.

Introduction

THE MATERIALS OF POETICS

Sylvia Plath's "Elm," drafted in April of 1962, illustrates several of the compositional techniques that she had cultivated over the past twelve years. Organized into fourteen three-line stanzas, the poem examines the elm's outward environment, its embodiment of emotionally charged experience, and its dialectical engagement with both knowledge and unknowability. Plath draws her readers into a narrative centered on the traumas that the elm has been forced to witness by alternating declamatory statements with questions, by infusing the poem's other inanimate objects with personality, and by repeating words that recur throughout her work: "horse," "stone," "scorched," "red," "burn," "shriek," "moon," "barren," "hooks," "snaky," and "kill." Readers' familiarity with repeated words, phrases, and images like these helps to increase the dramatic impact of this particular piece (Kendall, *Sylvia Plath* 201). Ted Hughes's "The Table," drafted sometime after the mid-1960s and published in his 1998 collection *Birthday Letters*, responds not just to the two writers' shared life experiences but to the materials with which Plath populates her own piece. "The Table" describes a desk that the poetic speaker built out of "a broad elm plank two inches thick," which he intended for his wife's work, but which evolved into a vehicle through which she resurrected their earlier problems. Rather than employing short, regular stanzas, Hughes narrates the poem's events in a long column of text divided about two-thirds of the way through by a single blank line. Using an approach more common in the work he published after the mid-1990s, Hughes describes the elm table's physical appearance and figurative value through a series of metaphorical scenes that gradually accumulate rhetorical weight. The living wood that Plath reads as witness to everyday grief—and as a receiver of "nuclear and chemical damage" (Brain, *The Other* 107)—is transformed in Hughes's piece into an object, a tool for taking the past apart and for reimagining art's familiar subjects as the sources of personal rivalry and division. Tracy Brain points out that the many drafts of "Elm" also underscore Plath's interest in environmentalism, a theme that the piece shares with much of Hughes's work and that "survives in trace within the metaphors, language and ideas that emerge" in the poem's final version (*The Other* 105). Hughes cites, in fact, "21 sheets of working drafts" and "a premature crystallization out of four densely crowded pages of manuscript" that led to the poem's published form ("Notes on Poems" 292), while Tim Kendall notes that the finished version "perfects themes and images with which Plath had been struggling for weeks" (*Sylvia Plath* 85).

Plath's and Hughes's poems also concentrate on the wood itself, which comes from a tree once common throughout North America before its decimation by Dutch elm disease. Hughes, a well-read amateur naturalist, might also have been familiar with elm's many practical uses, such as the construction of pre-twentieth-century water pipes, pilings, chair seats, wheel hubs, coffins, and shipping cases (Cwynar 1568). Both writers, in the course of their wide-ranging readings in mythology, are likely to have encountered stories of the tree's allegorical meanings as well. In Norse tales, for instance, the first woman, Embla, was created from an elm tree that Odin had endowed with a soul, Hoenir with the five senses, and Lodur with blood. The early modern English associated elms with elves and sometimes referred to the trees as "elven" ("Elm Tree" 494). In *The White Goddess: A Historical Grammar of Poetic Myth*, a study of central importance to both writers,[1] Robert Graves identifies the elm as corresponding to the letter A in the modern Irish alphabet (165). Among the members of the "tree alphabet," both the silver fir and the palm—which was "the Tree of Life in the Babylonian Garden of Eden story"—were originally known as *ailm* in Old Irish, but the term now designates the elm, revered in Italian history for the support it provided to grapevines (Graves 190). Many other examples of these contexts, natural and fabulous, recur throughout Plath's and Hughes's oeuvres.

This brief reading of "Elm" and "The Table" elucidates several of the compelling points of contact between Plath's and Hughes's poetics, as well as the techniques and subjects that separate them. While both writers find inspiration in personal circumstance, and they have written several poems that follow similar organizations and arguments, their work diverges in the use that they make of poetic materials: speakers, lyric subjects, material symbols, vocabulary, and syntax. In many cases, they pursue similar themes while framing radically different aesthetic perspectives. Their work also differs in its methods of revising and recycling earlier material. Steven Gould Axelrod has suggested, for example, that "Elm" borrows language and imagery from Sara Teasdale's poem "Spring Night" (155–56). In a more personally representative instance, Plath wrote a short piece entitled "Mr. and Mrs. Ted Hughes's Writing Table" while she and Hughes were on their honeymoon in Benidorm in 1956. While preparing lunch for Hughes's twenty-sixth birthday, Plath observed in their rented cottage a "heavy writing table of glossy dark polished wood" at which "Ted sat in a squarely built grandfather chair with wicker back and seat." She describes his "realm" at the table as "a welter of sheets of typing paper and ragged cardboard-covered notebooks" alongside a cascade of scrap paper, a bottle of blue ink, and their cookbook. In contrast, Plath's side of the table contains "tediously neat stacks of books and papers, all laid prim and four-squared to the table corners," her thesaurus, a birthday gift, and a sunglasses case that would be familiar to readers of *The Bell Jar* (*UJ* 259). Both this scene and a poem that she wrote a few months later about their time in Spain, "The Other Two," contain images that resonate with the elm tree's solid weight of knowledge and with the essential work that tables represented for both writers. In "The Other Two," the speaker imagines the happiness of a new marriage haunted by "two others" who "Performed a dumbshow in the polished wood" of their dining-room table (*CPP* 68). Ronald Hayman also notes that Plath's brother Warren, visiting the Hugheses at Court Green, helped Hughes to fashion "an enormous elm plank into a new writing table for Sylvia" (160), another dimension of their shared past that colors the poems' representations of the elm. The partnership between Plath and Hughes and the doubled functions of their table—practical and creative, manifest in both original wood and finished product—filter through their poems and the memoirs written by and about them.

FORMING INFLUENCES

Before she wrote "Elm," Plath's studies at Smith College and Cambridge centered her first published pieces in the modernist influences of Yeats, Auden, and early Roethke and Lowell. Linda Wagner-Martin describes her as "caught in mandates for reading—and, implicitly, for writing—that had traditionally inspired (male) writers" after she received the New Critical anthology *Understanding Poetry* as a high-school prize. In fact, she claims, "Plath and her contemporaries were indeed asked to model, to copy" such New Critical writers as Auden and Eliot (*Literary* 17, 84). Her later experiments with modernist style, in Christina Britzolakis's reading, "recover[ed] the resources of modernism within the empirical-formalist protocols of the New Criticism" by employing disjunctive, surrealist imagery ("Conversations" 170)—though, as Susan Van Dyne points out, she tended to compare even these famed precursors' work to Hughes's (20). After Plath and Hughes married and moved to Northampton, her attendance at Lowell's Tuesday-afternoon poetry workshop at Boston University, alongside Anne Sexton and George Starbuck (Stevenson 150; Clark, *Grief* 179), provided the first compositional strand that would connect her, for many, to the Confessional poets. In his now-famous review of Lowell's 1959 collection *Life Studies,* "Poetry as Confession," M. L. Rosenthal calls the book an example of "soul's therapy" written with a "self-therapeutic motive" (109–10). Though he does not link Plath's and Sexton's work to Lowell's in this review, Rosenthal describes "the secret self's inescapable drive to assure itself of continued life" in *Life Studies*, a theme that several mid-twentieth-century critics identify in Plath's late poetry. However, both Heather Clark and Christina Britzolakis make compelling arguments about the strategies Plath used to transform her biographical source material, which suggests that her approaches to composition transcend the outpourings of personal trauma and the psychoanalytic rhetoric commonly associated with Confessional writing. The *Oxford Dictionary of Literary Terms* describes the mid-century Confessional approach as "an autobiographical mode of writing" that focuses on "what were at the time of writing virtually unmentionable kinds of private distress." While this mode represents an essential step before the synthesis of personal revelation and social statement that characterizes much late-twentieth-century and early-twenty-first-century poetry, contemporary critics immediately recognized the risk of fostering a "romantic confusion between poetic excellence and inner torment" ("Confessional Poetry").

Most of the poets linked to this group, including Plath herself, openly rejected the Confessional label because of its associations with unregulated emotion rather than craft. In a 1995 conversation with Drue Heinz, Hughes pointed to the self-defeating effects of allowing personal revelation to dominate individual aesthetic style: "In poetry, living as a public persona in your writing is maybe even more crippling. Once you've contracted to write only the truth about yourself . . . then you can too easily limit yourself to what you imagine are the truths of the ego that claims your conscious biography" (69–70). Adam Kirsch, author of *The Wounded Surgeon: Confession and Transformation in Six American Poets* (2005), the only recent monograph that attempts a comprehensive assessment of Confessional poetry, describes the group's major accomplishments as "redefin[ing] our notion of what it means for a poet to write honestly" through "self-exposure," a refusal to treat private topics as taboo, and a courageous decision to "submit their most intimate and painful experiences to the objective discipline of art" (ix-xi). While this description acknowledges the presence of biographical elements in the work, it also names art itself as the writer's primary motivation. In keeping with this focus, Clark notes that, in turning away from modernist formalism, Hughes "situated himself within a British Romantic tradition that . . . preferred to explore states of mind rather than private, personal histories." For this reason, he urged Plath to frame her personal source material using cultural mythologies and metaphors rather than as direct renditions of her experiences (Clark, *Grief* 179–80). In a similar vein, Britzolakis describes the "controlled surrealism" of Plath's poetry from the 1960s, noting that over time she turned away from the chronological narratives associated with modernism in favor of "a series of hallucinatory images." These techniques reflect her interest in "the modernist and surrealist legacy of twentieth-century art" (*Theatre* 5), an affiliation that her own paintings and her ekphrastic poems confirm. Tracy Brain suggests that a viable alternative to reading Plath's work as Confessional would be to "place her as a writer who is concerned with such important public issues" as environmental pollution; as a result, her work "challenge[s] the arbitrary boundaries between 'literary' and 'scientific' writing" (*The Other* 84, 87). Scott Knickerbocker agrees, noting that "Plath expresses . . . the wildness and vitality she craved in nature through language itself"; she repeatedly opposed a "concern about industrialization and the destructive consequences of modern, technologized life" to a "love of nature" that was "interwoven with her self-reflexive concern for aesthetics" (4–5). This narrative of Plath's literary and cultural influences indicates that while her work's references to familiar details of her personal life seemed to position her work within a mid-century Confessional mode, her consistent interests in formalism and contemporary social issues diverged from merely emotional thematics. Instead, she cultivated a highly individual *ars poetica* that emerged from careful patterns of revision and reimagination.

Clark's, Britzolakis's, Brain's, and Knickerbocker's assessments also suggest that Plath's unique theory of artistic meaning relies upon some of the same compositional elements that define other mid-century groups. Paul Giles points out the many references to English and American landscapes that fill the work, which aligns her with other twentieth-century transatlantic writers like Thom Gunn; although she explores the ideological and social textures of both countries in the poetry, she does so "through ironic processes of transposition" that allow her to "render the national imaginary explicit and translucent" (108). Indeed, her writing often exposes "a collision between two distinct national traditions" that takes place through "a destabilization of national cultures as well as psychological identities" (Giles 110, 112). In keeping with this resistance to a unitary definition of national identity, Plath's work draws on a kind of self-conscious experimentalism characteristic of the

New York School. Roger Gilbert describes the "playful" and "mocking" aesthetic that poets like Frank O'Hara and John Ashbery pursued (567), which produces a lyric distance between speaker and subject akin to the detached, satirical perspective of poems like "Lady Lazarus." The antiwar protests of mid-twentieth-century poets Denise Levertov and Thomas McGrath provide another useful lens onto Plath's poetics, with their specific references to contemporary conflicts and their poetry's ontological reflections on "the responsibilities, political as well as artistic, of the poet" (Campbell 72): responsibilities that Plath articulated in many later poems like "Elm." In a manner similar to many other early-and mid-century poets writing on war, Plath considered both personal tragedy and large-scale genocide in her work but usually chose to represent them in metaphorical rather than literal terms. As Matthew Campbell argues, looking back to Adorno's injunction against poetry after the Holocaust, poets held a common "sense of the impossibility of closure, or of creating a form which will do the work of the epitaph or the elegy, and thus enable an adequate representation of the experience of war" (73). Several of Plath's 1960s poems make reference to the representational gap between the public and private experiences of tragedy, as do Denise Levertov's and Thomas McGrath's Vietnam poems. Plath's 1963 death also coincided with the emergence of the white second-wave feminist movement in America, which gained social traction with the publication of Betty Friedan's *The Feminine Mystique* (1963), Adrienne Rich's third and fourth collections of poetry, *Snapshots of a Daughter-in-Law* (1963) and *Necessities of Life* (1966), and Robin Morgan's edited anthologies *The New Woman* (1969) and *Sisterhood Is Powerful: An Anthology of Writings from the Women's Liberation Movement* (1970), among many other examples. Plath's consistent interest in domestic gender roles, which she explores in her diary entries and essays as much as in the poems, suggests that her work could have contributed significantly to the trajectories of second- and third-wave feminism. Britzolakis concludes that "Plath's poetry does not so much mythologize autobiographical details as put into question the notion of an autobiographical origin, as itself a 'myth' which must be endlessly reconstructed" (*Theatre* 65). The influences of modernism, neo-formalism, New York School poetry, war poetry, and feminist writings, among other possible approaches, expand the experimental potential and mid-century relevance of Plath's later work. These diverse contexts also contributed to Plath's conception of art's cultural functions.

Hughes produced poetry during his college years that, like Plath's, located its formal and ideological precedents in the work of modernists like Eliot, Auden, and Yeats. Leonard Scigaj, author of one of the earliest book-length studies on Hughes's work, describes him as a "modernist poet whose work supports the New Critical tenet that form and content are inseparable" (xiv).

Yvonne Reddick also notes his use of Gerald Manley Hopkins's "sprung rhythm," which, she suggests, lies "behind some of Hughes's most accomplished evocations of natural forces" (80). During his time at Cambridge, Hughes and the other poets who produced the short-lived *St. Botolph's Review* became devotees of the poetics that Robert Graves espoused in *The White Goddess*; like Graves, they rejected poetry currently in "literary fashion" and focused instead on "the primordial myths and ancient rituals that affirm man's animal instincts" (Middlebrook, "Caryatids" 162–63). While positioning his work as a continuation of these writers' commitment to aesthetic innovation, their poetry's collage-like allusions to ancient histories and languages, and even the "possibilities for reconstruction and 'translation'" that the New Critics saw (Brooker and Perril 22), Hughes developed an interest in classic Greek, Roman, Anglo-Saxon, and Norse mythology that unified his poetry over the four decades of his career. Like many mid-twentieth-century Western writers, too, he wrote verse that deliberately challenged the assumptions about the functions of art and the writer's responsibilities to his subject that underlay the work of his nineteenth-century predecessors. His first books, which concentrate on English national history and metaphorical portraits of animals, also point toward the intensive studies of specific English landscapes and the concern with ecological ethics that would center his work after 1970.

Much recent scholarship examines the environmentalist dimensions of Hughes's work, in fact, a focus that serves to distance Hughes from the ties to Confessional writing that both his relationship with Plath and his work in *Birthday Letters* and *Howls and Whispers* might suggest. Heather Clark reads his mid-twentieth-century allegiance with Robert Lowell, for example, as the result of "a profound desire to break away from the rigid formal verse that had reigned in the academy for so long" in favor of a new, more audacious energy (*Grief* 181). Steve Ely's 2015 monograph, *Ted Hughes's South Yorkshire: Made in Mexborough*, studies the influence that the thirteen years he spent in this small mining town exercised over his later work. Ely describes Hughes's relationship with John Fisher, an English teacher who helped him win a place at Cambridge and who remained a significant presence in Hughes's life until he died, arguing that his adolescent experiences in Mexborough "formed him as a poet" (4). Ely's detailed, comprehensive research on Hughes's daily life and personal interactions during this period helped him to determine, for instance, that "he had at least four significant encounters with foxes on Manor Farm [a nearby farm where he habitually walked and hunted]" (70), suggesting an obvious source for "The Thought-Fox" apart from the famous story of Hughes's Cambridge dream. Ely also identifies the environmental concerns that Hughes first articulated during these years (104), and describes the parallels that he repeatedly drew between human and animal needs as evidence of his interest in the philosophy of "social ecology" rather than "*direct* political engagement (191; original italics). As one means of challenging the label of social ecology, perhaps, Yvonne Reddick defines "four main strands of thought" in Hughes's ecological work that focus on the corrupting influence of rational thought on humanity, the categorical divisions between humans and animals sustained by Christian thought, the popular but false opposition between "nature and human technology," and the potential for a meaningful union between human and animal worlds (39). His work exists in relationship to the specific environments in which he has lived; he recreates their seasonal cycles and topological features in his poetry's thematic organization (Reddick 43, 47). In the environmentally focused 2018 essay collection *Ted Hughes, Nature, and Culture,* Terry Gifford assesses the mode of empirical observation that Hughes employs in his animal poems and his arguments on behalf of "the conservation benefits of hunting and fishing" (8, 15), while Danny O'Connor reflects on his mid-career turn away from animal poems to pieces that represent human beings in myth, elegy, and memorial (54). These ecocritical analyses, which represent only a sampling of the current scholarship, provide a useful lens through which to read Hughes's work without resorting to biographical revelation. Hughes himself speculated that all poetry has a confessional basis, which renders cultural and aesthetic contexts that much more useful: "Maybe all poetry, insofar as it moves us and connects with us, is a revealing of something that the writer doesn't actually want to say, but desperately needs to communicate. . . . If most poetry doesn't seem to be in any sense confessional, it's because the strategy of concealment, of obliquity, can be so compulsive that it's almost entirely successful" (Heinz 75). The contexts that shaped Hughes's poems helped him to construct a theory of artistic purpose independent from familiar tropes of Confessional writing.

Some Hughes critics have also examined the class-based dimensions of his poetry and their interaction with environmental concerns, particularly in relation to his *Crow* sequence. Paul Bentley describes a connection in Hughes's work between class as an element of "wildness" and personal freedom that originates in "the 'inner self'" (6)—a kind of "environmental revolution" (75). Using a slightly different approach than many of the ecocritical readings of Hughes's work, Bentley's argument recognizes "a fiercely idiosyncratic instance of the dialectic of nature and culture that all nature poetry, in the end, surely is" (16). Hughes sustains this dialectic by juxtaposing his studies of the natural world to portraits of people mythological, historical, and imagined. This duality is possible because of his interest in "the historical ideas about nature that underwrite . . . social stereotyping" (Bentley 49) and his ability to invert conventional metaphors and imagine instead "nature . . . as industry" (Bentley 55). This framework for reading Hughes's poetry engages not only its historical basis but also its environmental and socioeconomic concerns, all of which inform his theory of poetics.

Some critics locate aesthetic commitments similar to Hughes's in the work of the mid-century Movement poets; writers like Philip Larkin, Thom Gunn, Kingsley Amis, and Donald Davie, while reluctant to claim membership in the category themselves, produced work that relies upon a subtle use of wordplay, an air of worldly sophistication and detachment, and a general sense of social neutrality. Stephen Regan calls Movement poetry "urbane and academic," with a tendency toward a "shallow denial of human potential for change and development" (213), but he also acknowledges its expansion of the lyric and its later engagement with postwar British culture (215). However, in spite of his contemporaneity with Movement poets and his similar interest in the aftermath of the world wars, most assessments of Hughes's work agree that he was never considered a part of this group. Steve Ely contrasts the specific geographical basis of *The Hawk in the Rain* and its interest in the self with Movement writers' "hostility and scorn" toward what they saw as Romantic and modernist investigations of folklore, mythology, and spirituality (147–48); Bentley cites Hughes's own sense that he was "representing a new seriousness in poetry" in direct contrast to "a 'cosy' Movement sensibility" (28), suggesting that this affect allied him much more closely with "the restless spirit of the working-class Angry Young Men" (47). John Goodby labels Hughes's postwar efforts an intervention into "Apocalypse-influenced poetry" that predated and succeeded the Movement (180); rather than embracing the domestic comforts available after the war, as some of his contemporaries did, he chose to write outside the mainstream, with a "subaltern's awareness of the sham of bourgeois English liberal humanism" (189). Finally, in his study of Hughes, Plath, Thom Gunn, Geoffrey Hill, and Peter Porter, William Wootten defines this group as "the generation of poets born between 1929 and 1932 who succeeded and differed from the poets of the Movement" (xii). These analyses suggest that while Hughes read and remained aware of many other mid-century writers, some of his work's central concerns—including environmentalism and the postwar climate in working-class Britain—distinguished his work from the period's more visibly mainstream poetics. He was associated with Philip Hobsbaum's Cambridge reading circle, "the Group," at the time when he met Plath; heavily influenced by the ideas of F. R. Leavis, these writers devoted their time to analyzing both the work of new poets and their own compositions (Wootten 19–20). Though he did not remain part of the Group for long, Hughes quickly acquired an unblemished reputation among members of their circle, and they continued to read his work after he had left with Plath for the United States (Wootten 23).[2] In spite of his ideological divergences from the Movement and the Group, Hughes acknowledged their literary influences in his contemporary work.

READINGS ACROSS THE FIELDS

In part because of their work's many social and aesthetic contexts, Sylvia Plath and Ted Hughes continue to exercise an unshakeable hold over the imaginations and intellects of their readers. The long span of Hughes's career, Plath's intensely productive working life, and their seven-year marriage have given rise to a nearly countless array of critical studies, biographies, fictional homages, hagiographies, and public tirades. Hughes himself has claimed a large share of the critical interest centered on twentieth-century English poetry, far beyond the years that he spent living and working with Plath. Yet, in spite of the more than thirty poetry collections that he published, his numerous plays and translations and essays, the long period during which he worked as a commentator on the arts and as a judge of children's work, his fourteen years of service as the English poet laureate, and his other professional commitments, his ties to Plath have continued to resurface in the many public assessments of his work, both because of the circumstances of her death and because of the two collections that reflect on her life and work, *Birthday Letters* (1998) and *Howls and Whispers* (1998). As a result, some of the early literary criticism and several biographical studies of the two poets have focused on subjective interpretations rather than more precise analyses of their poetry's shared influences and compositional differences. As Jacqueline Rose notes, "No writer more than Plath has been more clearly hystericized by the worst of a male literary tradition" (28); because of the intense public scrutiny focused on her professional and private life, Rose argues, "it is impossible to read Plath independently of the frame, the surrounding discourses, through which her writing is presented" (69). Similarly, Diane Middlebrook asserts that "within the deterministic language of the story he tells in *Birthday Letters* can be discerned an explanation of fatedness that Hughes had absorbed from Robert Graves. Hughes's marriage was the doing of the White Goddess, who had laid claim to Ted Hughes through the agency of Sylvia Plath: Hughes had no choice" (*Her Husband* 27–28). Each of these texts, paradigmatic examples of the diverse scholarship that exists on the two poets, makes a unique argument within the fields of Plath and Hughes studies; both of them incorporate biographical readings of the poetry alongside discussions of its formal and thematic properties. Their structural approaches to assessing the writing focus on key elements of both writers' *ars poetica*, in contrast to much of the other early criticism on Plath's and Hughes's work.

Many of the first studies of Plath's work, for instance, attempt to identify evidence of her premature death in individual poems, thus diminishing her poetry's distinctive voice and precisely rendered imagery to a tool of emotional purge. A. Alvarez's *The Savage God: A Study of Suicide* (1970), which treats Plath's last months as an introductory case study to illustrate the book's other subjects, helped to establish this trend in Plath criticism. After noting in the book's preface that he believed he "had best look at suicide from the perspective of literature to see how and why it colors the imaginative world of creative people" (xiii), Alvarez asserts that "For Sylvia Plath it was an attempt to get herself out of a desperate corner which her own poetry had boxed her into" (xiv). While he does provide some unique insights into Plath's and Hughes's shared life in London, he attributes her breakdowns and suicide to the pressure on them both to produce successful work and to outperform one another. As he puts it, "At a certain point of creative intensity, it must be more unbearable for the Muse to be unfaithful to you with your partner than for him, or her, to betray you with a whole army of seducers" (15). For both Plath and Hughes, Alvarez implies, the poetry comments directly on private sources of inspiration.

Edward Butscher pursues a similar approach in *Sylvia Plath: Method and Madness* (1976). In his preface, he notes that he "occasionally" employs the term "bitch goddess" for Plath, since he saw it as "a fitting description of the persona who rages through the poetry of *Ariel* and *Winter Trees*."[3] Butscher defines this phrase in phallogocentric terms, describing the "bitch" as "a discontented, tense, frequently brilliant woman goaded into fury by her repressed or distorted status in a male society," while "the 'goddess' conveys the opposite image, a more creative one, though it too represents an extreme." Together, the terms connote "a long metaphorical association . . . with fierce ambition and ruthless pursuit of success" (xi-xii). Butscher makes this reference to Plath at least twenty times over the course of the book; in his readings, he often equates the poetic narrator with Plath herself, aligning, in one such example, a poem's inclusion of oppositional imagery with "the pattern of night forces tearing away at Sylvia's soul" (Butscher 297). Ronald Hayman makes a similar argument in *The Death and Life of Sylvia Plath* (1991; revised 2003), suggesting that his text's readings of her work in relation to her approaching death "will help to . . . inaugurate a new phase in her posthumous life" (xv). He begins by describing the period leading up to Plath's death, after which he attempts to link each stage in her career to her anticipated demise; he speculates, for instance, that Plath had "begun to think about her own death as the unavoidable sequel to [her father's]" (25), that her marriage to Ted Hughes represented "a relationship with the death that awaited her" (91), that even motherhood was not enough motivation to survive (135), and that she prepared for her death in her 1963 poems (191).

Butscher's and Hayman's work illustrates the tendency of some of the first Plath biographies, which tried to locate the poetry's impetus in the supposed traces it bears of her internal deterioration. Even Andrew Wilson's 2013 work, *Mad Girl's Love Song: Sylvia Plath and Life Before Ted*, proceeds from the premise that Plath's life was shaped by four primary forces: a desire to cohere her identity, especially through writing, which he sees as "the dominant pursuit of her brief life" (122); financial worries; a drive toward suicide; and a search for a "double" figure, someone who could reflect and confirm her own experiences, that began in college (235). Wilson asserts, for instance, that Plath's "self was constructed of a number of different personalities, some quite at odds with the others" (8), which reflect the sense that "she is more abject than sublime, more modern than romantic: her self is the site of all the horrors in the world" (Wilson 9). In terms of the writing she did to apprehend her own identity, Wilson finds that she understood "language, and specifically poetry, as part of her regeneration" (238). Most readers of Plath's work are familiar with the hypotheses set forward by Alvarez, Hayman, and Wilson. The value of these studies exists in their subjective examinations of Plath's motives for writing, which contrast with her investment in real craft and the long-term conclusions she drew about poetry's potential social relevance.

The most useful biographies of Plath have proven to be those that offer readers both verifiable history and careful literary interpretation. These studies illuminate some of the cultural frameworks that undergird her poetics and the roots of her mature compositional practices. Perhaps the most controversial among these works is Anne Stevenson's *Bitter Fame: A Life of Sylvia Plath* (1989), a book whose writing was influenced by the Hughes estate's commentary on the project and Stevenson's subsequent decision to revise her argument (Rose 93–94). Stevenson incorporates several accounts supplied by the couple's friends and family in an attempt to present a balanced portrait of their relationship and its dissolution. As she observes in her introduction, "I have avoided repetitious interviews with writers of published memoirs and with her American family [since] Mrs. Plath, in a final essay in Paul Alexander's collection, *Ariel Ascending*, indicates politely that she has said in writing all she wishes to say about her daughter" (xv). Stevenson's work is useful for its exceptionally detailed portraits of Plath's family and friends and its inclusion of materials not previously released by the Hughes estate. Her reading of the couple's relationship is more sympathetic toward Hughes than earlier biographies had allowed; however, Hughes's sister Olwyn edited the book heavily, while Ted Hughes spoke out against and discredited many of Stevenson's conclusions after the book's publication. Stevenson's experiences suggest that the most productive analyses of Plath's and Hughes's work are grounded in assessments of their poetic practice, not in the material of their day-to-day lives.

The biographies that followed Stevenson's attempt a more objective portrait of Plath's and Hughes's relationship and often include some insights into their working methodologies. Paul Alexander's *Rough Magic: A Biography of Sylvia Plath* (1991) traces the full span of Plath's writing career, from her first poems at age four (27) to her first national publication, "Bitter Strawberries" (66), through the ones she composed just before her death. Though he spends a significant amount of time on Plath's romantic history, Alexander also describes some of the major cultural and historical influences on Plath's work, including "Ted's avid interest in horoscopes, hypnosis, and mind control" (196), "concentration exercises" (238), linguistic experimentation (266), and political issues (270–71). Alexander assigns blame for Plath's death directly to Hughes but continues to explore the spiritualist techniques to which he had introduced her throughout the book (307). Connie Ann Kirk's *Sylvia Plath: A Biography* (2004; republished in 2009) notes that "[t]he mythology over what happened in Plath's last months and days grew to such proportions that it threatened to overshadow the poetry" (26); her assessment of Plath's life and work begins from Hughes's own efforts to champion her poetry. In *American Isis: The Life and Art of Sylvia Plath* (2013), Carl Rollyson assesses the iconic nature of Plath's posthumous legacy, labeling her "the Marilyn Monroe of modern literature" (1) and arguing that she embodied several different archetypes in her own and her loved ones' eyes, including a "primordial child of time," the "queen of the dead," "the universal mother," and the mythological Isis (chapter titles). He disregards many of the familiar anecdotes that fill the earlier studies in favor of elucidating the one-on-one interactions that shaped Plath's work.

One branch of Plath criticism, which continues to incorporate some biographical elements, reads her work's recurring themes as evidence of her investment in mythology and the fantastic. These studies, which include Judith Kroll's *Chapters in a Mythology: The Poetry of Sylvia Plath* (1976) and Jacqueline Rose's *The Haunting of Sylvia Plath* (1991), recognize such contexts as significant contributions to the evolution of Plath's writing style. Kroll argues that "her poetry is not primarily literal and confessional. It is, rather, the articulation of a mythic system which integrates all aspects of her work" (2). Among the many archetypal events and characters that influence Plath's work are "the ritually enacted destruction of the male," death-wishes juxtaposed to "a simultaneous wish for rebirth," and the dual appearances of true and false selves (Kroll 12–13). Jacqueline Rose, on the other hand, pursues the notion that Plath's work is characterized by "the circulation of fantasy" through her own particular "psychic processes" (x). By "fantasy," Rose means specifically "the forms of psychic investment which lie, barely concealed, behind the processes through which a culture—Western literary culture—evaluates and perpetuates itself" (1). One valuable element of Rose's argument exists in her dissection of Plath's language use; she notes that the poetry seeks to "confront us with the limits of our (and her) knowledge" (5). Many later readings of Plath's work draw upon the interactions among critical perspectives and upon biographical information; Rose suggests that accurate interpretation must emerge from this dynamic fantasy of artist and text.

Steven Gould Axelrod's well-received *Sylvia Plath: The Wound and the Cure of Words* (1990) creates such a "dynamic fantasy" by combining a Freudian reading of Plath's motivations for writing with insights into her work's formal and semantic elements. His text is one of the first in the field of Plath and Hughes studies to juxtapose sustained formal analysis to a consideration of the poetry's cultural implications. He examines her work's use of voice, its thematic treatments of "compulsive orality" (5), the personal needs it fulfilled (7), and its attempts to combat "effacement and erasure" by means of self-assertion (8). He labels Plath's representative composition a "domestic poem," which he defines as "one that represents and comments on a protagonist's relationship to one or more family members," which in her case often focused on her father (59). Claiming that Plath wrote specifically in response or even opposition to her literary forebears, Axelrod argues that her work constitutes a "feminization: a turning of male texts against themselves, an abduction of their language for the antithetical purpose of female inscription" and a way of participating in alternative traditions (71, 81, 99). He also investigates themes of doubleness in both Plath's and Hughes's work, which might, he suggests, have leveled their personal relationship and "eliminate[d] the rivalry between them," had it been pursued more successfully (179, 194). Here Axelrod models useful interpretations of individual poems and of Plath's signature tropes.

Some later studies of Plath's career enhance Axelrod's structural investigations by focusing on a cultural context or a social principle that organizes responses to her work. Karen Jackson Ford's analysis of Plath's anxieties about her roles as a woman, a chapter in her 1997 study *Gender and the Poetics of Excess: Moments of Brocade*, finds that Plath was weighted down by "the system of values that drove her to excel at conventional womanhood as well as at writing"; only writing itself offered an escape from these traditional duties (119). The personal pain that Plath depicts in her later poems, Ford argues, allowed her to cultivate "thematic excesses" through which to "redirect . . . her psychic, imaginative, and material resources" into a "new dedication to a single purpose—writing" (132). Likewise, in her study of privacy's cultural significance during the Cold War period, Deborah Nelson hypothesizes that "the confessional writing of the period," which for her includes Robert Lowell, Anne Sexton, Plath, and W. D. Snodgrass, presents privacy as a signifier for "isolation, loneliness, domination, and routine" (xiii). For Plath and Sexton specifically, these limits existed in the home and the family, "the very flux of middle-class life," yet the external threats posed by cold-war ideologies also permeated the familial space and could there be disclosed in a radical defiance of traditional domesticity (Nelson 75,

77). The political contexts that Nelson discusses here point to the broader social relevance of Plath's work. However, Robin Peel's *Writing Back: Sylvia Plath and Cold War Politics* (2002) does a more careful job of assessing Plath's response to political environments. Noting that though "Plath generally avoids direct reference to the issues, concerns and debates of the early 1960s," this absence "should not be taken as evidence that she remained unaffected by them" (30), Peel assesses the subjective, Romantic influences and the interest in "[r]ole playing and performance" that shaped Plath's early work (33, 36). Her gradual evolution away from Romantic reflection toward a performative detachment from her subjects speaks to a new sensitivity to "international [political] discourses," one which emerges more openly in her 1960s work (Peel 37, 99, 149). Peel argues that Plath attempts to assert control over her past and over current social discourses by "writing back" to them (Peel 153): he identifies compositional purpose in both her formal experimentation and her work's recurring concerns.

Many fewer biographies of Hughes have been written to date, but more of these studies than the earlier Plath ones temper personal narratives by pursuing literary criticism. Each of them presents useful insights into the formal and thematic innovations that Hughes created. Elaine Feinstein's *Ted Hughes: The Life of a Poet* (2001), the first comprehensive biography of Hughes, draws upon hitherto inaccessible archival records and interviews with close friends in order to discuss the major events of his life in concert with the evolution of his poetics. While acknowledging Plath's dominant presence in Hughes's life and her undeniable influence over his work, Feinstein treats her as just one among the many factors that contributed to his experiences and reputation. The book's short chapters and matter-of-fact assessments of Hughes's evolving personae illuminate both his personal tragedies and triumphs and the influence that they exercised over different stages in his poetics. Jonathan Bate's *Ted Hughes: The Unauthorised Life* (2015), a study that is more than twice as long as Feinstein's, provides additional insights into the social contexts of Hughes's work, the historical events that prompted specific compositions, and his publishing history in poetry, prose, and drama. Bate considers nearly every one of Hughes's most celebrated poems, the reception that each of his collections received, and the tension between environmental activism and laureate status that colored his last years. Though he concludes the book with the statement that "Sylvia Plath's death was the central fact of Ted Hughes's life" (566), he mitigates this personal focus here, as elsewhere, with a detailed close reading, in this case of "The Offers," the second-to-last poem in *Howls and Whispers*.

Some of the first critical explorations of Hughes's literary career make limited biographical references but focus primarily on analyzing individual poems and the contexts that inspired the work. Scholars Keith Sagar and Neil

Roberts established this approach in the early years of Hughes studies. In *The Art of Ted Hughes* (1975; revised 1978), Sagar assesses the central themes and formal elements that shape each of Hughes's collections through *Gaudete* (1977). He examines Hughes's imaginative influences, which, he argues, produce "charged poetry, visionary, revelatory poetry that sees into the life of things, that takes over where all other modes of apprehending reality falter" (Sagar 3). Roberts takes a similar organizational approach in *Ted Hughes: A Literary Life* (2006); his analyses of individual poems and Hughes's stylistic evolutions from book to book are founded on the notion that Hughes "felt increasingly that he was living in times when humanity had catastrophically lost connection with the sacred" (2). Both Sagar's and Roberts's work offers useful introductions to Hughes's published collections and to key poems. Leonard M. Scigaj's *The Poetry of Ted Hughes: Form and Imagination* (1986), in contrast, reads Hughes primarily as a modernist whose work up to the mid-1980s explored divergences between Western and Eastern cultural experience. He identifies several modernist concerns that persist in Hughes's poetry, including "an ironic juxtaposition of cultures ... that defines a current problem and provides an answer from the reservoirs of tradition," an affiliation with the formalist principles of the New Critics, and an investment in the psychoanalytic strategies of Carl Jung (Scigaj 10–12). This assessment of Hughes's career reflects a general tendency in the earlier criticism to look to historical models through which to read his work, rather than formulating a theory of his poetry's unique innovations. Later theorists like Steve Ely, Yvonne Reddick, Mark Wormald, and Paul Bentley favor contextual readings of Hughes's work that begin from his environmental activism, his arguments' consistency with proto-Marxist thought, and his challenges to English literary formalism, a tendency also seen in Sagar's and Roberts's post-1990 work.

Turning the Table has been guided in part by those studies of Hughes's and Plath's work that focus on the poetry's contextual influences while assessing its formal properties and recurring subjects. As these earlier critics' work does, this book centers on evaluations of the poems' structural innovations, their responses to social concerns and historical conditions, and their lasting impact on the history of modern poetry. In one key example of this type of criticism, Christina Britzolakis's *Sylvia Plath and the Theatre of Mourning* (1999) attempts to define the sources and effects of the "instability or doubleness" that Plath's language manifests (6). Her self-presentation is tied to her critique of American national identity and literary traditions; to acknowledge the traditions that precede her is to question and challenge them (Britzolakis 13, 43). This questioning takes the form of "a return of the repressed or 'raw' within the 'cooked' codes of formalism," a sense that it is impossible truly to represent the material world in poetic language, and a lyric *I* that can neither express itself fully nor connect with the greater world (Britzolakis 74, 83, 101). Such a lack of connection, Britzolakis suggests, signifies in Plath's poetry "a metaphoric return of the dead" that motivates her "theater of mourning": a move to "fragment or displace linear narrative, replacing it with the repetitive temporality of trauma" (104, 192). In *The Other Sylvia Plath* (2001), Tracy Brain assesses the various popular and critical perceptions of Plath that developed after her death. She argues that Plath's drafts uncover "a more complete picture of [her] intentions as a writer," which were always to work through "real political and material issues" and to produce "controlled, methodical, and carefully wrought" pieces (30, 37). Brain also points out the compositional influences that resonated between Plath and Hughes; as she argues, "this influence is rarely of one poet or poem over the other, but much more mutual, dynamic, and complex in its string of causes and associations," since the poems themselves gain meaning as "fragments of a continuing conversation" (191, 193). Lisa Narbeshuber's 2009 monograph, *Confessing Cultures: Politics and the Self in the Poetry of Sylvia Plath*, as Brain's does, looks at the ways in which Plath's work anticipates the feminist politics that emerged in the 1960s through "a new language, a new way of addressing the social scene" (60). Her interest in bodies and the social forces that gender them, Narbeshuber argues, issues from a type of "(social) fantasy" that helps to "construct the subject" (xxiii). Jo Gill's "Ted Hughes and Sylvia Plath" (2011), a shorter study of shared techniques and influences, assesses the major points of intersection between the two writers' work; she highlights the close attention both paid to English "voices and landscapes" (57). Gill calls *Birthday Letters* a "profoundly textual and highly tentative exploration of what it means to read and to write about one's own experience and that of others," rather than a mere response to the events that Hughes held in common with Plath ("Ted Hughes" 58). Each of these texts uncovers a different dimension of the writing practices that Plath and Hughes developed through their shared and separate lives.

In addition, Janet Badia's *Sylvia Plath and the Mythology of Women Readers* (2011) examines the ways in which Plath's readers have existed within a "long-established discourse about women readers" that positions them as "uncritical consumers, as Plath addicts, and even as literary cannibals" (2–3). Badia asserts that women readers traditionally have functioned as "a site of contest, a concrete ground on which those who wished to uphold the status quo could wage their resistance to broader cultural changes" (6). Reading Plath's work within this history, rather than as a product of biographical influences and formal strategies, reveals the "patriarchal ideologies" and recurring misrepresentations that have deformed current understandings of her work (Badia 23). This study represents a key intervention in the history of Plath reception because it shifts the site of critical analysis away from spectacle to cultural context. *Turning the Table* offers a similar redirection of critical attention toward the formal techniques and social factors that mark out Plath's and Hughes's work in particular ways. As a whole, Badia's and the aforementioned studies reveal many of the interpretive tendencies that have shaped current critical perspectives on Plath and Hughes. Many writers' early reliance on biographical and psychoanalytic readings of the poetry has been replaced by cultural-studies analyses and assessments of the work's contributions to the history of formal innovation. Still, the intellectual challenge and the aesthetic joy that the poetry continues to offer its readers make every stage of its reception history important. In recent years, scholars have returned to the analytical perspectives that Brain identified in *The Other Sylvia Plath*: the poetry's formal craft, its challenges to literary and aesthetic traditions, and its participation in contemporary social discourses.

Turning the Table contributes to a relatively small branch of criticism that examines the two poets' work in concert by working through these perspectives. In addition, this book reveals the underlying components of their compositional approaches by evaluating the patterns of revision that recur in each writer's early drafts, their divergent perspectives on similar subjects and themes, and the formal strategies that they borrowed from one another. These topics illustrate a strong formal affinity between Hughes's and Plath's work that is born of both coherence and opposition.

READING AND WRITING BETWEEN THEM

Relatively few critics have examined Plath's and Hughes's aesthetic collaborations and shared approaches to poetics, perhaps because "the critics are replicating the same rivalry that existed between the poets themselves" (Clark, *Grief* 4). To date, only five monographs exist that study the bodies of Hughes's and Plath's work as mutually influential and responsive to one another, all published over a forty-year span: Margaret Dickie Uroff's *Sylvia Plath and Ted Hughes* (1979), Diane Middlebrook's *Her Husband: Hughes and Plath—A Marriage* (2003), Antony Rowland's *Holocaust Poetry: Awkward Poetics in the Work of Sylvia Plath, Geoffrey Hill, Tony Harrison, and Ted Hughes* (2005), Heather Clark's *The Grief of Influence: Sylvia Plath and Ted Hughes* (2011), and Julie Goodspeed-Chadwick's *Reclaiming Assia Wevill: Sylvia Plath, Ted Hughes, and the Literary Imagination* (2019). Three of these texts assess Hughes and Plath as primary influences upon one another's work, while the other two position them as part of a broadly defined cultural context. In addition, Janet Malcolm's *The Silent Woman: Sylvia Plath and Ted Hughes* (1995) offers some insight into the difficulties of studying two such closely connected yet differently received writers. While Malcolm considers here the limitations of biographical writing specifically, her conclusions also apply to the interactions between creative and critical personae that are frequently explored in Plath and Hughes criticism. Malcolm interviewed Anne Stevenson and Jacqueline Rose while writing her book, looking for the roots of their biographies' reception histories, and while doing so concluded that the work of Al Alvarez and Plath herself had prepared the ground for the later popular views of Plath as martyred victim and Hughes as villain (23). *The Bell Jar* also established Plath as a proto-feminist model of willfully "unpleasant," "not-nice" behavior, while the many stories told about both writers' private conduct have accrued historical weight over time because there is simply no way to prove otherwise (Malcolm 32, 133). Because interviews comprise much of the source material for biographies, and because "both subject and interviewer [usually] give more than is necessary" (Malcolm 173), the author often risks producing a radically biased account of her subject—a danger multiplied in the case of Plath, whose chroniclers "have felt (consciously or unconsciously) . . . as if they had been given the right to act boldly, even wildly, where ordinarily they would be cautious and tread delicately" (Malcolm 184). Malcolm's study, appearing within the same time frame as these five works on Hughes and Plath, provides a valuable note of caution for critics: the moments of overlap between their compositions and their private lives that we analyze are always inflected by our own expectations as well.

Uroff's book was the first to advance the notion that the two poets could be productively assessed in tandem. She notes that "[t]hey had, of course, quite different needs" but remained "open to each other's work" (10), describing their idea of "poetry as a raid on the inner life, a breakthrough into taboo territory" (38). Both writers moved from traditional forms to more experimental works, in the course of which they exploited traditional mythologies as their major subjects (Uroff 59, 88). While Uroff identifies key contrasts between Plath's and Hughes's uses of physical landscapes, metaphor, and symbol (91, 97), she also credits Plath with a more incisive "psychological penetration" than Hughes and a greater interest in "the search for identity" (83, 124). Their work's common ground exists in its depictions of the natural world, its interest in natural and human energies, and specific uses of language—what Uroff calls "a new colloquialism which . . . is not a relaxation but a stiffening of diction" (212). This concentration on Plath's and Hughes's linguistic devices represents one of the first examples of sustained formal analysis in the field.

In contrast to Uroff's predominantly literary-critical focus, Diane Middlebrook's investigation of Plath's and Hughes's work emerges from the personal textures of their shared life and from readings of particularly resonant symbolic objects. She describes their habit of splitting the day between writing-time and childcare duties, for instance, as a routine that smoothed out "the evident differences in their dispositions"; to represent this compromise in material terms, Middlebrook characterizes their dining-room table (a precursor to the table that my Hughes epigraph visualizes) as both a shared worktable and "a dining table, to which they brought all of their appetites, including their aggressions" (92). Such symbols in Middlebrook's text often serve to highlight the differences in publication, reception, and temperament that other biographers have also noted. In one telling example, Middlebrook illustrates the contrast between Hughes's early success and Plath's struggle to gain notice in the U.K. through Al Alvarez, who hailed *Lupercal* as "an antidote to the 'gentility principle' that was stifling British poetry at the time," after which he offered *The Colossus* only a lukewarm review (131). Middlebrook's awareness of the influences that her subjects' personal lives exercised over their work enables her to make some unique connections as well, such as her observation that both *Lupercal* and *Ariel* were second books containing about forty poems each (218); Hughes himself interpreted Plath's manuscript arrangement of *Ariel* as "vivid evidence of her continuing attachment to the creative partnership that had flourished during their marriage" (Middlebrook 219).

Heather Clark's study appeared relatively soon after Middlebrook's, though with a critical focus much closer to Uroff's. Clark seeks to disprove the notion that Plath had drawn some of her best-known techniques from Hughes (2); rather, she asserts, they responded to one another's attempts to "remake" particular compositional strategies by "'misreading' and 'creatively correcting'" these techniques (8). Clark's argument proceeds from the premise that Hughes and Plath remain closely tied, both professionally and personally, because they suffered "Freudian melancholic failures of mourning"; she notes that they "sought to cultivate their own voices without recourse to the other's during their marriage, yet when they were left alone, it was the other's voice each could not forget" (9). For Clark, their shared "grief of influence" exists in recurring motifs of violence, competition, willfulness, and the subconscious (15, 46, 125); she comments that they "could not help borrowing images, cadences, and even words" from one another, though this constant exchange placed a strain on their relationship (110). During their period of separation, while Plath was composing the *Ariel* poems, she drew on a reservoir of emotional violence similar to that animating some of Hughes's work, yet, Clark argues, "her words are stronger, louder, more self-consciously vulgar" as she accomplishes her own poetic triumphs by, in part, satirizing his (151). Hughes, in turn, used his editorial work and his introductions to Plath's books as a means of reclaiming his own authorship (Clark 171). In the end, Clark suggests, their work with and against one another produced innovation: "in both *Ariel* and *Birthday Letters* engagement with the lost rival opened up new modes of expressive and aesthetic possibility" (240–41). Like Uroff and Middlebrook, then, Clark finds that the collaborations between Hughes and Plath produced specific stylistic, thematic, and ideological material.

Antony Rowland's and Julie Goodspeed-Chadwick's work offers different tactics for approaching Plath and Hughes collectively. Rowland's post-World War II study of Holocaust-influenced poetry defines his subject as "awkward poetics" because of its self-reflective perspectives, its use of "subtle irregularities," and its awareness of the gap between literature that witnesses the Holocaust directly and writings that respond to its history and aftermath (9–10). Rowland identifies in both Plath's and Hughes's poetry an engagement with precursors writing Holocaust-influenced pieces whose "subtle irregularities" are meant to "inaugurate creative tensions" (11). These irregularities can take the form of a poetic tone that conveys suspicion, a deliberately anti-aesthetic diction, or a consideration of a poem's ethical responsibility toward its subject (Rowland 13–14). Rowland describes a "camp poetics" in Plath's work that employs the familiar camp techniques of "[e]xaggeration, 'extreme metaphor and an emphasis on artifice," particularly in poems written between late 1962 and early 1963 (31). Hughes, in contrast, uses a "poetics of indirection" that condemns wartime atrocities in pieces that rely heavily upon violence and graphic imagery, such as the *Crow* sequence. Instead of satirizing participation in and spectatorship of the war, Hughes's Crow provides "'barbaric' depictions of war's barbarism, but not critiques of the critique of war" (Rowland 143). In Julie Goodspeed-Chadwick's study of biographical, cultural, and literary representations of Assia Wevill, in contrast, she reads the Plath and Hughes poems that were inspired by Wevill as a central influence upon her posthumous public persona. Goodspeed-Chadwick calls Wevill a "muse to Plath and Hughes," who nonetheless pictured her as an "abject" figure, a "scapegoat" who often bore the burden of misapprehension and blame in their work (11, 21, 25). Wevill allowed Plath to establish a recurring dialectic in her poetry between a positive, conventional femininity and an adverse, socially marginal femininity (Goodspeed-Chadwick 31–32). Hughes, on the other hand, punishes Wevill in his later works for "her death, for Shura's death, for Plath's death, for his own despair and trauma, and for her beauty and sexuality," using a "misogynistic rhetoric" that condemns her in terms similar to those Plath used (Goodspeed-Chadwick 55). Though Goodspeed-Chadwick asserts that his poems about Wevill both "establish an official (poetic) narrative of Assia's life and death" and "allow [him] the opportunity to act out and work through trauma" (57), she ultimately balances her censure of Hughes with his attention to Wevill's impressive "literary language abilities" (124). Both Rowland's and Goodspeed-Chadwick's cultural-studies analyses provide valuable insight into some of the social and personal contexts that motivated these collaborations.

These studies recognize that Hughes and Plath found common inspiration for their work even as they disagreed about that work's likely impact. As Hughes described their approaches more than thirty years after Plath's death, "our minds soon became two parts of one operation. We dreamed a lot of shared or complementary dreams," yet "Our methods were not the same. Hers was to collect a heap of vivid objects and good words and make a pattern; the pattern would be projected from somewhere deep inside, from her very distinctly evolved myth. . . . My method was to find a thread end and draw the rest out of a hidden tangle. Her method was more painterly, mine more narrative, perhaps" (Heinz 77). This passage offers readers two images that can be used to begin making sense of Hughes's and Plath's approaches to composition. Hughes suggests that Plath mined her pieces from extravagant collections of images, stories, and influences, leaving more potential material in waiting for future compositions, while he strove to locate a single idea that would unify the developing work.

TURNING THE TABLE: BORROWING, REVISION, AND COMPOSITIONAL STRATEGY

My study begins both from this rich array of literary and social contexts and from an analysis of key archival materials: drafts of some of Plath's and Hughes's earliest manuscripts, which reveal their emerging compositional strategies. After considering the factors that shaped each one's methodology for drafting and revision, I move to an evaluation of their work's most representative themes and organizational principles. Comparing the evolution of Hughes's aesthetic interests, formal techniques, and prominent themes with Plath's allows me to identify the points at which their compositional approaches overlap and the divergences between them. Plath's and Hughes's poetics incorporates a range of strategies for precisely capturing image, dialogue, character, space, occasion, and politics. The poetry's formal structures—often traditional in the early works but increasingly diverse as their careers progressed—help to articulate the authors' responses to contemporary cultural perspectives and to describe the challenges that writing itself poses to the formation of a coherent self. While Heather Clark asserts that Hughes and Plath "were more likely to view their partnership as a competition rather than a collaboration" (*Grief* 7), I contend instead that the draft techniques and compositional devices they hold in common, their mutual inclination to complicate and challenge shared themes in the poetry, and the material that they regularly borrowed from one another signal affinity much more clearly than challenge. I acknowledge the role that biographical information plays in shaping the events, characters, and themes of Hughes's and Plath's poetry, but my analysis focuses more closely on the work that the poets have done to craft individual pieces, to arrange the collections, and to articulate the aesthetics of composition more generally. Their published works speak to the many different cultural environments that they encountered during their lifetimes and demonstrate their contrasting interpretations of the same events and social conditions. The methods that both poets used while creating and revising drafts, however, illuminate their responses to one another's works-in-progress and the influences that each poet's writing exercised over the other's. Plath and Hughes worked so closely together during their marriage that their manuscripts served as each other's strongest literary inspiration. An early monograph on Hughes's work, Terry Gifford and Neil Roberts's *Ted Hughes: A Critical Study* (1981), admits that "it seems to us likely that the greater rhythmical freedom, compression and elliptical language of Hughes's poetry from *Wodwo* onwards owes something to the example of Sylvia Plath's later work" (22). Similarly, Margaret Dickie Uroff observes that, in his earlier work, "Hughes reveals close affinities to Plath's experiments in free association, surrealistic imagery, psychic explorations" (126). Clark notes, in turn, that "Plath looted Hughes's poetic corpus" ("Tracking" 101). Even after her death, Hughes's work in the late 1960s and early 1970s, and his 1998 publications, reveal the presence of Plath's signature rhetorical devices and stylistic traits in tandem with his own.

Plath experimented throughout her career with various forms of fragmentation, alienation, and automation, on the levels of both formal structure and theme. This particular aspect of her poetics was inspired by her critiques of late-stage industrialism and her oft-cited anxiety over women's professionalism—what Lisa Narbeshuber has called a "post-human perspective" that is prompted by an "alien moment" (viii, xi). The presence of both topical and formal fragmentation in her work allowed her to develop increasingly sparse structures, voiced in an imperative mode. At the same time, Plath moderates the moments that resemble personal revelation in her poetry through an accretive poetic vocabulary and a series of compositional methods, which develop across the span of her manuscript drafts, that produce sharply honed images and a detached sense of lyric observation. While it is essential to keep in mind, as Tracy Brain points out, the fact that Plath's work exists in many different variations through the poem's archival, published, and recorded versions ("Unstable" 34), careful analysis of these diverse renderings reveals that she continued to work at developing a distinctive voice and unique set of stylistic traits to the end of her life. The themes to which she habitually returned often issue from moments of personal or social trauma; however, she articulates the subjective burden of these moments using a lyric mode of address that resonates with "trauma theory's notions of testimony" (Keniston 150). Giving voice to such ordeals does not signify an unmediated outpouring of emotion in her work; rather, her interpretation of the lyric represents a unique method for depicting experiences whose long-term effects remain unknown.

Hughes, on the other hand, who was invested in English national and natural landscapes from the beginning of his career, cultivated his creative aesthetic through environmentalist arguments; metaphorical renderings of animals; revisions of familiar social and cultural narratives; investigations of the mythic possibilities of Robert Graves's moon goddess; postmodernist samplings from a range of Western mythologies; and one particular poetic narrator, Crow, who gives voice to the ontological uncertainties that plague human creativity. As Brian McHale has noted in his study of the ideological dimensions of postmodernist fiction, one characteristic of this historical period in literature is the text's tendency to minimize epistemological concerns, "as the price for foregrounding ontology" (*Postmodernist* 11); indeed, McHale asserts, the same shift occurs in long poems of the period, which tend to "treat the discourses circulating around them . . . as *objects for exhibit* rather than as *means of expression*" (*Obligation* 11; original emphasis). Hughes tends to articulate ontological questions through treatments of the writer's life and considerations of the limits that the self's inward anxieties place on his attempts to produce meaningful work. While many of his popularly cited works also engage with themes and tropes that are readily identifiable from Plath's oeuvre, these pieces often comment, more precisely, on the philosophical and ideological burdens of writing. In the poems, Hughes tends to equate the solipsistic nature of relationships, for instance, with the professional stresses that fracture the self, rather than concluding that such ties are in themselves the ultimate goals of art. His recursive treatments of animal, human, and geographical bodies function as investigations of the poet's aesthetic and social responsibilities: not just to represent the patterns of his own life but to think conscientiously about the broader designs that shape human existence.

Both Plath's and Hughes's drafts, techniques for revision, and shared thematic material reveal not only their treatment of cultural traumas but also their explorations of the writer's responsibilities to the self, to society, and to literary tradition. William Wootten describes these mutual interests in terms of the new "'seriousness'" that their work articulated (xiv). While they approach their primary interests via a diverse range of compositional techniques and thematic frameworks, both of them ultimately figure these interests as metonyms for the broader challenges of writing itself. Plath's and Hughes's struggles to formulate a poetics that accounted for their unique approaches to language use while reflecting the complexities of their source material, both personal and national, translated into philosophies of the *ars poetica:* the purposes and functions of artistic communication. Following a tradition that originated in Horace's own first-century *Ars poetica*, Plath and Hughes attempt through specific compositional principles and strategies for revision to demonstrate the "instructional potential" of poetry as well as its fitness for allegorical and even play-based meaning (Reed). As Sandra Faulkner understands it, the *ars poetica* "articulates the art" of writing itself (223); it focuses on "the importance of embodied experience through attention to the senses," a representation of that experience that is both "precise" and "conditional and partial and interested in approximations of something like truth." At the same time, an effective *ars poetica* portrays writing as a process that requires "discipline, persistence, and attention to craft" (Faulkner 224). Both Hughes and Plath work through rigorous compositional techniques as they draft their work, and both struggle at times to capture subjects that are by nature imprecise, yet neither writer's poetry is didactic. Rather, the poetry attempts to grapple with the motivations behind the act of composition itself and the social, cultural, personal, and other effects that poems can achieve.

The four central chapters of *Turning the Table* examine the compositional techniques that both Hughes and Plath developed through their early writings, their draft manuscripts, and the books that concluded their careers. Using archival materials from four of the primary libraries that hold their papers, I define the writing strategies that they established in their drafts, the eventual divergences between their approaches, and the dominant themes that emerged in the course of their aesthetic and real-life collaborations. Like Heather Clark, I note that "Plath's and Hughes's dialogue [in the poems] . . . consistently resists a reading in which one always refashions or revises the other's work in the same way" (*Grief* 10). They rewrite one another's poetic situations and figures in palimpsest-like fashion, borrow and quote from individual poems, and annotate the values, contexts, and events that motivate their writing. Diane Middlebrook describes, for instance, the ways in which Hughes's "words activate [Plath's] own distinctive poetic method" ("The Poetry" 158); the "calls and responses" they produced in response to monumental occasions such as the birth of their daughter Frieda ("The Poetry" 160); and the "creative appropriation" that Plath practiced "aggressively" after her separation from Hughes ("The Poetry" 169). Their individual poetics, even when tied to mutually familiar schemas for composing their work, came into conflict when they confronted questions of literary inheritance and succession: whose work mattered, in what ways, and why? In order to answer these questions, all four chapters of *Turning the Table* center on the imitation, exchange, quotation, and response strategies that they used in creating new material while in dialogue with one another: what Heather Clark has referred to as their tendency to "loot . . . each other's poems" in the course of participating in "a long and intense dialogue fueled by both rivalry and grief" (*Grief* 2–3). These compositional techniques, which originated in their drafts and culminated in the poems of *Ariel,* the *Crow* sequence, *Birthday Letters,* and *Howls and Whispers*, diverge from poetic tradition by modeling new approaches to the art of poetry in rhetoric, form, theme, and cultural commentary for future readers.

In chapter 1, "Revision and Transformation in Hughes's Early Work," I investigate some of the many shared compositional elements that appear in Plath's and Hughes's work in order to uncover the sources of Hughes's most commonly recurring poetic structures and rhetorical techniques. Beginning from a discussion of Hughes's "The Thought-Fox" and Plath's well-known response, "Burning the Letters," I argue that the two pieces' formal similarities reflect the nature of their shared work life, even during periods of conflict. I then turn to *The Hawk in the Rain* to illustrate some of the specific formal strategies and themes that emerged in Hughes's work from this period, including animals as metaphors for human ambition, artistic production, and the physical consequences of war. I underline the significance of Hughes's interests at this time by evaluating representative drafts from the book. Next I argue that in *Lupercal*, Hughes's second published collection, he continues to explore the artist's recurrent anxiety over production as well as his work's historical precedents. Many individual poems in this volume center on material objects with a particular cultural resonance. Hughes embeds them within specific mythologies or ties them to the English landscape in order metaphorically to reject the literary world and its social expectations.

Chapter 2, "Figures and Flowers: Plath's Approaches to Draft and Revision," assesses Plath's early compositional techniques. I begin by looking at two versions of an unpublished poem, "The Bronze Boy," as a means of uncovering her first drafting methods. This analysis, which is tied to several pieces in her posthumous collection *Johnny Panic and the Bible of Dreams*, also reveals the emergence of her signature poetic vocabulary, including neologisms, portmanteau words, and recurring adjectives. In conjunction with these semantic elements, she employs a range of formal traits, several pseudonyms that reflect her anxiety about self-presentation, consistent efforts to cut out narrative excess, and strategic uses of repetition-with-a-difference. These drafts also include rhetorical strategies characteristic of Plath's later work, and they focus on themes that persist across the body of her work. In order to illustrate the evolution of these compositional techniques, I present a case study of "The Rabbit Catcher," which exists in several draft versions in the Smith College papers. Plath's formal strategies in this poem allow her to pose a challenge to the lyric tradition and to offer a critique of language's inadequacy at moments of violent personal witnessing. I conclude the chapter by looking at Plath's drafts of "Words heard, by accident, over the phone" and "Words" as two instances in which she pares down her own language in order to produce a sharply focused assessment of the enduring effects of creative discourse.

My third chapter, "Silent Partners: *Ariel* and *Crow*," asserts that these two poem sequences, written in close succession, highlight each poet's apprehensions about not only artistic legacy in general but also their own work's lasting merit. I begin by discussing the longstanding controversy over the arrangement of the three published versions of *Ariel*, which I argue ultimately renders the sequence a central example of the long poem. These different renderings offer three contrasting perspectives on the relationship that Plath understood between aesthetic statement and the poetic narrative. I examine poems that are unique to the arcs of *Ariel 1* and *Ariel 2* in order to define the progress of central themes across the work;[4] these variances also reveal Plath's characteristic poetic vocabulary and syntactic techniques, which contribute to *Ariel*'s recurring meditations on present uncertainty and future promise. Next, I identify Hughes's Crow poems as a loosely unified sequence by tracing the character's poetic lineage from W. B. Yeats's Crazy Jane character through Amiri Baraka's blues-influenced Crow Jane and John Berryman's semi-autobiographical Henry. Hughes attempts to give Crow coherence by positioning him within familiar mythologies, yet the character's elusive nature suggests that he most closely embodies the shortcomings of artistic representation: an issue with which *Ariel* also engages. By examining the formal and thematic affiliations between individual poems from *Ariel* and *Crow*, I reveal the sequences' sources of artistic inspiration as well as the complex figurative language on which both poets rely. Though Hughes uses allegory grounded in specific political concerns, the two collections ultimately seek to illuminate the purpose of the writer's art itself.

The book's fourth chapter, "'This is the last': Words Between Them," examines Plath's and Hughes's work within similar thematic material and historical contexts. Her work reveals that Plath shares Hughes's interest in ancient mythologies as a means of reading archetypal structures in real-life events. I illustrate this shared element of their poetics through a reading of Plath's "The Lady and the Earthenware Head" in comparison with Hughes's "The Earthenware Head," and by assessing the ways in which Hughes's "The Shot" responds to Plath's "Lady Lazarus." The most striking example of this type of exchange in their work occurs in the dialogue between her bee poems and his most broadly conceived response to her work, "The Bee God." I also discuss the public furor that accompanied *Birthday Letters*' appearance in England and note the aesthetic concerns that define the collection. Hughes's drafts of these poems, which were only recently acquired by the British Library, provide invaluable insights into his composition and revision processes as well as his profound concern with order and organization. I argue that the book elucidates the final stages of his ongoing collaboration with

Plath by confirming the themes and compositional techniques that they held in common throughout their careers. To illustrate these elements of the book, I discuss hitherto unknown aspects of the *Birthday Letters* papers, including Hughes's diagrams and the letters in which he evaluates both the book's reception and the poems' contexts. *Birthday Letters* describes a series of metaphorical geographies that Hughes's work shares with Plath's in key poems such as "A Pink Wool Knitted Dress," "Visit," "The Afterbirth," "Fever," and "Being Christlike." By comparing her syntactic and semantic strategies from the 1960s poems to the pieces that he drafted over the succeeding decades, I provide evidence to support the notion that Hughes incorporated some of Plath's approaches to writing in his new works. The techniques of his final poems draw upon recognizable aspects of her poetics. I conclude the chapter by examining the poems of *Howls & Whispers* that help to complete the conversations begun in *Birthday Letters*, alongside some of Hughes's final unpublished letters.

Because of their work's close formal affiliations and, at times, radically divergent approaches to similar subjects, I believe that we can best understand Hughes's and Plath's poetry by examining the points of intersection between their work. Their shared aesthetic, which arises from a unique combination of structural innovation, philosophical reflection, and cultural insight, reflects a mutual decision—albeit one that each writer reached at a different point in time—to transform the confessional impulse, the biographical matter that serves as one source of the poetry's themes and allusions, into a window onto the *ars poetica* instead. How, Plath and Hughes ask, does the poet arrive at a particular juncture of idea, setting, and occasion? What rhetorical modes and compositional devices, retrieved from a deep wellspring of experience and memory, best help to achieve accurate expression? What world does the poem's voice finally identify? These questions point us toward the poets' manuscript drafts, which reveal each writer's notion of "the art of poetry": precise language that assembles a characteristic set of images, and poetic speakers whose voices give shape to the writer's overall body of work. This creative discourse enables the construction of poetic narratives centered on ontological investigations of the self and its social contexts, as well as instructions geared toward the act of writing in and of itself.

NOTES

1. Hughes sent a letter to Graves on 20 July 1967 thanking him for "your poems and for the White Goddess—which I regard as the chief holy book of my poetic conscience (confirmed, again, after the Festival). Somebody [English teacher John Fisher] gave me a copy when I was 17" (*LTH* 273).

2. Wootten notes that Hughes had submitted some of Plath's poems to Hobsbaum in order to gain her admission to the Group, but he did not accept her—due, he speculates, to "Hobsbaum's short-sighted and, it is fair to surmise, sexist, dismissal of her work" (102).

3. Plath herself employs a version of the term in a journal entry dated July 20, 1957: "Virginia Woolf helps. Her novels make mine possible. . . . Make her enigmatic: who is that blond girl: she is a bitch: she is the white goddess" (*UJ* 289).

4. In keeping with the usual critical practice, I will refer to Plath's original arrangement as *Ariel 1* and Hughes's edition as *Ariel 2*.

Chapter One

Revision and Transformation in Hughes's Early Work

Ted Hughes, as both husband and renowned contributor to modern English poetry, participated in many of the same historically resonant events that Sylvia Plath did. While the work he published after Plath's death signaled some interest in personal revelation, he honed at the same time a poetic vocabulary of recurring images, thematic preoccupations, and syntactical complexities. His and Plath's work manifested many of these elements in common, both in the work they produced during the 1960s and in the poetry that Hughes composed after her death. The two of them took part in a years-long conversation about the difficulties of creation: both in terms of marriage and family relationships, and with regard to the challenges of refining an original voice. The resulting work demonstrates a uniquely interactive poetics, one in which they examine their respective roles as well as the expectations each holds of the other. Evidence of personal and professional rivalry exists in one poet's borrowings from and revisions of the other, yet their direct responses to one another and the work's changing contexts also illustrate the degree to which their rhetorical styles, motivations for writing, and formal techniques overlapped and mirrored one another's. The material that Plath and Hughes quoted, shared, and inspired in one another's work underscores the contradictory nature of poetic composition itself and poses challenges to their literary precedents.

One famous dimension of Plath's and Hughes's shared creative life exists in the responses that they created to the material versions of one another's work. In some cases, these texts comment directly on the work that appears on the page's verso, while in others they offer insight into the incidental issues that motivated the writing. The Emory papers contain, for instance, an early draft of "Full Moon and Little Frieda" that Hughes wrote on the back of the first page of Plath's "Tulips" in typescript; he also wrote a list of conditions that were making life difficult for the couple in the same group of drafts from *The Hawk in the Rain*. These conditions include "things coveted" and "I'm cold all the time" (MSS 644 – Box 59, folder 66). Several of the uncollected poems that Hughes composed in the 1960s appear in the Emory drafts, including "Lines to a Newborn Baby," which he wrote on the pink Smith College memorandum paper familiar to scholars of Plath's work; he also used the versos of her "Black Rook in Rainy Weather," "Metaphors," "All the Dead Dears," "This Earth Our Hospital," and "The Bed Book" to finish sketching this piece. One of Hughes's draft stanzas for "Lines," "We lean / Over you like masks hung up unlit / After the performance" (MSS 644 – Box 82, folder 18), which became the final lines of "To F. R. at Six Months," closely resembles "We stand round blankly as walls," from Plath's "Morning Song" (*CPP* 156). Hughes also drafted "My Uncle's Wound" on Smith College memo paper as well as on an envelope addressed to the couple, on the verso of two manuscript pages of *The Bell Jar*, on the back of a draft of Plath's "Widow," and on the verso of a letter to Plath from Anthony Thwaite at the BBC, dated 3rd May 1961, which gives details about her upcoming appearance on an episode of *The Living Poet* (MSS 644 – Box 83, folder 20). Finally, Hughes drafted "On Westminster Bridge" on the reverse sides of typescript pages of Plath's "The Smoky Blue Piano," "Tulips," "A Prospect of Cornucopia," and "Stone Boy with Dolphin"; Emory grouped these papers with an unfinished letter that Hughes wrote to Aurelia and Warren Plath, also on Smith memo paper, explaining that Sylvia had been out of the hospital for a few weeks (MS 644 – Box 83, folder 43). Among the drafts of the *Wodwo* poems held at Emory is also a handwritten copy of "Song of a Rat," which, along with "The Howling of Wolves," is one of the only poems in the book that was written just after Plath died rather than in the months before (Bate 251; Webb 36). On the back of this poem's final page is a letter Hughes had written to an estate agent, expressing his interest in selling Court Green "after the recent sudden death of my wife" (MSS 644 – Box 60, folder 13). These points of physical contact between Hughes's and Plath's work testify to the attention they paid one another's writing as well as the opportunities that both had to comment on or borrow material. In some cases, these doubled documents illuminate the personal experiences—such as a child's birth, a hospitalization, or Plath's death—that undergirded Hughes's compositions.

In the most oft-cited example from their collective oeuvre, Plath sketched her first draft of "Burning the Letters" (1962) on the back of a typed copy of Hughes's 1957 poem "The Thought-Fox" (Rose 142; Bundtzen, *The Other Ariel* 68).[1] Hughes had written his own poem in bed after spending the evening with a fellow poet, though in public conversation he also tied it to a dream he had had two years before the poem's composition (Bate 94; Middlebrook, *Her Husband* 9). In the course of working on a college essay, he dreamed one night about "a figure that was at the same time a skinny man and a fox walking erect on its hind legs" and that looked as though "its body and limbs had just now stepped out of a furnace. Every inch was roasted, smouldering, black-charred, split, and bleeding. . . . It came up until it stood beside me. Then it spread its hand—a human hand as I now saw, but burned and bleeding like the rest of him—flat palm down on the blank space of my page. At the same time it said: 'Stop this—you are destroying us'" (Hughes, *WP* 9). Yvonne Reddick also suggests that Hughes's interest in the writings of D. H. Lawrence would have led him to study Lawrence's 1922 novella *The Fox* (86), while Steve Ely describes the "four significant encounters with foxes" that Hughes had while spending time at Manor Farm in Mexborough (70–71). The conjunction of these various origins helps to explain the poem's enduring popularity among Hughes's readers. Indeed, Neil Roberts posits that "the fox . . . was Hughes's totem animal or shamanic spirit" (*Literary* 65); images of foxes recur throughout *The Hawk in the Rain* and *Lupercal*, as well as in other collections, in poems as diverse as "Roarers in a Ring," "Crow Hill," and "Sunstroke." Susan Van Dyne describes "The Thought-Fox" as his "visionary equation of his own poetic genius with the mysterious powers of nature" (41), a quality that lays the poem open to intense critical scrutiny. Like Plath's later poem, Hughes's piece speaks through a first-person lyric; its singular focus allows mention of the poetic tenor only twice, in the first and final stanzas. The "thought-fox" itself represents the inspiration behind a piece of writing; the poem works by "entwin[ing] the *act* of writing with the *action* of the animal written about" (Webb 35). Hughes's opening observation that "Something else is alive / Beside the clock's loneliness / And this blank page where my fingers move" (*CPH* 21) is articulated through a carefully delineated poetic subject. The animal manifests as nose, eyes, and footprints that appear one at a time under the speaker's gaze. As Roberts points out, the poem intentionally separates the fox's emotions from its body, producing a "figurative displacement of the fox's natural fear on to its shadow, leaving the fox itself free to represent a bold venturesomeness" ("Cambridge" 30). At last, however, in the sixth stanza, the fox's intrinsically wild nature intrudes upon the scene. The poem concludes with a sharp contrast between the civilized atmosphere associated with composition—the clean page, the quiet space—and the animal's unregulated disposition. Hughes ties the frustrations of the writing process to its sudden materialization, the unpredictable qualities that define the natural world: "Till, with a sudden sharp hot stink of fox / It enters the dark hole of the head. / The window is starless still: the clock ticks, / The page is printed" (*CPH* 21). The fox stands in for the intricate processes of creation, the moment of inspiration, and the final sense of writerly satisfaction. In a piece created for the BBC's *Listening and Writing* program, Hughes notes that "The Thought-Fox" "does not have anything you could easily call a meaning," since it, as an extended metaphor, "is both a fox and a spirit." Hughes felt that the poem's success as a piece of writing could be measured by the fact that "every time I read the poem the fox comes up again out of the darkness and steps into my head"; he speculates that "long after I am gone, as long as a copy of the poem exists, every time anyone reads it the fox will get up somewhere in the darkness and come walking towards them" (*Poetry in the Making* 20). While the poem allows the reader to interpret the fox as both an avatar of the creative process and an inhabitant of the nonhuman world, Hughes's commentary attaches significance to it primarily as an aesthetic object, one whose presentation he has tried to perfect in the interest of illustrating the instructive possibilities of composition.

In contrast to Hughes's hermetically conceived *ars poetica*, Plath's "Burning the Letters" was motivated by a deeply personal event, her discovery in June of 1962 that Hughes was having an affair with Assia Wevill. After this revelation, Plath "invaded his attic study, gathered assorted papers and 'stuff,' and burned them" (Bundtzen, "Poetic Arson" 239). Her poem is fifty-six lines long, comprising four extended stanzas, in contrast to his six tidy stanzas of four lines each. In spite of these formal differences, there are, as Clark notes, many resemblances between their work; she argues that this poem in particular "inaugurates a phase in which Plath borrows from Hughes's poems, distorting both his voice and images to fashion her own art" ("Tracking" 102). Brain argues that it exists "at the extremity of the most fundamental and physical sense in which Plath's work is related to Hughes's" (*The Other* 205), while Van Dyne notes the "permeable page" on which she composes the piece (34). The drafts through which she shaped her words reflect her "efforts to recast each of the central images of persecution, silencing, and torture to give the speaker the controlling force in the action and the last word in a battle that involves the record of their poetry no less than the history of their marriage," through images of dogs and Joan of Arc, which were erased from the poem's final version (Van Dyne 35). Kendall points out that she did not write another surviving poem for more than six weeks after this one, which illustrates the importance of this particular piece: she possessed a "tendency to write her poems in batches, punctuated by long poetic silences" (*Sylvia Plath* 104). Plath's speaker takes a lyric stance, as in "The Thought-Fox," but here the poem's dominant image is literal rather than metaphoric. Beginning with the "old / Letters and their death rattle," the speaker condemns not only "cardboard cartons the color of cement" but also "the eyes and times of the postmarks." What she wants, what the fire can offer, is "an end to the writing," to "The spry hooks that bend and cringe, and the smiles, the smiles" (*CPP* 204). Here Plath borrows an image from the 1961 "Tulips," in which a hospital patient longs for release from "My husband and child smiling out of the family photo; / Their smiles catch onto my skin, little smiling hooks" (*CPP* 160).[2] "Burning the Letters" thus recalls two different periods of Plath's history, both of which emphasize the speaker's desire for escape. Though the earlier "hooks" signify only personal attachments, the image's second use also suggests alien intrusions into family life, which the speaker chooses to eradicate through violence rather than negotiation. Plath's poetic speaker addresses a broadly imagined theme of burden and responsibility through the piece's representation of infidelity. The poem's literal reference to their private life and Plath's decision to write on and over Hughes's piece suggest that he stole her professional inspiration by violating her trust. However, the poetic elements that Plath includes in her re-creation of this situation signify, more importantly, a direct critique of the *ars poetica* that Hughes advanced on the reverse side of the page.[3]

Signaling a disruption of Hughes's familiar tenors and vehicles, Plath names multiple animals in the poem: the speaker calls herself a "Dumb fish / with one tin eye" who must "poke at the carbon birds in my housedress" because "They are more beautiful than my bodiless owl" (*CPP* 204). These images resonate with Hughes's familiar metaphors for creative energies, though Plath's creatures possess inorganic traits of "tin" and "carbon." As Heather Clark has pointed out, "Ariel" also responds directly to "The Thought-Fox"; its opening reference to darkness, its setting in the natural world, and the contrast that it sketches between interior domesticity and events taking place outdoors all speak back to Hughes's piece (Clark, *Grief* 160; "Tracking" 104–08). As in "Burning," too, Plath searches in "Ariel" for an accurate representation of "the act of writing itself" ("Tracking" 102). Plath's first response to "The Thought-Fox," though, shows the speaker attempting to tie now-static images of animals to the sentient nature of the letters themselves, "papers that breathe like people" and to betray only traces of their contents, including "a name with black edges" (*CPP* 204–05). Charged with her own angry energy and with the letters' false sentiments, she takes them out of the house to a place "Between the yellow lettuces and the German cabbage"[4] in the garbage, thus reclaiming the house for her own by emptying out the evidence of her partner's presence. The speaker draws an additional connection between the German cabbage's "weird blue dreams" and the paper fragments' "foetus"-like enfoldment among them, both of which connote an illogical, wrong state of being (*CPP* 205). Here Plath positions the revelatory text of the letter as a natural product, something that might grow out of the earth or from a womb, but the surrealist juxtaposition of these images works to undermine the validity of writing itself.

Though she initially drafted her piece on the verso of his, Plath's poem is not animated by a direct response to Hughes's piece until the final stanza. The speaker declares herself in powerful terms: "Warm rain greases my hair," she notes, and "My veins glow like trees." These descriptions of the speaker's physical state contrast with the detachment that Hughes's speaker evidences. She possesses the ability to tear apart her partner's words, quite literally, through the control she assumes over his texts. Here Plath responds to Hughes's titular fox by envisioning a scene in which one predator is overpowered by another, stronger one: "The dogs are tearing a fox. This is what it is like— / A red burst and a cry / That splits from its ripped bag and does not stop." As in Hughes's carefully controlled illustration of poetic creation that emerges from the mind's eye like a fox in the forest, Plath's central image does not gain full dramatic force until the end. The graphic images she employs surpass the passive "sharp hot stink" in favor of blood and spilled guts, an agony that "splits" and "does not stop." Rather than imagining the fox as arbiter of the creative process, she pictures it "With the dead eye / And the stuffed expression"; it is remembered and carefully preserved, but as a relic instead of a living, breathing agent.[5] In fact, Plath's speaker accuses Hughes's fox of poisoning the very landscape around it: "Dyeing the air, / Telling the particles of the clouds, the leaves, the water / What immortality is. That it is immortal" (*CPP* 205). Literary significance, she implies, should be earned rather than forcibly taken. The carnage that the poem depicts also resonates with Plath's other descriptions of childbirth. In "The Rabbit Catcher," for instance, she characterizes the trapper's snares as "Set close, like birth pangs" (*CPP* 194), while in "Three Women" she describes a delivery room as "a place of shrieks . . . not happy" and a mother herself as "a garden of black and red agonies" (*CPP* 180). The visions of bodies ripping and blood bursting that conclude "Burning the Letters" contribute to the vocabulary that Plath assembled not only to describe childbirth but also to signify the sacrifices that authentic writing demands. Ultimately the poem argues that the sacrifices this speaker makes for her art are realer, more rooted in the body's experiences of pain and danger, than are observations made from a distance.

Some readers have interpreted the violent event at the core of this poem, which Plath contrasts with both the stillness of death and the false life that taxidermy imparts, as an assessment of her relationship with Hughes and an indictment of his poetic skill. Yet "Burning the Letters" and "The Thought-Fox" share a remarkable number of formal elements that recall the compositional techniques both writers developed in the course of their earliest drafting and revision processes. Both of these poems are written in present tense, from a third-person perspective. The two pieces also use alliteration and end-stopped lines in order to sustain a tension between narrative progress and the speaker's feelings of hesitation and uncertainty. Plath's and Hughes's descriptions of the fox even incorporate enough paratactic sentence constructions that they seem to anticipate Ron Silliman's theorization of the Language poets' "new sentence" (90–91). Yet the fox serves very different rhetorical and ideological functions in the two pieces. For Hughes, the fox is a kind of psychopomp, leading the poetic narrator through the untried landscape of creation to a point of intellectual revelation. It operates as confirmation of the narrator's insights into the outside world as well as proof of the writer's own literary acumen; these inter- and extra-textual purposes signify in archetypal rather than specific terms. In Plath's poem, on the other hand, the fox is an object rather than a subject, and its implied disembowelment suggests a challenge to patriarchal literary traditions. Its "dead eye" and protestations of immortality suggest, rather, that its death freezes a particular moment in time without preserving its vitality.

These contrasting perspectives on the fox's rhetorical purpose illustrate diverging views on the *ars poetica*. Plath extended her contemplation of the animal's potential for artistic representation in "Lyonnesse," which she finished on 21 October 1962, more than two months after "Burning the Letters." This later piece imagines a male subject whose vast features form the outlines of this mythical land. Both the "white, high berg on his forehead" (*CPP* 233) and the "Sea of his eyes" recall Plath's "Colossus," yet his earthshaking movements point, in the broader context of Arthurian mythology, to the decisions that the poet makes while shaping a sentient creation. The poem concludes by noting the near impossibility of success. In spite of the fact that "[h]e'd had so many wars," the subject does not truly know how to act without the poet's guiding presence: "The white gape of his mind was the real Tabula Rasa" (*CPP* 234).

The analogous elements of "The Thought-Fox" and "Burning the Letters" illustrate some aspects of Hughes's and Plath's shared work life. Throughout their marriage, Plath scheduled work-sessions into their days to ensure that they each had ample time to write. Both poets alternated teaching with reading and writing early in their married life; later on, they negotiated the regular hours, conditions, and workspaces that could enable them to produce new material for magazines and competitions while caring for their children and working on improvements to Court Green. By drawing on a common pool of not only lived experience but also social history, writerly innovation, and literary study, they created unique poetic vocabularies and an arsenal of compositional strategies that inflect both Plath's 1962–1963 poems and Hughes's 1998 collections. These strategies did not evolve organically, but emerged piecemeal, over time, as a result of poetic conversations begun and ended, questions left unanswered, and shared experiences to which Hughes returned in the years after Plath died. While part of his intention in creating recursive versions of these scenarios in later poems may have been to resolve longstanding internal or personal conflicts, he also argues in these pieces that specific compositional techniques and carefully shaped narratives can reveal new insights into the purposes of writing itself. Hughes finally locates the poems' real meaning in the contested ground that they inhabit. Lyric accuracy does not exist on one side of an opposition but in the struggle between the two, which Plath's evolving ideas in "Lyonnesse" also illustrate. This methodology was well-suited to the negotiations of intellectual and creative identity in which several of his earliest poems participate.

FINDING VOICE AND BODY:
THE HAWK IN THE RAIN **AND** *LUPERCAL*

Hughes's first two collections, *The Hawk in the Rain* (1957) and *Lupercal* (1960), introduce some of the poetic themes, compositional techniques, and forms that defined his career. Several of the poems in the former work function as blazons, for instance, in which a creature's individual parts create an extended metaphor. Terry Gifford and Neil Roberts call this approach "not a series of statements but of re-enacted encounters and adventures" (18). "The Thought-Fox" is the most famous example from the book, but the title poem, "Macaw and Little Miss," "The Jaguar," "The Horses," and "The Dove Breeder" all investigate both the intrinsic and the symbolic properties that animals possess, aligning them with their historical representations and suggesting a still-unrealized metaphoric potential. Hughes investigated these properties further in a series of line drawings included in the 1957 manuscripts held at the Lilly Library. His draft of "Parlour Piece," for instance, is accompanied by a sketch of a bird leaning down to peck at the ground, next to two clawed hands. This image may be intended to illustrate the poem's vision of "Stillness, silence, the eyes / Where fire and flood strained" (*CPH* 25): a love shared by two partners who sit wordlessly rather than risk its eruption. The drawing that adorns Hughes's draft of "Vampire," on the other hand, includes a tiger growling up at the sky and a slim black panther whose body is so long that his head appears on the next page, which contains an apparently unpublished "Autobiography of Thomas Nashe." These animals give life to the "fusty carcass" of "Vampire," which leaches away the poetic speaker's life-force until "This grinning sack is bursting with your blood" (*CPH* 39). Perhaps their silent outlines are meant both to embody the negative energy that this parasitic guest expends and to offer resistance against him. Hughes also includes a sketch of an astrological wheel on the back of a draft of "Two Wise Generals" in the same collection. The appearance of this particular image suggests that he might have been anticipating the future conception of his and Plath's children, or that he meant to reflect on the thoughtless decisions that enable history-altering events—as in the poem's final lines, "Both / have found their sleeping armies massacred" (*CPH* 47). These sketches, though brief and incidental, demonstrate the multiple dimensions in which

Hughes imagined his poetic subjects and foreshadow the major revelations that Hughes's sketch for *Birthday Letters* would bring to light.

Animals remain a central source of the imagery in *The Hawk in the Rain* and later collections, as these illustrations indicate. Hughes notes that animals recur throughout his work "because they were there at the beginning. Like parents" (Heinz 81), a statement that testifies to their fundamental value in the poetry. Yvonne Reddick notes the "remarkably vivid" evocations of British geographies that Hughes created in the book, though he worked on it while living in America (117). The animals' anthropomorphic traits resonate with these poetic landscapes and render them apt vehicles for Hughes's speculations on writing's social relevance. "Famous Poet," for instance, suggests the self-doubt that accompanies creative endeavors; it begins with a challenge to "Stare at the monster: remark / How difficult it is to define just what / Amounts to monstrosity in that / Very ordinary appearance." The speaker, confronting a recalcitrant public self, describes what he sees as "Nothing there / But the haggard stony exhaustion of a near-/ Finished variety artist." He attributes this physical and psychological damage to the stresses of his work, but Hughes mitigates the imbalance between the writer's labor and public demands by introducing a startling image at the poem's end. Here the *ars poetica,* aiming this time to diminish the imagined burden that artistic creation assumes, pictures the "famous poet" as a "Stegosaurus, a lumbering obsolete / Arsenal of gigantic horn and plate / From a time when half the world still burned, set / To blink behind bars at the zoo" (*CPH* 24). The hopeful, rather inept persona that Hughes sketches here—with direct reference, perhaps, to his own emerging reputation—concludes as a kind of satire, a relic from a dead era. Here Hughes's character is caught between desire for a more successful life and his own propensity for self-sabotage. In a discussion of Hughes's use of simile, James Castell emphasizes his tendency to exploit "the range and ambiguity" of the device; indeed, he links his "understanding of a nonhuman dimension in poetry" directly to "the formal techniques that he deploys when writing" (88, 91). The simile is effective in works like "The Thought-Fox" and "Famous Poet" precisely because it is "an active and independent" literary device but also "leads as much to misrecognition as to insight" (Castell 99). The speaker of "Famous Poet" articulates the doubt and uncertainty that plague every writer in striking terms; yet, as Jonathan Bate has noted, this poem was one of the "less successful" pieces from the book (168). The ambiguous perspective on poetic legacy that this piece offers suggests that, at this early moment in his career, Hughes had not yet fully imagined the social roles that the poet might play.

A few other poems in *The Hawk in the Rain*, including "Secretary" and "A Modest Proposal," employ animal metaphors in order to explore the range of human reactions to thwarted ambition. In "Secretary," for instance, the speaker anticipates how an unbidden touch would make the title character "shriek and weeping / Crawl off to nurse the terrible wound." Rather than expressing empathy with her hurt, he describes her movements at work in bestial terms, comparing her retreat to "a starling under the bellies of bulls" and her escape homeward as a "scuttle. . . down the gauntlet of lust / Like a clockwork mouse" (*CPH* 25). Steve Ely notes that Hughes wrote the poem "for or about Edna Wholey," sister to his friend John and an early love interest of his (174).[6] Much like the "typist" in Part III of *The Waste Land*, who "is bored and tired," lacks the energy to forestall her unwanted suitor's advances, and finally "Paces about her room again, alone" after the deed is done (Eliot ll. 236, 254), this secretary "Goes to bed early, shuts out with the light / Her thirty years, and lies with buttocks tight, / Hiding her lovely eyes until day break" (*CPH* 25). Eliot's anonymous woman is treated with an indifferent contempt consistent with the work's overall structure, which positions a host of female figures—among them the mythical Belladonna, Eliot's first wife, Vivienne Haigh-Wood, and a woman vampire—as symptomatic of modernity's encroaching desolation. The typist's loveless encounter with her "young man carbuncular" (Eliot l, 231) functions less as a portrait of a specific woman's disappointment than it does as a condemnation of modern tendencies to value profit and pleasure over intimate connection. The experiences of Hughes's secretary figure also hold a metaphorical significance. Though Tracy Brain points out that, in a poem that examines male interactions closely, "there is a reciprocal loss—of the woman herself—to the poem's speaker" ("Feminism" 94), the secretary's physical description originates in Hughes's tendency to exploit animals' expressive potential. Her actions and self-presentation depend upon the metaphoric use Hughes makes of birds, foxes, cats, and other beasts in the book: as one of his earliest characters, she is articulated through the images that first comprise his poetic lexicon.

"A Modest Proposal," which appears just two pages later in *The Hawk in the Rain*, offers a more specifically developed metaphor that draws an analogy between human decisions and wild animals' instinctual acts. The interactions of these poetic antagonists illustrate, through a compositional framework similar to that of "The Thought-Fox," the tremendous work that an artist puts into new creation. Hughes introduces his poem's subject first as "two wolves, come separately to a wood," who are "Distracted by the soft competing pulse / Of the other." Their progress toward a fixed goal takes place along a path through the woods—in the form of an active competition between natural enemies who seek both to undermine each other's efforts and to gain their journey's final reward. Each "wolf" is motivated by a "painful burning of the coal in its heart" and bears without complaint the "rage hoarse in its labouring / Chest after a skirmish" as well as "the rents in its hide" (*CPH* 27). Their competition is marked by a "red smelting of hatred" and a lust for "a mad final satisfaction," which suggests the triumph that only a writer's acknowledged masterpiece can bring about. However, the poem's final stanza upsets the narrative that its first two-thirds traces; the real leader in this race is the "great lord," who hunts both wolves, both writers (*CPH* 28). What the conclusion to this *ars poetica* suggests, in contrast to "The Thought-Fox," is that a wild battle within the forest—a struggle to capture and tame one's inspiration—can be cut off by the tired expectations of poetic convention. Though the wolves are not given distinct identities, they bow to a patriarchal tradition, its power underlined by repetition of the word "great." As in "Famous Poet," this poem ties creativity to brute physical power, suggesting that the vital force out of which art is born exists primarily in bodily exertions, rather than in the mind, psyche, or emotions. The *ars poetica*, at this point in Hughes's career, signifies poetic meaning produced through the sheer force of will and body.

Hughes continues to investigate the corporeal processes by which meaning is made in some of the later poems in *The Hawk in the Rain*. These pieces tend to associate artistic production not just with the atavistic instincts of animals but with the often violent public strictures that law and war impose. They also illustrate Hughes's efforts "to create poetry with a material body by employing language . . . dense with dental, plosive, and guttural consonants, and with alliteration and assonance" (Gifford and Roberts 35). In "Law in the Country of the Cats," for instance, Hughes reframes the wolves from "A Modest Proposal" as two men who "meet for the first time in all / Eternity and outright hate each other." This time, they come together "As dog and wolf because their blood before / They are aware has bristled into their hackles." They refuse to share in the usual "humble brotherhood of man" because competition has blocked their potential communion. Hughes suggests that two men who meet like this, two writers whose philosophies clash, will inevitably destroy one another. After "that moment's horrible pause / As each looks into the gulf in the eye of the other," violence erupts, and the victor claims his reward. Hughes describes the battle between them as "a flash of violent incredible action" that results in "one man letting his brains gently to the gutter." Though the man left standing concludes the poem by confessing to his crime—"'Let Justice be done. I did it, I'" (*CPH* 41)—Hughes offers no alternative to this preordained conflict. The survivor has committed murder, but his work has also withstood the threat that the other's writings posed to his legacy. Neil Roberts calls this poem an "inferior" specimen of Hughes's work and suggests that it typifies an approach that disappears in the later books (*Literary* 23). Yet its poetic traits indicate the dynamic nature of Hughes's aesthetic beliefs, which evolved over time. In *The Hawk in the Rain*, the repeated clashes between humans, or between beasts, simulate the excesses of creative energy expended in the service of art. These scenarios inevitably carry with them an element of brutality, a fundamentally physical conflict that links creation with destruction. Hughes's poetic characters do not perform their work in solitude; they require external antagonists against whose creations they can react. They draw conclusions about aesthetic creation and the world in a reactionary manner, rather than as the result of inner contemplation. In a conversation with Ekbert Faas, Hughes defines this kind of conflict carefully, as a "strong, specific, positive violence" that produces a "recognition of the operation of divine law in the created things of the natural world" (*WP* 255, 259). The confident manner with which each of these characters approaches his fight—whether in the guise of fox, dinosaur, wolf, cat, or another animal—signals his sense of mastery within the social world, a self-assurance about his rightful place, and his ability to manipulate those with whom he comes into contact.

The last several poems of *The Hawk in the Rain* refer to the armistice at the end of World War II. Hughes's descriptions of the brutal physical price exacted by hand-to-hand combat resemble the steadfast critiques of wartime politics that World War I poets Siegfried Sassoon and Wilfred Owen advanced. At the same time, his use of metaphor and sometimes absurdist imagery draws the reader's attention to the style and aesthetics of wartime struggles, rather than making a direct political critique. As a result, narrative focus draws inward as these pieces' narrators assert their identity in the midst of a chaotic, anti-intellectual world. "Bayonet Charge," for instance, features a soldier who is "hearing / Bullets smacking the belly out of the air" and experiencing the unique pain of a "patriotic tear that had brimmed in his eye / Sweating like molten iron from the centre of his chest" (*CPH* 43). Yvonne Reddick points out the Hopkins-influenced "sprung rhythm" that filters through this piece in order to "evoke natural forces" and to create a kind of "rhythmic enjambment" (80). Unlike Sassoon's and Owen's narrators, this protagonist does not reflect upon the real human cost of the conflict around him, nor does he display compassion toward his unseen foes. Rather, he attempts to locate himself as a tangible physical participant in the whirlwind of combat, wondering "In what cold clockwork of the stars and the nations / Was he the hand pointing that second?" He observes the wildlife around him rather than his fellows, noting the point when "the shot-slashed furrows / Threw up a yellow hare that rolled like a flame / And crawled in a threshing circle, its mouth wide" (*CPH* 43). This narrative interest in the natural world is consistent with the rest of the book's subjects, yet the hare resonates with the English countryside, rather than with English personnel sacrifices. As a result, this particular image unsettles the poem's title—and foreshadows the recurring interest in rabbits that Hughes would trace through such poems as "The Rabbit Catcher" and "The Afterbirth." Roberts suggests that this off-kilter focus represents "the suspended sense of temporality in a man going through an extreme crisis" (*Literary* 29), though Hughes does not resolve the moment of disaster. That moment is doubled in a handwritten draft of the poem that appears in the Emory archives, in fact; according to Hughes's original version, the second stanza begins by noting that "In bewilderment he almost stopped" (MSS 644 – Box 59, Folder 1). In the published form, the line reads, "In bewilderment then he almost stopped—" (*CPH* 43). The differences between these two iterations, although small, point to the importance Hughes places on narrative timing here. The poetic speaker pauses on "then," and suspends his motion briefly at the line's concluding dash, but the poem's energy continues onward to the question that drives its next two lines. Hughes's revision also completes the line's pentameter and enables its imperfect trochaic pattern to continue after the dactylic interruption of "bewilderment." After the new version of this line sustains the speaker's participation in the "charge" itself, the piece's most obvious marker of humanity appears in its concluding lines, where he reminds us of the terror that drove soldiers onward: fleeing past the hare, the soldier discards everything he once valued, his sense of "King, honour, human dignity, etcetera / Dropped like luxuries in a yelling alarm" (*CPH* 43). Perhaps, the poetic narrator suggests, humanity and national identity are indulgences that military combat cannot accommodate. Instead, Hughes's character leaves the wilderness behind, that seat of poetic inspiration and violent battle, in favor of surviving the conflict. This particular vision of England is marked by hostility and bloodshed, rather than creation, yet Hughes includes this perspective to indicate the pain that must be endured before the poet can accurately represent the land.

Hughes published *Lupercal* just a few years later; in keeping with the animal metaphors and anxieties over control and creation that permeate *The Hawk in the Rain*, this collection shares a name with the cave in which Rome's twin founders, Romulus and Remus, were suckled by a female wolf. In a letter to Olwyn, Hughes notes that "the Feast of Lupercal was a Roman festival held on 15th of February, in honour of Zeus as a Wolf. Nobody knows how it originated, but it came from Mt Lycaon in Greece, & combined sacrifices of goats & of a dog" (*LTH* 148). Margaret Dickie Uroff points out that the poetry from this period illustrates the sources of several of the thematic interests that Hughes and Plath shared; both read deeply, for instance, in early ecological literature, from which they developed several familiar tropes (100–01). The collection begins, in both "Things Present" and "Everyman's Odyssey," by expressing uncertainty about the creator's ability to make his ideas new, to produce meaningful art. Hughes's modernist inspirations are visible in this volume's nod to Ezra Pound's admonition, often repeated in *The Cantos*, to "make it new."[7] Like William Carlos Williams, too, Hughes seems to subscribe to the notion of "no ideas but in things";[8] in "Things

Present," his poetic narrator attempts to represent "All things being done or undone" by his own hands. These accomplishments acquire worth from their tangible nature: the narrator works to "Embody a now, erect a here" but with "no shoes, / Honour, or hope." This concrete evidence of existence serves as a poor substitute for the wealth, property, and reputation that the speaker's heritage has lost. He calls himself a "tramp in the sodden ditch" (*CPH* 59), suggesting that he now makes his way alone and unencumbered—at the cost of his lineage's rightful inheritance. This phrasing assumes that he deserves the land and names that his forefathers possessed and that they sacrificed their very bodies in the service of maintaining their holdings. But his interest exists in a strange isolation that does not acknowledge the other social factors that have also played a role in the history. For Hughes, at this point in his career, "Things Present" signifies the ability to hold onto inherited rights. He shares with Plath a profound investment in the materiality of poetic objects—their potential for symbolic resonance and their contribution to an objective correlative—but locates their significance, for now, in persistent traditions rather than in aesthetic transformation.

A similar argument can be made about "Everyman's Odyssey," whose title already implies participation in the classical epic tradition. Beginning with an apostrophe addressed to Telemachus, Hughes's narrator invokes the historical properties of the Homeric epic in order to pay homage to the efforts that Odysseus's son made both to find his father and to efface even the memory of his mother's suitors. Hughes underscores the patriarchal inheritance that this history implies by all but eliminating Penelope; she appears only as "Your mother, white, a woe freezing a silence" who "Parried long their impertinence with her shuttle." The narrative focus falls instead on her son, who sees his father's lonely weapons as "great blades [that] shook light at you like the sea." He is moved to act against the strange men who now fill his house by his "father's honour" (*CPH* 59), a prize that he envisions as "a sword in the scabbard of your body you could not draw." This image originates in the ancient Greek epic tradition, yet it also recalls the pen, a literary object that is commonly opposed to the sword. Hughes suggests here that the writerly articulation of Odysseus's honor is as important, and difficult, as the act of winning it. These two struggles undergird the relationship between Telemachus and Odysseus in the poem's final stanza, in which the son first witnesses "How the father arrives out of the bottom of the world" (*CPH* 60), in a nod to the story's epic origins, and then sees him avenging himself on Penelope's potential lovers. On the one hand, Hughes's attention to Western mythological precedents positions his work in relation to some of the major modernist epics like *The Waste Land*, *The Cantos*, and H.D.'s *Helen in Egypt*. On the other, however, he is writing well after the peak of high modernism, at a historical moment that witnessed both American civil-rights movements and emerging second-wave politics on both sides of the Atlantic. His narrator's desire for revenge, articulated through a story that focuses on the instrument of vengeance itself, renders the piece a metaphorical commentary on the poet's efforts to write his work into and beyond established traditions. Hughes's title, which describes Telemachus's experience as an "everyman's odyssey," suggests that anyone can participate in the many revisions of the original *Odyssey* that followed Homer; the poem serves as proof of developing artistic acumen.

Hughes's interest in classical mythologies, which remained strong throughout his career, informs *Lupercal* indirectly, though many of its poems pay closer attention to England's landscapes and, especially, its wildlife. As in *The Hawk in the Rain,* Hughes locates power, beauty, and insight in animal traits, often focusing on the expressive possibilities of a single creature's movements and physical appearance. This strategy allows him to form precise portraits of English country life that also function, at times, as meditations on contemporary social conditions or on the writer's struggles with creation. The collection's title points backwards in time nearly two thousand years to the founding of the most famous empire in the West; consequently, the animal poems identify the inhabitants of a modern-day Lupercal as undeniably English and tied to the terrain itself. Through the title, Hughes links Roman policies to Britain's own imperialist practices. While most of the book's animal poems do not endow the natural world with human qualities, they do tie animals' everyday actions of hunting, rest, combat, and feeding to humans' ineluctable need to assert dominance over their surroundings. As Hughes himself noted in a letter to Olwyn, the book's overarching theme is "God the devourer... which is brainless & the whole of evil" (qtd. in Roberts, *Literary* 50). As a series of potential metaphors for the act of composition, too, these animal images link creative practices to life's most basic functions.

In "Hawk Roosting," which contains one of Hughes's most oft-cited examples of animal as metaphor, the poetic subject sits in the top of a tree, imagining the source of its next meal and reflecting on the world. Neil Roberts has called this poem an explication of Hughes's understanding of the law, through critiques of both contemporary ecological policy and English political attitudes toward Ireland (*Literary* 49). Like many of Hughes's animal subjects, this hawk is a predator, focused on his relationship to the beings around him. In a typescript draft held at Emory, Hughes portrays an evolution in the hawk's perspective on the world he occupies that takes place between the beginning of the third stanza and its end: though he notes that "It took the whole of creation / To produce my foot, my each feather," in this early version, he ends the stanza with the conclusion that "Now I hold Creation in my foot" (MSS 644 – Box 59, Folder 9). The shift from "creation" to "Creation" in the draft articulates the hawk's own transformation from a creature who inhabits the natural world among countless others to a sentient being who understands the power he can exercise over a human-defined concept of existence. Hughes's decision to capitalize both instances of "Creation" in the published poem excises this moment of transformation; the hawk remains a citizen of the political rather than the natural sphere throughout the piece.[9] He also changes the end punctuation of "To produce my foot, my each feather" from a semicolon to a colon. This shift indicates the hawk's purposeful mastery over both his body and his environment instead of a tolerance for his place. In the end, the hawk's attitude toward conquest is clinical: "I kill where I please because it is all mine. / There is no sophistry in my body: / My manners are tearing off heads— / The allotment of death." As an avatar of imperialism, and a potential signifier for the processes of artistic innovation, the hawk calmly assumes total power and complete acquiescence from its subjects. It deals in violence, taking aggressive action and considering no appeals to reason. The poem concludes with the observation that "The sun is behind me. / Nothing has changed since I began. / My eye has permitted no change. / I am going to keep things like this" (*CPH* 69). These four paratactic, end-stopped lines resonate like a proclamation, or an enactment of evolutionary principles; the hawk's drive to kill reiterates its instinct for survival.

Hughes makes no overt statement in the poem that links this attitude to traditional English nationalism; the hawk's traits produce, rather, admiration and fear in the observer. In it, Hughes creates a symbol of violent mastery whose elevated perspective, both physical and ideological, enables the speaker to reflect upon the productive potential of the scene before him. He may decide to destroy his subjects, or add to them. The piece remains a controversial one in Hughes's oeuvre, though he claimed in an interview with Ekbert Faas that he imagined "in this Hawk, Nature is thinking" (199). The hawk's actions in this piece, and its resonance with other animal figures like the wolf and the jaguar, complicate this rather neutral perspective, however. In a 1965 interview with BBC producer George MacBeth for an Edinburgh Poetry Festival edition of *Poetry Now*, in fact, Hughes noted that the poem was inspired by the idea that "the truth kills everybody." The specific insight here is that we exist within "a totalitarian system" but the poem doesn't operate according to "random, or civil or elemental violence," but in terms of "Peace" (qtd. in Bate 165). The hawk itself is not aware of its own mortality, so it is not troubled by the violence that it exercises upon its prey (Bate 376). These observations suggest that the poem's strongly limned images represent animals' literal power, but Hughes also encourages readers to contemplate the consequences of human actions through the eyes of a potential creator, a poet.[10]

As another dimension of his emerging sense of the *ars poetica*, Hughes examines the work of some of his famous poetic precedents in pieces like "Nicholas Ferrer" and "Wilfred Owen's Photographs." These pieces illustrate not only Hughes's early attempts to understand the nuances of English history but also the types of stories that contribute to his poetics. The former piece imagines the social contexts of Ferrer's life; this bishop, a distant ancestor of Hughes's on his mother's side (Middlebrook, *Her Husband* 64), was burned for teaching what the English church termed blasphemies. The latter poem offers—through a reference to Owen's war poetry—a subtle critique of Parliamentary attitudes toward military discipline. The other portraits of human action in *Lupercal*, many of which attempt to imagine the role that the artist can play in the political world, occur in the course of Hughes's reflections on contemporary art and world politics. In "A Woman Unconscious," for example, the poetic narrator observes the ominous fact that "Russia and America circle each other" as evidence that "there no trusting (trusting to luck) / Dates when the world's due to be burned." The woman of the poem's title endures "a lesser death," her state of being "numb beyond her last of sense" a metaphor for the stunned and threatened world around her (*CPH* 62). While few Hughes critics have discussed this piece, its resonance with contemporary Cold War politics ties it to current events and may give readers insight into the writer's social beliefs. Its metaphorical treatment of Cold War confrontations resonates with the difficult interactions in which the writer must also engage.

Hughes considers the burden of personal and cultural truths that the writer sometimes shoulders in poems that touch on, however briefly, familiar stories of mythic archetypes. His "Witches," for instance, which appears near the end of *Lupercal*, demands comparison with the many other poetic faces of female intelligence that permeate Western literary traditions—among these, Christina Rossetti's "Goblin Market" (1862) and Anne Sexton's contemporary "Her Kind," from *To Bedlam and Partway Back* (1960). Hughes's piece distinguishes itself in its attempt to discredit some of the archetypal stories that define women's creativity as a source of social resilience. Both Rossetti and Sexton draw on longstanding cultural mythologies—a Christian story of sin and redemption versus the martyrdom that women who dared to pursue exceptional lives often faced—in order to align their poetic narratives with a counter-history of women's accomplishment. "Witches," in contrast, asks whether these extraordinary figures had merely imagined all their accomplishments and concludes, almost paradoxically, that "our science says they did. / It was all wishfully dreamed in bed. / Small psychology would unseam it." Hughes suggests here that cultural counter-histories struggle to resist the dominant narratives imposed by "science" and "psychology"; these narratives do not lack meaning but are often severed from mainstream belief-systems. In Tracy Brain's reading of the poem, she argues that the speaker "mourns the loss" of "women's witchery" and desires a return of the particular "inexplicable power and creativity" that women possess ("Feminism" 95).

However, the poem's tone and diction undermine this rather hopeful analysis. The speaker attributes everyday ill fortune to the fact that "we are devilled"; the women who imagine that their "feet dance while their heads sleep" are constrained by their society to act otherwise in public (*CPH* 80). Plath's writing from the same period as Hughes's includes legendary creatures like the titular "Goatsucker," as well as the mythologically- and biographically-influenced "Electra on Azalea Path," "The Beekeeper's Daughter," and "The Colossus." Like Hughes, she pursued a modernist interest in the classical stories as a means of providing readers insight into current events; both she and Hughes focus on women's existence at the intersection of public spectacle and private experience. As a metaphoric representation of the writer's craft, the poetic speaker in "Witches" attempts to become an active participant in longstanding cultural mythologies—in order to intervene in the stories that preceded hers.

Hughes's interest in reworking mythologies at this point in his career is, in part, a dimension of his emerging *ars poetica*. In attempting to define the issues that confront the artist, Hughes's poetic speakers sometimes turn away from the struggles for reputation and dominance that his animal characters embody. They seek, instead, to resist the systems that constrain aesthetic production. These critiques spring from nationally defined spaces; Hughes investigates the ways in which English patriotic history and English landscapes help to articulate ideal approaches to craft. In both "Historian" and "The Perfect Forms," for instance, anxieties over historical precedents and the worth of one's tangible accomplishments produce narratives fraught with unresolved conflict. These poems contain images derived from human anatomy that, literally divorced from the body politic, suggest that the speaker sees the world in fragmented, dissociated terms. As a consequence, Hughes imagines "the eye and the head" functioning like "an underworld," as in "Historian" (*CPH* 67), or, in "The Perfect Forms," which presents an ironic vision of Christian influence, Socrates "Smiling, complacent as a phallus" alongside the "Visage of Priapus." This vision of aesthetic ideals relies upon classical figures from world mythology in order to illustrate the difficulty of creation itself. "No better," the poetic speaker notes, "for the fosterings / Of fish, reptile and tree-leaper throughout / Their ages of Godforsaken darkness." These efforts to create "the perfect forms" result only in a "monstrous-headed difficult child" that is still supposed, by its observers, to issue from "the kingdom of heaven" (*CPH* 82). In contrast to these failed efforts, the "Historian" who is meant to record such creations finds that "The decisive random of chance / Was concealed skill of his choice"; this trait enables "Word breathed into a wig / To raze like Attila" (*CPH* 67). Hughes indicates here that the writer's actions shape his own fate and that of his art. These images, as in pieces like "The Thought-Fox," illustrate artistic innovation through English landscapes, classical philosophy, and literary traditions. In both his early drafts and in the published versions of these poems, Hughes explores the creative possibilities of diverse perspectives, subjects, and forms. Yet it is not until he begins engaging directly with individual Plath poems that his work explicitly defines a mature theory of poetics.

The compositional elements that Hughes and Plath share—an interest in locating their work within familiar poetic landscapes, a focus on the metaphoric potential of animal imagery, anxiety about artistic production itself, investment in the material qualities of the poetic object, borrowed phrases, and a constantly evolving poetic vocabulary—illustrate the enduring weight of the short time they shared as creative partners. At the same time, the styles, tones, and themes of their work diverged, particularly as each came to terms with the nuances of his or her individual *ars poetica*, or theory of poetry's potential for writerly instruction and performance. These differences indicate that Plath's work registered shifts in influence and motivation that departed significantly from Hughes's by the end of their time together.

NOTES

1. Tracy Brain notes that Plath's manuscripts for this poem also appear on the verso of Hughes's typescripts for "Toll of Air Raids," "A Fable," "Cradle Piece," "Unknown Soldier," and "Poltergeist" (*The Other* 203–04).

2. See my discussion of Plath's revisions to the "Tulips" manuscripts in chapter 2.

3. Susan Van Dyne also notes that Plath drafted "A Secret," "The Applicant," "Daddy," "Eavesdropper," "Medusa," "The Jailer," "Lesbos," "Lyonnesse," and "Amnesiac" on the reverse sides of Hughes's handwritten draft sheets of his unpublished radio play *The Calm* (9–10, 33–34).

4. Van Dyne glosses this image as an orchid, symbolic of Hughes's affair with Assia (38).

5. This sense of the fox as relic is a theme in Plath's 1956 story "The Wishing Box," in which the narrator Agnes's husband, Harold, dreams that "a red fox ran through his kitchen, grievously burnt, its fur charred black, bleeding from several wounds"; this dream, which he suffered before they met, is followed by another just after their marriage in which the fox is healed. Harold also dreams about a "giant pike" (*JP* 215–16), which inevitably recalls Hughes's "Pike," from *Lupercal*.

6. Bate notes that Philip Hobsbaum speculated—apparently erroneously—that the poem was inspired by a woman named Rosemary Joseph. Bate describes Joseph as "a shy, plain schoolteacher poet" who later published a poem called "Baking Day" but cautions against too easily linking the virginal subject of the poem and their friend. Hughes himself was wary in this period of relying too heavily on first-hand experience (Bate 88–89).

7. See, for example, Pound's Canto LIII, one of the "China Cantos," which includes the line "Day by day make it new" (265).

8. Williams repeated this idea throughout his own epic poem, *Paterson*, which serves in part as a directive to poets creating new work in the age of modernism. In Book I's "The Delineaments of the Giants," for instance, the speaker commands the reader to "Say it! No ideas but in things" (9).

9. In a letter to Ruth Barnhouse Beuscher dated 30 July 1962, Plath called this piece "pure ego-Fascist," a reflection of his beliefs in the "advantages of destruction" (*LSP2* 803).

10. Margaret Dickie Uroff identifies thematic affinities with Plath's work in "Hawk Roosting" (158–59) and in Hughes's "Cadenza" (180–81) as well.

Chapter Two

Figures and Flowers

Plath's Approaches to Draft and Revision

During her time at Cambridge's Newnham College, Plath sometimes walked through the grounds to visit a statue of a little boy holding a dolphin, a copy of Andrea del Verrocchio's *Putto with Dolphin*. As she describes it in her journal, "the bronze boy, whom I love, partly because no one really cares for him" stands "in the semi-circle of the privet hedge, bearing his undulant dolphin, smiling still, balancing on one dimpled foot." This first mention of the statue, which Plath wrote about on 19 February 1955, connotes isolation and cold; the boy is dusted with snow and shadowed by the nighttime trees. He serves in the role of touchstone for her hectic everyday routine, but she also cares for him, regularly "brush[ing] . . . the snow from his delicate smiling face" as he stands "there in the moonlight, dark, with snow etching his limbs in white" (*UJ* 200). Plath notes in the next paragraph that this image intensifies her desire to have a child with then-boyfriend Richard Sassoon, yet she tempers this idea with a reflection on what she sees as Sassoon's physical limitations. The statue offers her a kind of comfort but reminds her at the same time of personal disappointments that are not likely to be resolved. She attempts to come to terms with the statue's complex emotionality in an entry dated ten days later, reframing Sassoon's creative voice as the dolphin boy himself: "you gave me your image, and I made it into stories and poems; I talked about it for awhile to everyone and told them it was a bronze statue, a bronze boy with a dolphin, who balanced through the winter in our gardens with snow on his face, which I brushed off every night I visited him" (*UJ* 216). The similar phrasing and action in these two passages are striking, as though Plath revises her initial description of the statue in order to render it more precise. While the first allusion highlights the loneliness she feels in England, separated by distance and state of mind from Sassoon, the second suggests her attempt to cultivate a new perspective on the situation. Such acts of revision, writing out and re-envisioning even relatively commonplace events and observations, would become one of Plath's signature approaches to composition. Her attention to various acts of caretaking, coupled with her apparent disappointment in Sassoon's potential, also point to the varying uses that she made of source material, like her visits to the statue, in order to assure her proficiency in several different literary genres at once.

Plath established her practice of producing and keeping multiple drafts of her poems with her early juvenilia; many of the poems she wrote before 1956, even those never published, exist in forms that may vary by only a capital letter or two, or by entire stanzas. Steven Axelrod labels this period in her writing life a "transitional" one, in which she "struggled with the verbally playful and imagistically precise poetry of Dickinson, Moore, and Bishop" (129). Her responses to both literary and real-world stimuli resulted in pieces in which she experimented, sometimes more successfully, with a range of compositional techniques. The emotional and creative resonance of the Newnham College statue, for example, inspired an unpublished poem, "The Bronze Boy," which exists in two distinct versions in the Lilly Library archives. In the first attempt, Plath not only captures the statue's physical presence but also signifies his mythological resonance. The poem's four stanzas depict the boy's stillness and beauty, a monument to the statue's aesthetic legacy, before considering his lonely endurance as a symbol of bygone histories. Certain phrases recall the journal entries; Plath describes "the bronze boy who stands / Naked in the garden" in the first stanza and concludes by observing that "The bronze boy stands defying centuries / With his heroic eyes gone blind with leaves." As in her journal, here she expresses admiration for his steadfast existence. This draft of the poem casts the statue in sunlight rather than evoking the persistent dark that overshadows the accounts in her journal—perhaps because his presence now signals enlightenment. He is a witness to the literal leaf-showers of autumn, as "a hundred thousand leaves / Came sliding down his shoulder blades," though the passage unmistakably recalls the weight of human history and knowledge as well. Another contrast exists in the "Warm years of sunlight [that] lie upon his lips," rather than the blanket of snow that Plath remembers brushing from his arms. This shift in setting might indicate a more optimistic perspective on the history that the statue represents, yet she ultimately ties his figure to disappointed expectations. Revising her vision of the garden statue, she imagines the bronze boy's poetic presence as deceptive; he "never grieves" but communicates "clear delusive reason" and, again, is unable to see through "heroic eyes gone blind with leaves" (Lilly Library Plath mss. II. Writings: Poetry—B [Box 7A], Folder 8). Though this poem's allusions to interpersonal dynamics are subtle, Plath's portrayal of the boy as not only an emblem of historicity but also a figure both deaf and blind to outside forces anticipates the sense of an *ars poetica* that continues to emerge in her later work.

Plath's second draft of "The Bronze Boy" offers a more concise perspective on the statue's symbolic meaning in thirteen rather than the original fifteen lines. The revision also reacts to a series of handwritten comments present on the initial typed draft, most likely written by one of her English professors at Smith, Alfred Young Fisher. In a letter to Aurelia dated 23 April 1954, Plath notes that Fisher "has offered to coach me privately next year in writing poetry" (*LSP1* 735); she enthuses about his tutelage in several letters over the next seven months or so and continues to credit him with inspiring her drive to write.[1] In partial response to her reader's inclusion of scansion marks in the first and second stanzas, Plath cut five lines from the original and added one, producing a single five-line stanza from the first and second stanzas of the original. Among the lines she cut is "Warm years of sunlight," while she amends "clear delusive reason" to "bronze enduring reason." While her revisions probably acknowledge the commenter's directive to "Work through to an incisive development of both meaning and imagery" (Lilly Library Plath mss. II. Writings: Poetry—B [Box 7a], Folder 8), they also recast the boy's poetic persona as fixed and stoic, a reflection of his physical properties, rather than in the rather piquant terms that the first draft suggests. Plath's conclusion to the revision relies more heavily on the image of falling leaves than did the first draft; she depicts him "stand[ing] kneedeep in centuries / remembering a thousand autumns." The leaves that cover him again signify the burden of history, but he still manages to rise above it, emerging solidly from the detritus around him. The line Plath cut earlier returns in the "years of sunlight warm upon his lips," while the one adjective eliminated from the poem's final line removes the mythic cadence of the initial draft, returning it to the realm of everyday despair. In Plath's final version, his responsibility to the past has overwhelmed his legacy: "and his eyes gone blind with leaves" (Lilly Library Plath mss. II. Writings: Poetry—B [Box 7A], Folder 8). The alterations that Plath made in the poem's second draft reveal early signs of her revision process. Here she chooses to focus her descriptive lens on physically quantifiable images rather than on subjective associations. The poem's link to her journal entries demonstrates her ability to translate a particularly strong image from its real-world context to a poetic situation, where it undergoes a series of transformations before reaching its final state of signification. The poem itself enacts the activity of revision, as Plath tries on several ways of understanding the statue's meaning before settling on its simultaneous gesture toward the future ("sunlight warm upon his lips") and imprisonment within the past. This vacillation between an investment in present aesthetic conditions and a dissatisfaction with her environment's social potential continues to develop in her post-Cambridge writings.

As she does with thematic and formal material from some of her other early work, Plath returns to her encounters with the bronze boy statue in two later pieces of writing: a letter to Richard Sassoon on 1 March 1956 and a 1957 story, "Stone Boy with Dolphin." She wrote this letter just a few days after her encounter with Hughes at the *St. Botolph's Review* party; its tone is reflective and nostalgic. Though it had been more than a year since she first wrote about the statue in her diary, here she uses it to explain the reasons why their relationship must end: "you gave me your image, and I made it into stories and poems; I talked about it for a while to everyone and told them it was a bronze statue, a bronze boy with a dolphin, who balanced through the winter in our gardens with snow on his face, which I brushed off every night I visited him" (*LSP1* 1117). After this rumination on the sources of inspiration, Plath returns to the image of the boy with the dolphin one final time, in "Stone Boy with Dolphin." This story, which Hughes chose to include in *Johnny Panic and the Bible of Dreams*, is also the only "sizeable fragment" of her prose written before *The Bell Jar* that later readers can still access (Hughes, "Introduction" 1). Plath includes some descriptive passages in the story that derive from the journal entries and the poem. The main character, Dody Ventura, notes that "she had taken to brushing snow from the face of the winged, dolphin-carrying boy centered in the snow-filled college garden"; more specifically, he is "poised on one foot, wings of stone balancing like feathered fans on the wind, holding his waterless dolphin through the rude, clamorous weathers." In a gesture that mirrors Plath's from two years earlier, Dody "[n]ightly after snows . . . scraped the caked snow from his stone-lidded eyes, and from his plump stone cherub foot" (*JP* 181). "Stone Boy with Dolphin" focuses on Dody's lukewarm experiences in dating while she is a student at Cambridge; Plath repeatedly presents the title image as a reminder of the guarded inner life that Dody turns to in times of disappointment. While venturing out with a friend, Hamish, Dody thinks of her chosen sexual innocence as a means of "nun-tending her statue. Her winged stone statue with nobody's face" (*JP* 185); she imagines during her first physical encounter with the roughly attractive Leonard—a thinly disguised version of Hughes—that the statue's "Stone-lidded eyes crinkled" before it "cracked, splintered, million-pieced" (*JP* 191). The story concludes with Dody sneaking back into her college dormitory after Hamish takes her home from Leonard's party. She can think only of "the unbreakable stone boy in the garden, ironic, with Leonard's look, poised on that sculpted foot, holding fast to his dolphin, stone-lidded eyes fixed on a world beyond" (*JP* 204). By this point in her writing career, a year after meeting and marrying Hughes, Plath had reframed the story of her encounters with the boy statue with reference to his characteristic affect, suggesting that his words and expressive strategies had not only replaced Richard Sassoon's but also motivated her forays into prose. These recursive uses of material—quoted from the original source, revised, and approached from new perspectives—anticipate some of the compositional strategies that Plath developed in her early poetry as well. As Tracy Brain has noted, "Plath habitually turned to a previous piece of writing—usually her own or Ted Hughes's—to revisit or argue with the earlier material, or as creative inspiration" (*The Other* 106). Kathleen Connors agrees, observing that she "returned to her former works at regular intervals to mine them for new art, look into her past, and assess her creative progress" (5); one such instance can be seen in a Smith College painting, "Two Women Reading," a piece for which Plath had already completed a sketch in her senior year high-school history notebook (Connors 36). This methodology—recursive uses of the same material, new perspectives captured through shifts in punctuation and rhythm, images foregrounded through sparse phrasing and symbolic representations—gives us insight into the strategies that emerged across her career and her priorities as a writer.

REVISION AND IDENTITY IN PLATH'S JUVENILIA

Plath works through recursive revisions of original material in "The Dead," a sonnet she wrote while in residence at Smith's Lawrence House (and one of the only examples of juvenilia discussed here whose text Hughes chose to include in *The Collected Poems*).[2] Of the six drafts she preserved, three contain substantial revisions: she wrote corrections in pencil to one, while another adds capital letters to the beginnings of the lines, and the third includes handwritten revisions by Alfred Young Fisher. The poem provides a characteristic example of Plath's tendency to practice traditional forms, while its title points to her modernist roots, recalling Joyce's famous story of the same name. Unlike Joyce's metaphorical usage, though, Plath describes here literal corpses that are "Couched in cauls of clay as in holy robes" and "Rolled round with goodly loam." Her poem sketches a vision of the afterlife without faith or redemption; instead, its inhabitants "loll forever in colossal sleep" that even "God's stern, shocked angels" cannot interrupt (*LSP1* 731). Fisher wrote comments on the manuscript that call specific images into question, including "apple-lobed world" and "some bulb-like bloom" (Plath mss. II. Writings: Poetry—D [Box 7a], Folder 10); these nearly surrealist juxtapositions set the tone for later poems like "Moonrise" and "The Moon and the Yew Tree," which also frame the natural world through metaphors whose tenor and vehicle coexist uneasily. Plath deliberately sets her poetic subject and the object to which it is compared at odds using words—like "bald," "terribly," and "idiot"—that will continue to recur throughout her oeuvre. While Plath had not yet amassed a body of poems large enough to distinguish her particular poetic vocabulary when she wrote "The Dead," its images demonstrate the early development of her diction. Fisher criticizes the poem's "earlier incursions into horror" and warns her against being "too lavish both in auditory and usual imagery" (Plath mss. II. Writings: Poetry—D, Box 7a, Folder 10), but the drafts show that she continued to push her language's expressive capacities to its limits. Critics like Margaret Dickie Uroff, Steven Axelrod, and Adam Kirsch have identified linguistic imitations of predecessors like Robert Lowell and Theodore Roethke in Plath's work. Kirsch calls Roethke "Plath's model" for her work in the late 1950s (254), while Uroff notes that although she had "written poems heavily influenced by Lowell and Roethke . . . she simply took from them the encouragement she needed to develop in her own way" (37). Axelrod describes the "tropes" that Plath borrowed from her predecessors, among them the inspirations for her work on doubles such as "Eliot's striding and rising 'shadow,'" "Roethke's 'shadow pinned against a sweating wall,'" and "Yeats's 'image, man or shade'" (217). Plath worked to reshape these influences in early experiments in formalism like "The Dead."

Professor Fisher also provided comments on Plath's "Sonnet: To a Dissembling Spring," which is preserved in four drafts, the last three of which differ substantially from the first. The comments here encourage her to "[c]onsider the problems of development which the sonnet presents," commending in particular the poem's thematic transition in lines 3–4 and its concluding couplet. Fisher awarded Plath an A- on the poem (which, the note reads, is "the first I've given in poetry") (Lilly Library, Plath mss. II. Writings: Poetry—T, Box 8, Folder 4); however, the piece's subject and central images suggest that it functions more as a means by which to practice the form than as a real effort toward original expression, as the journal entries and the poem on the bronze statue are. Plath noted in a letter to Aurelia on 5 May 1953 that she was "not caring for the poem, and wanting to write over the whole thing to save the last two excellent clinching lines." The final two lines are "Again we are deluded and infer / That somehow we are younger than we were" (*LSP1* 609). "To a Dissembling Spring" represents a paradigmatic example of the experiments in style and form that characterize Plath's work from this period. Their emergence syncs with her poetry's first commentaries on the responsibilities and labors of the writer herself.

Another of Plath's idiosyncratic stylistic devices grew out of her tendency to create portmanteau words meant to capture a unique poetic occasion. The first examples of this type of experiment appear in her work as early as 1949; many of these words help to articulate the difficulties of composition and an emerging sense of the writerly self. One example, "ode on a bitten plum" (a poem that she had written in 1949 and later sold), includes "smokeblue" and "rainwet," though these are later amended to hyphenated words (Lilly Library, Plath mss. II. Writings: Poetry—N-O [Box 8], Folder 1). She also drafted undated poems entitled "Chef d'oeuvre," a pun linking cooking to the craft of writing (Plath mss. II Writings: Poetry—C [Box 7a], Folder 9), and "neveryou" (Plath mss. II. Writings: Poetry—N-O [Box 8], Folder 1). "Doomsday," a 1953 villanelle that also seems to have served as a formal exercise, employs internal rhymes by juxtaposing "And all the actors halt in mortal shock" with "The streets crack through in havoc-split ravines." The poem's metrical regularity also underlines the significance of the rhyme in the repeated lines "The doomstruck city crumbles block by block" and "Our lucky relics have been put in hock."[3] Though the poem's metaphorical description of catastrophe lacks the sparse phrasing and metaphorical precision that exemplify Plath's better-known work, the portmanteaus of "doomstruck" and "havoc-split" demonstrate her typically compact, dense articulation (Lilly Library, Plath mss. II. Writings: Poetry—D [Box 7a], Folder 10). Similar imagery appears in the story "Stone Boy with Dolphin," written four years later. Here Dody Ventura describes the windy weather in which she first meets the mysterious Leonard as filled with "Flags of havoc"; quoting a poem he has just delivered, Dody says, "'Patch the havoc,'" to which Leonard responds, "'Not all their ceremony can patch the havoc'" (*JP* 190). The distinctive sound of "havoc," repeated three times within five lines of the story, inevitably recalls the sound- and image-experiments of "Doomsday." This story also includes a selection of other phrases that resonate with the earlier poem, including "the smoke-burdened air of the party" (*JP* 192), "Hark, hark, the dogs do bark," and "a clocked bonged out. Bong" (*JP* 194). These careful juxtapositions and simple repetitive rhymes prepare the ground for the sparse, declamatory phrasing of the *Ariel* poems. Plath is already practicing a careful economy with her creative material by this stage in her career, recycling especially resonant imagery. As in her stage-by-stage revisions to "The Bronze Boy," both in poetic form and in her journal and letters, the poem relies upon unsettling metaphoric juxtapositions. These surrealist images, and the gradually altering material in which they are couched, contribute to the clearly limned voice that would emerge in her later work.

In addition to her experiments with revised material and portmanteau words, Plath's juvenilia include many poems with lines that are longer and denser than the relatively sparse verse of the *Ariel* poems. This tendency reflects both the varied styles that she tested out and the elements of imitation and re-imagination that the manuscripts reveal. During this period, she also experimented with varying line lengths by shifting different poems' enjambments; perhaps as a means of deciding on a piece's desired effect, she highlights these semantic changes through variations in capitalization, punctuation, and left indents. Her close attention to such stylistic and syntactic details illustrates one of her poetry's most significant legacies: the vital role that subtle shifts in language use play in communicating the evolution of the philosophies that her poetic speakers articulate. The first draft of "Twilight," for instance, which exists in two versions in the Lilly Library archives, contains ten lines while the second includes only eight. While the first draft incorporates the title into the poem's text and the second does not, there is only one other difference in wording between them, an added "all" in the final line of draft two. Draft one eschews capitalization entirely, except in the opening line and in the first-person pronoun:

> Twilight:
> to know that I
> am free to sleep
> oblivious,
> yet in the deep gray corridor between
> a dream
> and waking,
> to muse upon a memory
> that I would keep
> from forsaking.

Draft two adds a capital letter to the beginning of each line and changes the line breaks:

> To know that I am free to sleep
> Oblivious,
> Yet in the deep
> Gray corridor between a dream
> And waking
> To muse upon a memory
> That I would keep
> From all forsaking. (Plath mss. II. Writings: Poetry—T [Box 8], Folder 4)

Here Plath exchanges the iambic dimeter of the first draft's initial lines for a more conventional iambic tetrameter. This shift demonstrates her consistent interest in metric regularity; she also employs three instances of rhyme that underline the poem's relatively mundane subject. Though this poem does not reveal any tension between the speaker and a lyric object, it provides a way for her to explore the roles that line breaks and meter play in making meaning.

In addition to the development of some of Plath's characteristic compositional devices in these early pieces—neologisms and portmanteau words, reused material, repeated words, regularized meters, and dissonant, almost surrealist imagery—she experiments here with markers of personal and professional identity. Among the drafts of her poetry written between 1947 and 1957, she includes three pseudonyms that suggest a keen interest in imagining a new version of her creative self. She attributes "A Ballad," the first two drafts of "Fog," the first four drafts of "Go Get the Goodly Squab," "In Passing," "Lonely Song," "Song of a Superfluous Spring," and "Spinning Song" to "Sandra Peters," for instance; she gave the author's name for the early sonnet "Doom of Exiles" as Alison Arnold. She also typed on the title page of the unpublished manuscript collection *Circus in Three Rings* that it was "by Marcia Moore" (Lilly Library, Plath mss. II. Writings—*Circus in Three Rings*, Box 8, Folder 7). Many artists have similarly identified themselves, but Plath's three alternative selves here resonate with other familiar biographical details. Both her friend and Smith College roommate, Marcia Brown Stern, and Marianne Moore may have inspired the Marcia Moore pseudonym; the latter's one encounter with Plath and Hughes is the subject of Hughes's *Birthday Letter* poem "The Literary Life."[4] All three names' trochaic rhythm also recall the autobiographical heroine of *The Bell Jar*, Esther Greenwood. Most importantly, the names demonstrate that Plath laid claim to her identity from the start of her writing career. She not only cultivated an assortment of distinctive compositional techniques but also imagined what labels might best fit her own sense of self.

Plath evidenced a similar concern with self-presentation in the types of proprietary markings she made on draft copies. Some manuscripts—such as "April Aubade," which she wrote at 4 Barton Road in Cambridge; *Circus in Three Rings*, which she wrote at Smith College's Lawrence House; "The Grackles," written at 26 Elmwood Road in Wellesley; and "Snakecharmer," which she composed while living at 9 Willow Street in Boston—include handwritten details about geographical location and current occupation. Others bear her initials, a fuller version of her name (such as the "Sylvia Plath Hughes" that graces the manuscript of "Full Fathom Five"), or a dedication; she labeled "Have You Forgotten?," drafted in 1948, with the letters "P.N.," for Perry Norton, the older brother of her high-school boyfriend Dick Norton.[5] She also signed "Candles," written in December 1960, "for Mrs. Prouty / with love / Sylvia" (Lilly Library, Plath mss. II. Writings: Poetry—C [Box 7a], Folder 9). Olive Prouty, who helped to fund Plath's college education, remained a close friend until Plath's death (Bronfen viii). In a manner similar to Hughes's tendency to recycle paper from other aspects of his work, too, Plath often drafted her work on Smith College memorandum paper; the aura of her formal education and first professional position seems to infuse much of her creative identity. These pink manuscript drafts remain one of the most familiar archival sights for Plath scholars.

In the early manuscripts, Plath also employs compositional techniques that resemble jazz improvisation: she tries out sampling and repetitions-with-a-difference as important preliminary steps to the poetic borrowing and imitation that would become central strategies in some of her later poems. "In Passing," from 1949, contains the phrase "wet black boughs" (Plath mss. II. Writings: Poetry—G-I [Box 7a], Folder 12), which might have been lifted straight from Ezra Pound's "In a Station of the Metro." Her "Incident" recalls Countee Cullen's poem of the same name, while "Spring Again" (1948) could be an indirect tribute to William Carlos Williams's "Spring and All." Plath's themes and rhetoric in "Voices" also suggest that she borrowed more substantial material from her precursors while she was working out her own style. In this case, the last stanza of the poem's first draft contains the lines "I have spent my days / Listening to the murmur / Of voices / In another room" (Lilly Library, Plath mss. II. Writings: Poetry—U-Z [Box 8], Folder 5); this passage recalls the fifth stanza of "The Love Song of J. Alfred Prufrock," which ends with "I know the voices dying with a dying fall / Beneath the music from a farther room" (Eliot 5). The connection to Eliot also underlines the influences that New Critical writers exercised upon her early poems. In addition, Plath's 1959 "Poem for a Birthday" has often been compared to the poems in which Theodore Roethke explored personal trauma, such as the sequences of the 1958 collection *Words for the Wind* (Middlebrook, *Her Husband* 109). Finally, drawing from similar sources of inspiration, Plath's "Epitaph in Three Parts" recalls Thomas Gray's "Elegy Written in a Country Churchyard" in setting, theme, and mood.

Plath's three years of honors English study with high-school teacher Wilbury Crockett introduced her to many of these writers and encouraged her emerging interests in socialist politics, community service, and socially responsive writing (Connors 49). He argued, in fact, that writing could be "a means to advance" social justice (Hammer 151), and he required his students to read more than forty works of classical literature each year (Wilson 60), much of which exercised an influence on Plath's developing style.[6] She believed that he had "fostered [her] intellectual life" throughout high school (*UJ* 65); close friend Philip McCurdy called her a "'crocketeer,' one of Crockett's intellectuals," who also "'loved learning' and 'responded particularly well to Crockett's classes'" (qtd. in Wilson 63). Though Plath often imitated admired predecessors in order to find a place for her work within an already familiar poetic landscape, she also sought real-world sources and goals for her work. Both aspects of her poetics demonstrate the scope of her background knowledge and prepare the ground for her later poems that addressed Hughes's work directly; these pieces would draw upon borrowed material in order to voice a critique, rather than positioning her writing within an already established field. Robin Peel suggests that her poems "need to be considered as a series of texts, each one a reworking of its predecessor" since "each is certainly a new text in its own right, but one which clearly and deliberately draws on what has gone before" (156). Thus her techniques of borrowing, revision, and imitation would enable Plath to challenge artistic conventions that she saw in both Hughes's work and the more general community of writers.

Plath's work eventually exercised a significant influence over others' writings as well, as several critics have noted.[7] In some of these cases, images that first appeared in her poetry seem to resonate with her contemporaries or with later writers, as Roethke's did with hers, but her poetry also inspired others to incorporate elements of her work into their own. In one instance, she chose to end her most famous tribute to motherhood, "Morning Song," with an image that reappears in the work of former teacher Robert Lowell. "Morning Song" concludes with the child's voice: "And now you try / Your handful of notes; / The clear vowels rise like balloons." This image captures the delicate boldness of a baby whose voice rings forth purely, with no history or social ties; the poem's simple diction suggests the mother's awe at this new life, an emotion that compensates for her sense that she is "cow-heavy and floral / In my Victorian nightgown" (*CPP* 157). Readers familiar with Lowell's work in his 1959 National Book Award-winning *Life Studies* and its companion volume, the 1964 *For the Union Dead*, will recall his allusion to contemporary racial tensions in the latter collection's title piece. Reflecting on Boston's changed landscape since the Civil War, the speaker observes the ways in which human violence resurfaces with every new public conflict. In spite of the age's technological advances, he notes that "When I crouch to my television set, / the drained faces of Negro school-children rise like balloons" (Lowell 72). Though Plath had studied with Lowell at Boston University much earlier than this poem was drafted, in 1958 and 1959 (Clark 179), his foreword to the 1965 edition of *Ariel*—in which he calls her "one of those super-real, hypnotic, great classical heroines" (vii)—indicates that he retained a fascination with her work. Lowell reframes this striking image to comment on the most divisive social issue of his day, lending it a political acuity that it lacks in Plath's poem. However, her original image preserves the child's innocence—an inversion of the "drained faces" that Lowell's poetic speaker describes—in order to recuperate the poem's other images of the new parents' weariness and uncertainty. The baby's initial comparison to "a fat gold watch" and her lonely, "bald cry" are mitigated by her voice's "clear vowels," the obvious miracle of her attempts to communicate (*CPP* 156–57).

Another clear example of Plath's influence over her contemporaries can be seen in Anne Sexton's "Sylvia's Death," which was first published in the January 1964 issue of *Poetry* magazine, less than a year after Plath's death. Although Sexton might seem to fuel the belief that she and Plath are self-defined Confessional writers with this piece, it serves as a carefully structured tribute to some of Plath's familiar strategies and images, and as a recognition of the unique talents that they each possessed. Plath had sent Sexton a letter in August 1962 congratulating her on *All My Pretty Ones*, which she called "superbly masterful, womanly in the greatest sense, and so blessedly unliterary" (*LSP2* 812). "Sylvia's Death" includes several instances of Plath's signature repetitions, iterations of both objects and exclamations. Sexton addresses her subject using a lyric voice, apostrophizing her absent friend in a manner that recalls the most traditional uses of the device: "(O Sylvia, Sylvia, / where did you go / after you wrote me / from Devonshire / about raising potatoes / and keeping bees?).” These familiar references to Plath's domestic life at Court Green are couched in a style that closely resembles her own, including short lines, frequent enjambments, and occasional parentheses. Sexton's image of Frieda and Nicholas, "two children, two meteors" (224), echoes Plath's "two children, two roses," from "Kindness" (*CPP* 270), while several words that recur frequently in Plath's oeuvre are scattered across the poem: "dumb," "terrible," "sleepy," and "mole" (Sexton 224–26). Sexton concludes with an intimate picture of Plath that, again, mirrors her diction but also acknowledges the impact her work has already had on the world, literary and otherwise: "O tiny mother, / you too! / O funny duchess! / O blonde thing!" (226). Like Lowell and Hughes, Sexton learned from Plath's idiomatic syntax and borrowed some particularly effective imagery. The fact that these poets drew inspiration from passages of Plath's work testifies to the powerful originality of her compositional techniques.

DIALOGUE AND DEBATE IN THE LATER WORKS

Lowell, Sexton, and Hughes incorporated material from Plath's work into individual poems using several different compositional approaches. As Plath worked through drafts of her mature poems, she drew on some of the same strategies for rewording individual pieces and intensifying her work's rhetorical impact. In her early drafts of "Tulips," "Thalidomide," and "Kindness," for instance, she focuses on subtle shifts in punctuation and rhythm and crafts sparsely populated lines as a means of foregrounding central images. Taken together, these strategies contribute to a distinctive vocabulary through which Plath began to articulate the positions on creation and artistic responsibility that represent a key dimension of her mature style. As Scott Knickerbocker has pointed out, the images of nature that often appear in these pieces illustrate "her use of poetic devices as a response to her environmental concerns and sympathies," which help to articulate her "*ars poetica* and philosophy toward language in general" (9).

"Thalidomide," alternately titled "Half-Moon" in seven of Plath's handwritten and typed drafts, displays at first a dense wordiness seen more often in her pre-*Ariel* writings. The first draft found in Holograph no. 2 in Smith's Sylvia Plath Collection contains ten lines that have been partially or fully crossed out during the revision process. "Spidery, unsafe," the line beginning the fourth stanza of the poem's published version, is followed in this holograph by "The zoo's bird-eater, big abortion! / That abortion! / Hair-legged hand of a big man," all of which Plath has struck through. These original lines link the poem's genesis to a specific setting and agent, both of which she eliminates in order to allow for indeterminacy in the final version. This revision also removes indicators of specific animals, allowing bestial signs to emerge gradually through the remaining "Knuckles at shoulder-blades" and "two wet eyes and a screech": her subject is named, in the end, only "the thing I am given" (*CPP* 252). In contrast, Plath's early drafts of this passage include more physical details and names, as though the speaker were attempting to delimit the drug's bodily effects and to tie them to a particular level of intelligence, an attitude, a racial identity, and even a gender: "I am making a place in the heart / For the thing I am given, the [illegible] bloodclot / The suicide, the idiot, / two blue eyes and a screech, / The wrong side of the moon and the teeth that hurt / The swell of perilous slumber" (Holograph 2). Though reading this passage with the deleted phrases intact recalls Plath's taxonomic approach in poems like "Daddy" and "In Plaster," their elimination enables her to depict the aura of the "thing" rather than the subject itself. Such a symbolic rather than literal methodology marks the development of Plath's mature style. In an article examining the analogic relationship between allegory and psychoanalysis, Barbara Johnson notes that "[p]ersonification and anthropomorphism," features present in this early draft of "Thalidomide," "are also identifying marks of allegory—excessive, rather than inadequate, rhetorical representation." In this reading of the preliminary versions of Plath's work, then, the "thing I am given" is not just "an object of representation" but "either a representation obscured or an unrepresentableness represented, an unspeakableness spoken" (Johnson, "Allegory" 67). As she attempts to capture the essence of her poetic subject, Plath identifies its unrepresentable nature through these multiplying, repetitive images. Though she decided to eliminate some of the images' rhetorical excess in the final version of the poem, Plath's drafts give us additional insight into the concerns that continued to inform her poetics, particularly the stresses of creative and personal relationships and the purpose of one's existence.

Adding another rhetorical technique to her compositional arsenal, Plath experiments with the expressive possibilities of description and Althusserian interpellation in Holograph 2's second draft of "Thalidomide." In this version, Plath follows "two blue eyes and a screech" with "The moon's backside

/ ~~The swell of perilous slumber.~~ / Smiles and perfections, a slumber / ~~Perilous, thin as an eyelid~~. / A slumber of accident and indifference / You turn and turn. / Perilous, thin ~~as an eyelid~~. / Dark fruit! / ~~An eyelid, a leaf of ice~~. / O unholy light, of accident and indifference / Child's eyelid, / ~~A leaf of ice!~~ / ~~It turns and turns~~ / White spit / Nothingness! Black ox!" This draft provides a fascinating example of Plath's revision process, which includes repetitions-with-a-difference—what Christina Britzolakis has labeled "a compulsive, magical, or gnostic ritual" (*Theatre* 54)—as she searches for the correct visual and narrative placement of phrases and individual words. Certain phrases—including "thin as an eyelid" and "leaf of ice"—did not survive in the published version, despite their multiple incarnations here. This approach to figurative language, which attempts to pinpoint a unique emotional experience through an accumulating series of metaphors and similes, is more common in her earlier work. Many of her later pieces incorporate relatively simple but often surrealist adjective-noun pairs instead. These repeated references to "eyelid" and "backside" anticipate the fixation on bodily experience that recurs throughout her work, often as a means of representing the creative process itself.

In order to achieve the regular two-line stanzas and short, sparse lines of the final version of "Thalidomide," Plath cuts phrases that offer several perspectives on the same aspect of her subject, choosing instead to limit the poem's descriptive phrases to a single snapshot of each drug-deformed feature. This draft ends on the same type of exclamatory note present in many of the October poems, though the final images of her subject that she offers—"Nothingness! Black ox!"—are absent from the published version. These phrases suggest a self-contradictory perspective on the poem's theme, an abortive offspring that both fades from sight and solidly occupies space: one that not only demands the speaker's attention but also subverts her potential role as mother and creator. This paradoxical view is aligned with at least one famous poem on the hope and fear associated with the writing process: Anne Bradstreet's "The Author to Her Book," which imagines her work as "Thou ill-form'd offspring of my feeble brain" (221). Plath's own views on the near impossibility of producing satisfactory work also appear in the "establishments which imagined lines / Can only haunt" of "Poems, Potatoes" (*CPP* 106), and in "Stillborn," whose "poems do not live: it's a sad diagnosis" (*CPP* 142). As Susan Van Dyne has noted, "Plath was determined to prove that writing and maternity were both inherent expressive needs of female sexual identity"; though she sought out and reveled in both, she found them to be "fearful ordeals with uncertain outcomes" (6). Since she saw "making poems and making babies [as] persistent metaphors for each other," Plath seems to have wondered whether "their inevitable separateness questions rather than affirms her identity as their maker" (Van Dyne 144–45). Poems like "Half-Moon/Thalidomide," "Poems, Potatoes," and "Stillborn" render this concern an extended metaphor for the artistic uncertainty that the *ars poetica* is meant to redress.

Plath's goal while working through these drafts seems to have been to sharpen her focus on the physical act and tangible effects of writing. In fact, in the 4 November 1962 typescript of "Half-Moon" that appears next in the Smith collection, she introduces the new images that will ultimately sustain the poem's conclusion. These images resonate with the concerns about desire, isolation, and creativity that she follows throughout both her own work and her poetry's intertexts. Crossing out "A slumber, / Perilous, thin, / O unholy night, / Child's eyelid, / White spit / Of accident and indifference! / Nothingness! Black ox!," she tries again with "Sleep" alone, then with "Imperilled [sic] sleep, / Fearful as an eyelid" and then finally with "Sleep, perilous" and "Sleep, thin as an eyelid. / O white spit." Only the last of these phrases remains untouched on the page, underscoring her interest in the traumatic consequences that difficult articulations enact upon the body itself. As Van Dyne notes, these carefully parsed images reflect Plath's interest, after her children's births, in "fragmented body parts, hyperbolically reduplicated but never become fully human"; her revisions gradually render the poem's images "less appealing" and intentionally foreclose any sort of "sentimental response" (153). Rather than concluding with "Black ox!," too, a specific image that diverges from the poem's other more figurative representations, she adds in three images that resonate with other texts. "The dark fruits revolve and fall," the speaker notes, "O moon-smoke, / Unholy light! / The glass cracks across, / The image / Flees and aborts like dropped mercury." Though Plath ultimately chose to cross out the second and third lines of this passage, in their original form these poetic visions suggest a distance from the subject, something viewed through an instrument. This sense of allegorical meaning is appropriate to Plath's literary antecedents here, which may include Christina Rossetti and Alfred, Lord Tennyson. Rossetti's most famous work, the 1862 long poem "Goblin Market," describes the material consequences of giving in to temptation through a story of two young sisters who meet a group of goblin-men selling magical fruit. Their "dark fruits" threaten the life of one sister, Laura, until her stronger-willed sister Lizzie rescues her by physically resisting the goblins' attempts to stuff the fruit into her mouth. Plath also references Tennyson's poem "The Lady of Shalott" through the "glass [that] cracks across." In Tennyson's Arthurian narrative, the Lady is imprisoned in a tower, embroidering tapestries and watching the world go by through a window reflected in a mirror mounted on the wall. It is not until Lancelot comes riding past that she forgets she is bound to remain apart from the world of men, looks directly out the window to admire him, and suffers her fate. As Tennyson puts it, once she turns her back on the mirror in order to gaze out the window, "The mirror crack'd from side to side; / 'The curse is come upon me!' cried / The Lady of Shalott" (24). Both poems remind their readers that yielding to self-indulgent pleasures is dangerous, yet—using figurative imagery that suits their Romantic origins—they also indicate that one only gains true moral insight through personal risk. Here, through Johnson's notion of "excessive rhetorical representation," Plath explores the isolation that women creators experience—whether they are writers or mothers, or both. The poem concludes that punishment, here imagined as deformity rather than as offspring or a creative invention, will result.

In the five succeeding typescripts of the poem, now titled "Thalidomide," Plath makes more subtle changes to her gradually narrowing portrait of physical transformation. She cuts "All night" from the start of the third line of the second typescript, for instance, in order to bring forward the final lines of this stanza, "Your dark / Amputations crawl and appal [sic]." These revisions unmoor the poetic narrative from the usual markers of time, drawing readers' attention instead to the erratic movements and sounds that her subject produces. The poem's focus thus reverts to the speaker's experiences with physical damage and lack. From "Flower faces that / Shove into being, dragging / The lopped / Blood-caul of absences" she eliminates "flower" in the third typescript, and there also makes the important decision to revise "two blue eyes and a screech" by substituting "wet" for "blue." This adjustment removes identifiable personal markers, deliberately rendering the subject ambiguous.

Written in November 1962, just after the furious outpouring of "October poems," the drafts of "Thalidomide" suggest Plath's slowly evolving perspective on a type of creation that is misguided or deceptive. The malformed efforts that the speaker identifies occur in a realm beyond her control, but they profoundly affect her physical capabilities. Plath's editorial decisions here focus on both the tactile experiences of invention and the factors that misdirect it. The final title fixes the poem within a particular historical moment but shifts the narrative attention away from its medical definition to a more general sense of failed creation. In this poem, Plath complicates conventional perspectives on the experiences of both writing and parenting itself, perhaps anticipating Adrienne Rich's famous 1976 critique in "Motherhood in Bondage." Her evolving composition process, as articulated in the drafts of "Thalidomide," reflects a dissatisfaction with the controls exerted upon women's ability to create, whether literally or figuratively. As Rich argues, "the pressure on all women to assent to the 'mothering' role is intense" and defiance of that role means "to challenge deeply embedded phobias and prejudices" (197). While Plath's 1963 death meant that she produced all her work before the widespread emergence of second-wave politics like those Rich espouses, she addresses similar problems through this piece's ambivalent attitude toward motherhood and, by extension, the literary advances through which writers challenge established tradition.

Plath's "Tulips" offers another rich illustration of her attempts, through the drafting process, to locate a series of precise analogues to the experiences of the working poet. In the earliest handwritten draft from 1961, she titles the poem "Sickroom Tulips" and tries out several versions of the poem's central images; these repetitions-with-a-difference resemble those in the first drafts of "Thalidomide." The long, dense lines of "Sickroom Tulips" enable Plath to explore the everyday details of a domestic setting in tension with the speaker's desire for independence and self-driven innovation. The first stanza, whose initial line survives intact in the final version, includes material that would become the published first and second stanzas of "Tulips." Plath's speaker observes, "Look how white everything is, the walls, my bed / Tight white with its sheets a light blanket for the line and eyelid / And my head opens like a pupil between the pillow and sheet-cuff. / Stupidly as a pupil, it has to take everything in" (Smith Autograph 1). These lines exist in altered form in stanza one of the published poem, which limits the white imagery to just three lines: "Look how white everything is, how quiet, how snowed-in. / I am learning peacefulness, lying by myself quietly / As the light lies on these white walls, this bed, these hands." The famous image that pictures the poetic speaker lying in bed as a "stupid pupil" begins stanza two, at line 8: "They have propped my head between the pillow and the sheet-cuff / Like an eye between two white lids that will not shut. / Stupid pupil, it has to take everything in" (*CPP* 160). In her revisions to this first draft example, Plath defines the room's fittings, the "walls" and "bed," as sources of comfort through their utilitarian impersonality. The passage personifies an inanimate object, endowing it with jarringly alien traits, in order to underline the disjunction the speaker perceives between the inert fact of her history and her physical desire to work alone. The speaker feels a sense of disconnection from her family life; in rejecting those ties, she seeks an alternate vision of herself.

In the third and fourth stanzas of "Sickroom Tulips," Plath auditions images of "my overnight bag like a black patent leather pill box" and the speaker "Hanging onto my name and address stubbornly as money" (Smith Autograph 1), neither of which appears in the published poem. Though she alters the first of these images to "My patent leather overnight case like a black pillbox" and the second to "Stubbornly hanging on to my name and address" (*CPP* 160–61), the corrections underscore the significance of her narrator's personal possessions while eliminating a simile that links her private experiences in the hospital to the social world of interaction and exchange. Again, these editorial decisions indicate Plath's interest in paring down excess as well as claiming an independent space for the poem's speaker; she eschews discordant images (a "black patent leather pill box") in favor of describing the most basic actions necessary for survival. "They have swabbed me clear of my loving associations" (*CPP* 161), the third line of the third published stanza, is absent from this first draft; instead, Plath tries out and rejects such images of purging as "I watched my identity recede: they tied up my hair / In a gauze bandage they taped / My wedding ring to my finger with white adhesive" (Smith Autograph 1). In these lines, all of which Plath crossed out in this draft, the speaker lists specific personal effects. The lines that replace them (which also appear on the draft page), "I watched my teasets, my bureaus of linen, my books / Sink out of sight and the water went over my head" (*CPP* 161), remove the source of pain from the speaker's own body, distancing her trauma from her immediate experience so that she can grapple with its narrative implications. The draft of the fifth stanza of "Sickroom Tulips" also includes a passage cut before the final version, "Bouquets are for arrivals, departures or sweet connecting / And I have gone and come, but I'm not back yet" (Smith Autograph 2). Plath's decision to cut these lines is consistent with the poem's overall mood, which grows out of the speaker's desire to detach herself from both personal and social spheres and to disappear, instead, within the anonymity of the hospital environment. The confidence with which Plath endows the final version of her speaker, after working through the drafts, suggests that this detachment helps to produce effective self-expression, a key element of the composition process. In a discussion of Gwendolyn Brooks's poem "The Mother," Barbara Johnson notes that some women poets have reworked apostrophe's lyric function in order to position absent children in the position once occupied by the general dead. Critics have traditionally understood apostrophe as both distancing the speaker from the lyric object and calling into question language's ability to describe experience accurately; the difference for Brooks's speaker and for Plath's is the painful "vividness of the contact" between speaker and object, the inability to achieve a distance from the lost loved one ("Apostrophe" 32). Jonathan Culler adds that apostrophes "serve as intensifiers, as images of invested passion," and as devices "spontaneously adapted by passion" that signify, "metonymically, the passion that caused [them]" (60–61). Plath does not address a missing child directly in these lines, yet the speaker's attempts to distance herself from her immediate surroundings and to redirect her internal emotions inform the poem's lyric message. In Britzolakis's terms, Plath's use of apostrophe in this and similar poetic situations marks her "investment in metaphors of lyric voice," in order to "vivify inanimate objects" but also to "ward off the narcissistic fear that one will *not* see oneself reflected in objects" (*Theatre* 106–7). The repeated addresses that Plath's speaker makes to the tulips gives them life while emphasizing her anxiety about the restrictions they may place on her.

These first few revisions to "Sickroom Tulips" seem to have been relatively minor ones, aimed at clarifying the relationship between the speaker's physical trauma and her growing tendency to observe her situation, so that she can learn how to facilitate her own creative interpretation of the world rather than allowing herself to become immersed in it. As is evident in the drafts, Plath struggled especially to articulate the poem's eighth stanza, in which she draws a comparison between the tulips' aggressive color and the disruptive noises around her. Here her repetition-with-a-difference strategy illuminates the difficulty of identifying the sources of the speaker's antipathy, the moments when she decides to distance herself from her family and the social environment in order to create something alone. Crossed out in this first draft are "Even now the air snags and clamoring for attention / There they stand, with the air snagging on them / The way stream water snags on some rust-red engine"; Plath allowed "Now the air snags and eddies around them as a river / Snags and eddies round some sunken rust-red engine" to stand as the following lines, and she repeats them again in the final version of this passage on the same page (Smith Autograph 3). The revisions she makes by cutting "clamoring" and by reorganizing the poem's final stanza reimagine the tulips as threatening yet inert, conveying an innate sense of menace. The speaker's position as witness to the poetic scene allows her to achieve distance from it; she controls the terms of its narration rather than yielding to it by "sharpen[ing] the dichotomies in the poem" and by delaying the tulips' appearance to the very end (Van Dyne 92). After the first line of the final stanza, "The walls, also, seem to be warming themselves," Plath crosses out "For the tulips are egotistical" and "The tulips are dangerous" (Smith Autograph 3), choosing figurative language instead: "The tulips should be behind bars like dangerous animals; / They are opening like the mouth of some great African cat" (*CPP* 162).[8] These lines express a desire to limit the tulips' agency. Plath creates a sense of control over this symbolic intrusion of the social world by framing the flowers in figurative terms and by choosing the analogues that best contain their obnoxious traits.

Most of the comparative language that Plath employs to describe the tulips suggests that they are dangerous, yet she also indicates that they only threaten the speaker. The final revisions to the draft of "Sickroom Tulips" preserve the sense that the poetic narrator seeks to cut herself off from emotion: Plath first writes, "The water I weep comes from another country" (Smith Autograph 3), before amending it to the final version, "The water I taste is warm and salt, like the sea / And comes from a country far away as health" (*CPP* 162). As in her re-visions of the tulips themselves, she deletes a phrase with literal meaning in favor of a figurative representation; the two similes that conclude the poem underscore the speaker's detachment. Though she weeps, the speaker does not express sadness, and she names her illness without wishing for a return to good health. Wagner-Martin reads this revision as a shift away from the "faintly nostalgic mood of 'another country' to a comparison with her touchstone . . . the sea" (*Literary* 67). These changes also suggest that the speaker seeks to redirect the energy that the tulips' violent presence conveys. Isolated, divested of the weight of familial expectations, she focuses instead on the new uses to which she can put her mind. In its final form, the poem thus argues that an alien setting, in this case the hospital bed, allows the poetic speaker to pursue her own thought, independent of society or the home. As an *ars poetica*, the piece models a rupture in the patterns of everyday life as a necessary precursor to creation. Wagner-Martin also describes it as "more of a sounding board for her current state of disarray than it is a finished or polished philosophical prolegomenon" (*Literary* 70); the poem and its drafts try out some of the expressive techniques that contribute to Plath's overall approach without committing to a single, overarching statement on the nature of successful art.

This draft of "Sickroom Tulips," originally held in the Woodberry Poetry Room of the Houghton Library collection at Harvard, is preserved with a letter from Plath to former curator John Lincoln Sweeney, in which she describes her work as emerging "out of my weekly holocaust of draft sheets" (Smith Autograph Letter). The poem was evidently drafted during a happily productive period in Plath's and Hughes's marriage; she writes to tell Sweeney of their recent purchase of Court Green, and the letter's verso contains a poem by Hughes, written to Frieda at six months of age. A later 1961 draft, by which time Plath had amended the title to "Tulips," contains a few minor revisions that adjust adjectives and adverbs to suit the poem's final version. It was first published in *The New Yorker* on 7 April 1962; Plath records this information at the top of a typescript produced at her 3 Chalcot Square address in London. She also makes a handwritten note at the page's left margin, "New Yorker / Mermaid Festival 1961 / March 18, 1961" (Smith Typescript 1). This annotation records the fact that Plath read the poem at London's Mermaid Theatre as part of a "Poetry at the Mermaid Festival"; eleven other poets were also featured on the program, including Hughes. Interestingly, though the poem makes reference to well-known autobiographical details from Plath's life, the markings on its drafts capture the professional success and creative energy that Plath enjoyed during this period. The revision strategies that she evidences here—including shifts to symbolic rather than literal representations of her poetic subjects, repetitions-with-a-difference, increasing semantic ambiguity, and a focus on her subject's potential for commentary on the act of writing itself—recur throughout the poems she wrote between October 1962 and February 1963. These later poems register, in addition, Plath's growing tendency to articulate her subjects through carefully crafted allegory rather than metaphor.

One key example of Plath's investment in allegorical representation exists in "Kindness," which she wrote in February 1963. Her revisions to the drafts of this piece center on "Dame Kindness," a figure whose ironic depiction may comment on the distinctions between professional and personal relationships. Originally imagined as "Godmother Kindness," the titular character first "sips" and then "glides" "about my house"; the mirrors in which she is reflected "Ripple with smiles" in the first handwritten draft and then "Are filling with smiles" (Smith Holograph). Though these alterations are relatively small, they illustrate the poem's allegorical functions: both to annotate the situation in question and to distance oneself from it. As Barbara Johnson has observed, allegory always has a Manichean structure, in which one term is "segregated" from the other in either racial or sexual terms ("Allegory" 67–68). Plath depicts no direct interactions between people in the poem; instead, they see the reflections of each other's smiles under the watchful eye of a proper "Dame." Plath points to the empty nature of superficial "kindness" with the observation that "she is so nice!" The properties of Dame Kindness, a metonym of social propriety, are articulated through reflective surfaces, including mirrors, "blue and red jewels," windows, crystals, and silks. Only the poem's fourth and final stanza is written on the draft page without revision: "And here you come, with a cup of tea / Wreathed in steam. / The blood jet is poetry, / There is no stopping it. / You hand me two children, two roses" (*CPP* 270; Smith Holograph). These images tie creative work to domestic life; the two poetic characters' interactions are reduced simply to passing symbolic objects—children, roses—from one to the other. Though this stanza contains one of Plath's most famous statements on the act of composition itself, the poem retains a dimension of controversy. She extracted an image from Hughes's radio play *Difficulties of a Bridegroom*, broadcast on the BBC on 21 January 1963, in which "a man driving to a sexual liaison sees a rabbit in the road and accelerates to kill it; on arrival in the city he sells the dead animal for two shillings and buys two roses for his mistress" (Middlebrook, *Her Husband* 172). In Plath's poem, this gift undergoes a Medea-like transformation into children. Additionally, Hughes chose to include "Kindness" in the 1965 version of *Ariel*, yet it was not present in Plath's original layout for the book (and thus does not appear in *Ariel 1*). The second typescript of the poem contained in Smith's collection includes Plath's final London address, 23 Fitzroy Road, at the top. We know, therefore, that it was written during the couple's final separation, just before Plath's death, and its drafts may reflect an incomplete version of the piece, rather than a final vision. However, the speaker's actions—rejecting the superficial offerings of "Dame Kindness," listening to "the cry of a child" (*CPP* 269), pouring forth poetry, receiving tea, children, and roses from an unnamed partner—add to the body of Plath's commentary on poetry's instructive, self-reflexive functions.

ACTION AND AGENCY:
THE CASE OF "THE RABBIT CATCHER"

As I discuss in more detail in chapter 4, several of Hughes's later poems, especially those collected in *Birthday Letters* and *Howls and Whispers,* respond to certain of Plath's poems by annotating the narratives she describes, as in pieces like "The Earthenware Head" and "The Shot," while others reimagine the story she told or offer a contrasting perspective on the same scene. Though *Birthday Letters* was published in 1998, thirty-five years after Plath's death and thirty-three years after Hughes edited the first edition of *Ariel*, it engages with specific passages from poems that she wrote as early as 1957, not only reflecting Plath's aesthetic and rhetorical choices but also casting her subjects in new terms. Plath's drafts from 1962 and 1963 illustrate the unique compositional strategies that she had consolidated before this period. At the same time, her poetic subjects—born in part from the strong emotions that she associated with Hughes as well as the daily struggles she faced in caring for two young children alone, in an isolated house in the English countryside—inflect the manuscript pages with a sense of urgency. The drafts' many strike-throughs leave her rejected phrases almost fully visible while demonstrating the complex strategies she used to create her pieces. Hughes incorporates several of these strategies and meditates on her aesthetic preoccupations in his 1998 collections.

"The Rabbit Catcher," which Plath began in May 1962, presents a paradigmatic example of her approach to composition. Many critics, including Tracy Brain, Heather Clark, Jo Gill, Diane Middlebrook, Yvonne Reddick, and Jacqueline Rose, have commented on the ties between this poem and Hughes's companion piece, also titled "The Rabbit Catcher." Middlebrook speculates, for instance, that "no poem by Sylvia Plath or Ted Hughes is more dense with literary resonance than the poems they titled 'The Rabbit Catcher'"; Plath's poem describes, she claims, the means by which "[her] creativity has been enthralled by marriage to the man she identified with D. H. Lawrence" ("Creative" 256, 262). Hughes's piece, on the other hand, engages in "dialogue with . . . its resistance to him, and where it was coming from" (Middlebrook, "Creative" 264). In a slightly different take on Lawrence's influence, Tracy Brain argues that Plath's female narrator borrows some language from Lawrence's "Love on the Farm" but instead of opposing her to the man she desires, "dramatizes her ambivalent fear of, and desire for, the man" through depictions of his hands and the objects they use (*The Other* 127). As a part of the general critical consensus on the poem's historical significance, Jacqueline Rose describes its draft and publication process as a metonym of "the sexual confrontation which it represents at the level of theme," noting that Hughes excluded it from the 1965 edition of *Ariel* (135). Yvonne Reddick also identifies Hughes's attempt to correct Plath, suggesting that "repeated images of pursuit and hunting, drawn from Hughes and Plath's shared poetic mythos, show that Hughes wished to redress the image of him as a sadistic hunter" (302). Heather Clark's reading views Hughes's poem, in fact, as a reversed or mirrored perspective on the poetic situation: he "portrayed Plath as she portrayed him at the end of her 'Rabbit Catcher'—as a cruel and merciless hunter" (*Grief* 233). Sarah Churchwell sees the poem, in the most abstracted critical terms, as "a palimpsest of Hughes's reaction to Malcolm's discussion of Hughes's reaction to Rose's reading of Plath's poem" ("Secrets" 133): in other words, as an intervention in the public history of Plath's poem more than an independent work in its own right. In her piece, Plath interrogates the English landscapes in which her marriage had begun to disintegrate, reading the country's characteristic traits as signs of the speaker's stifled creativity; Hughes, on the other hand, turns the poem's emphasis away from rabbit-catching as a metaphor for personal wrongs to the practice's historical roots. Jo Gill sees this disparity as evidence of "a crisis of cross-cultural communication" between the two writers, which Hughes dramatizes as a conflict between "naïve, idealistic American and experienced and embattled Englishman" ("'Exaggerated'" 167–68).

"Snares," a draft that represents an early version of "The Rabbit Catcher," locates its momentum in an object rather than an agent; the revision shifts narrative focus from the creature(s) being captured to the responsible party. In Plath's conceptualization, the poem's "snares" represent not just the traps in which she sees helpless rabbits writhing but also the poetic speaker's sense of entrapment in a relationship whose terms she did not define. After sketching the poem's setting, Plath crosses out first "These freedoms / And the open gate stenciled Private" and then "These freedoms astonished me" before settling on "These freedoms flew through me," a line absent from the poem's published version. Similarly, she tries out "The wind met objects, the hill and the sea" before choosing to keep "The wind met objects and quickly / Deflected itself, the hill and the sea / Still as sheet metal, and stiff" (Smith Holograph no. 2, p. 1). The repeated phrases Plath includes here elucidate a distance that is forcibly imposed. The personification that animates the passage also underlines the symbolic significance of these natural events; the rapid movements of the wind and the rigid surfaces it meets foreshadow tension in the speaker's world.

With each successive revision of "Snares," Plath cuts out ambiguity and impersonal descriptions in order to portray a landscape defined by brutality, one whose natural elements conspire to inflict harm on the inhabitants. As Jacqueline Rose has suggested, in pieces like this one, "Plath's writing unsettles poetic syntax in such a way as to disturb any simple location of agency or causality" (129–30). Tim Kendall adds that this kind of "fusion with the natural world in *Ariel* is at once terrifying and exhilarating" (*Sylvia Plath* 30). Her careful attention to diction and syntax underline her concern about the exact message that the landscape means to convey to the poetic subject and the strategies that she uses to interpret it. The manuscript contains several lines that have been struck through:

> Only played with their glittery lights
> The clouds couldn't snuff
> Not snuffing that stable eye
> Neither touching nor snuffing that eye
> Stable, it steadily
> Shone at the blue heights
> Neither touching nor snuffing the eye
> That looked out, from the back of the sky when they were by, stable and sturdy
> Yellow and steady
> The perfect constancy
> At loops of metal, ankle-high.

After cutting this meditation on the scene's witness, Plath chooses instead much more concise wording: "The clouds kept up their bluffs / Snuffing the eye / That looked out when they were by, yellow and steady / With an old constancy" (Smith Holograph no. 2, p. 1). At this point, an actor appears in the poem for the first time, if only through personification; the clouds take on the kind of malignancy that Plath will assign to the gorse—a plant that signifies regional English identity—that populates the later drafts of the poem. She also incorporates pathetic fallacy, as the sun connotes a loyalty to the poetic subject that the poem's human characters lack. Each of these poetic figures operates within a dialectic, gesturing toward both the beauty of the material landscape and a dissolving interpersonal bond that the speaker also witnesses. This first draft of "Snares" ends with an animosity toward the natural world, and the people that walk through it, that is fully realized in the final version of "The Rabbit Catcher." In the poem's concluding stanza, the narrator notes, "I, too, moved on wires, / A flat personage in the gorse / Dragged and chastised within fears / A force / [illegible] / Than wind, than rocks—and in my heart / Snared nastier than in the dirt / Pushing me like a wind, and stopping me, like a rock" (Smith Holograph no. 2, p. 2). The struck-through lines here gesture toward an ambiguous being that manipulates the speaker against her will. Though this figure's purpose and identity remain vague at this point, Plath's revisions to "The Rabbit Catcher" eventually center narrative attention on the obstacles such forces pose to the speaker's self-sufficiency and creative power.

Plath apparently rejected this draft of "Snares," with the exception of a few images that appear in altered form in "The Rabbit Catcher"; it was never published as an independent poem in any volume. This piece's disappearance from her oeuvre may signal that Plath saw "The Rabbit Catcher" as a more accurately realized depiction of the poetic situation of "Snares." The second poem focuses on agency and actors rather than reflecting an unpopulated setting, in part because the poetic speaker identifies the scene as the site of her emerging voice. In the Smith holographs, the last stanza appears on the same page as the first recognizable text of "The Rabbit Catcher" (Holograph no. 2, p. 2). The initial draft of "The Rabbit Catcher" contains many fewer revisions than does "Snares"; she adjusts the second line from "The wind stuffing itself into my mouth" to "The wind gagging my mouth," and the fourth and fifth lines from "Blinding me with its glare, its terrible chambers / Opening on the open faces the glitter of knives" to "Blinding me with its lights, the lives of the dead / Unreeling in it, spreading like oil" (Holograph no. 2, p. 2). The shift here from stuttering repetitions to short, forceful verbs and the new assonance and alliteration echoing between "lights" and "lives" emphasize the actions that the speaker confronts at the poem's start. These two passages remain in the piece's final version; Plath removes the manmade objects that motivate her initial metaphors, choosing instead to illustrate a hostile landscape with which the speaker grapples directly. These revisions also point to the speaker's emerging agency: though the landscape resists her, she tests its limits and defines its nature.

The drafts of both "Snares" and "The Rabbit Catcher" reveal that during her revision process, Plath makes line-by-line corrections in order to cut away repetitions and figurative language. This type of revision helps her to construct a sparse, densely resonant, intricately meaningful language. The changes that she made to the second stanza of the published "Rabbit Catcher" illustrate this distinctive interaction between linguistic and expressive innovation. Here she explores the gorse's aura of spite, testing out a series of metaphors and similes that align it with ritual moments in human history. Gorse is a low bush with branching thorns that flowers near the end of the summer in Britain. Its tenacity—it flourishes even in soil affected by salt spray and supports a wide variety of bird species—and self-protecting nature both tie it to the land and repel human contact. After trying and rejecting "The hemlock of," she confines her description to "its black spikes / The extreme unction of its yellow candle-flowers," which links the gorse to Christian final rites. She also changes "they had the beauty of an atrocity" to first "They had the beauty of a clean killing" and then "They had an efficiency, a great beauty; / Like a clean killing" before eliminating the references to killing altogether. Before arriving at the stanza's final line, a simple "They were extravagant, like torture," a shortened form of the published version, she experiments in addition with "They were a sordid experience, like torture / They were final, like a bad accident / They were final" (Smith Holograph no. 2, p. 2). Plath ultimately cut the extended descriptions of the gorse, choosing instead to define it as ambiguously threatening. Similarly, in her description of the paths leading up to the rabbit-catcher's snares in the next stanza, she strikes through "Without apparent motive, the paths / plunged into this hollow from many directions / They burned in the hot sun; they were innocent. / With no apparent motive" (Smith Holograph no. 2, p. 3). Her final version, "There was only one place to get to. / Simmering, perfumed, / The paths narrowed into the hollow" (*CPP* 193), removes the paths' personification and focuses on their sensory impact instead. These decisions foreshadow the revelations about creation and identity that appear in the poem's second half.

The central subject of "The Rabbit Catcher" comes into focus in the second half of this third stanza, which introduces a complex set of repetitions framed in figurative language: a new version of the device meant to underscore "poetic language as something ritualized, rhetorical and incantatory, conscious of its status as performance" (Kendall, *Sylvia Plath* 149). These similes and metaphors not only describe the physical violence that Plath's speaker perceives in the rabbit-catcher's snares but also illuminate the external restrictions that have limited her ability to read the world accurately. The first perspective that Plath tries out notes that the snares "effaced themselves into the air—little loops of emptiness. / But significant: they had a significance. / T̶h̶e̶y̶ ̶m̶u̶l̶t̶i̶p̶l̶i̶e̶d̶ ̶i̶n̶ ̶m̶y̶ ̶s̶i̶g̶h̶t̶, subtractions, subtractions! / Closer and closer, like birth pangs, / J̶e̶a̶l̶o̶u̶s̶, with nothing to think about / But what they are missing, and how to get it: / W̶h̶a̶t̶ ̶t̶h̶e̶y̶ ̶w̶o̶u̶l̶d̶ ̶c̶l̶o̶s̶e̶ ̶o̶r̶ ̶w̶o̶u̶l̶d̶ ̶b̶e̶ ̶/̶ ̶S̶q̶u̶e̶e̶z̶i̶n̶g̶ ̶l̶i̶f̶e̶ ̶a̶f̶t̶e̶r̶ ̶l̶i̶f̶e̶,̶ ̶k̶e̶e̶p̶i̶n̶g̶ / Zeros, shutting on silence" (Smith Holograph no. 2, p. 3). The cuts that Plath makes here eliminate some of the snares' individual actions; the rhythmic repetitions of "significant" / "significance," "subtractions, subtractions!," and "Closer, closer" imbue the snares instead with a deadly but anonymous purpose. This change focuses narrative attention on the speaker's actions rather than on her surroundings, shifting lyric focus from inanimate objects to an agent.

When Plath's revisions reframe the snares as inert elements of the landscape, she cuts out their owner as well in order to make space for the actions that the speaker takes. In the published version of stanzas three and four, she notes that the snares have "almost effaced themselves— / Zeros, shutting on nothing / Set close, like birth pangs" (*CPP* 194). When she is working through this image in the holograph draft, Plath at first places her narrator in an intimate relationship with the snares, juxtaposing the tactile sensations associated with giving birth to the snares' appearance of silent indifference:

"The absence of shrieks oppressed me. / ~~The absence of shrieks was like the silence of God.~~ / The ~~steel rings~~ wires slid into silence. / I saw the hands of the man behind them, / ~~And his mind, loving its alley of looped wires / Thinking all day of the brides of nothingness / Fashioning the doors of silence, strong, ingenious~~ / Dumb, blunt, ~~always about to arise~~ / in love with the death-shriek" (Smith Holograph no. 2, p. 3). After comparing the snares' poised threat to a woman's agony in birth, the speaker attributes their menace to a kind of puppeteer, "the man behind them," who produces death, not life. Their silence suggests not that they are pregnant with potential but that they are "in love with the death-shriek." Plath's edits here eliminate both the rabbit catcher and God from the poetic narrative. Left alone within a hostile landscape, the speaker is able to derive her own meaning from the situation.

Plath reimagines the snares' expressive connotations several times during this draft process, only arriving at the final version of stanza four—"Set close, like birth pangs. / The absence of shrieks / Made a hole in the hot day, a vacancy. / The glassy light was a clear wall, / The thickets quiet" (*CPP* 194)—halfway down the fourth holograph page. The snares now appear in relation to one particular day and within a regionally specific outdoor setting; a range of sensory input fixes their threat in space and time. They are separated from the poetic narrator by "a hole," "a vacancy," and "a clear wall," yet these very silences, the "absence of shrieks" and the "quiet thickets," suggest that the speaker resists the process of birthing or becoming that they attempt to impose.

In the fifth stanza of this draft of "The Rabbit Catcher," Plath tries out two versions of a domestic space that moderates the wild setting of the preceding lines. The poem's shift toward more homely qualities signifies the speaker's growing ambivalence about the natural world. Though Plath keeps the first two drafted lines—"I felt a still business [sic], an intent. / I felt hands round a tea mug, dull, blunt"—in the poem's published form (*CPP* 194), she explores and then crosses out several more similes. "~~And deaths~~," the speaker observes in the draft version, "~~sad and common as laundry, common and small. / Wrung throats expect those hands / Muffle me like gloves. How they awaited him! / Opening their tea roses. / How they opened their scalded roses! / Their colors broke open! / Thumbing death like old women / Staking out death like artisans~~" (Smith Holograph no. 2, p. 4). Plath's decision to excise these similes helps to moderate the poem's overall emotionality. Though she often uses exclamation points effectively, perhaps most notably in "Words heard, by accident, over the phone," "The Swarm," "A Secret," and "Kindness," here she eliminates three such moments of emphasis, leaving only one in the final version. This change narrows the speaker's focus to the revelations about creation that she can derive from her private life; a single image, the "hands round a tea mug," now stands in for the "laundry," "gloves," "tea roses," and "old women." Here, rather than examining the rabbit-catcher's métier in relation to the larger world, she interprets the rabbits he captures as a signifier of the productive energy she has lost. The speaker reads his betrayal, of the rabbits and of their relationship, as evidence of his attempts to stifle her. The three lines that ultimately conclude this stanza—"Ringing the white china. / How they awaited him, those little deaths! / They waited like sweethearts. They excited him" (Smith Holograph no. 2, p. 4)—draw the narrative focus away from the speaker's anxious anticipation of the rabbit-catcher's approach to the effect that his actions have on her. By making this narrative shift, Plath suggests that the rabbit catcher pursues not only the demise of his rabbits but also the more profound deaths of his comfortable home and the speaker's own autonomy and capacity for work. The complex extended metaphor that Plath fashions here comparing the traditional English practice of rabbit-trapping to unequal domestic relationships locates the roots of the speaker's unhappiness in the suppression of her potential creativity.

The published version of "The Rabbit Catcher" concludes with a sixth stanza that is absent from the first Smith holograph draft. It does not appear until the first partial typescript of the poem, in which the narrative skips stanzas four and five completely, continuing with a version of stanza six: "And we, too, had a relationship— / Deep driven pegs, tight wires between us. / I, aware of my impotence / It might cause him a morning's anger. / I imagined his body blocked off my vision—solid and faceless. / The pegs were too deep to move, but I buried the prop stick" (Smith Holograph and Typescript, revised, p. 5). Both this initial version of the stanza and its published iteration expose the restrictions that have cut the speaker off from self-expression; in the latter, the rabbit-catcher's "mind like a ring / Sliding shut on some quick thing" (*CPP* 194) effectively destroys her ability to act independently. Plath suggests through this passage that the creative life can be stifled by "tight wires," "deep pegs," and "prop stick": manmade objects meant to control rather than release. The alterations to her draft strike out some of the speaker's agency and produce a more objective portrayal of the trap. Rather than describing the wires, pegs, and stick as tools of the trade, she chooses in the published version to frame these elements as impediments to artistic expression. The final lines of the poem appear on the second page of this holograph-typescript draft, again with some variations from the final form. Plath initially writes, "And we, too, had a relationship— / Tight wires between us, / And pegs too deep to uproot: his mind a ring / Sliding shut, continually, on a long scream death-shriek. Some hurting throat thing. / The constriction making killing me also" (Smith Holograph and Typescript, revised, no. 2, p. 5). This draft version assigns blame to the speaker's partner alone, gleaning its expressive impact from what Middlebrook has described as "[t]his privileged knowledge of the way hunting and killing informs her husband's creativity" ("Creative

Partnership" 263). Yet the first version of the poem's conclusion draws a clear connection between the operation of the catcher's mind, "sliding shut, continually, on a long scream" (or "death-shriek"), and the "absence of shrieks" that she observed earlier in the poem. The drafting strategies that Plath employs here shift narrative focus away from the emotional associations of the traps to their metaphorical resonance. This portrait of a personally and culturally significant location, which also functions as a metaphor for repressed creativity, adds to Plath's commentary on the *ars poetica*. Her poetic speaker remarks upon the traps' history in order to critique the belief-system that supports the practice of rabbit-catching, finding in this resistance to literal entrapment an apt metaphor for her call for unfettered self-expression.

Plath's revisions to "The Rabbit Catcher" demonstrate the evolution of her later compositional strategies, many of which would shape the *Ariel* poems. Several of the passages' final versions emerge through repetitions with a difference, for instance, lines that attempt to capture an ideally crafted image by reiterating it in multiple subtle variations. In "The Rabbit Catcher," she also sharpens the focus on her poetic subject by eliminating irresolution in the lyric voice, and she hones her typically spare expressive style by excising inconsistent metaphors and simple repetitions. In order to represent the rabbit-catcher's snares more accurately within their English landscape, she eschews the temptation to attach human attributes to the surroundings, focusing on the rabbit-catcher's tools rather than on the speaker's meditations on her circumstances. Plath treats concrete everyday objects as metonyms of the tension between two strong wills, one focused on control and the other seeking free self-expression; she employs a strategy that Diane Middlebrook identifies in her college work, giving "the female 'object' . . . a consciousness, a subjectivity" in order to unsettle "the legacy of male dominance in art" ("Caryatids" 166). The poem gains additional force from assonance, rhyme, and strong anapestic, trochaic, and spondaic beats. Her revisions enable Plath to advance a challenge to the English landscape and, through the alternate perspectives on the scene that she thus creates, the lyric tradition itself: she opposes, in other words, the "culture of gentility," which A. Alvarez defined in his famous essay "Beyond the Gentility Principle," that had characterized much pre-1960s American and British poetry (Wootten 112–13). The piece that she ultimately creates relies upon deliberate emotionality, focused imagery, and expressive brevity, as do many conventional examples of the Western lyric mode, but in this case Plath centers her poetic message on external conflict as a metaphor for the writer's struggle to produce. This resistance to conventional methods of storytelling and the speaker's insistence upon pursuing her own creative potential represent key elements of her mature *ars poetica*.

WORDS: THE "BLOOD-JET"

While Plath's best-known commentary on the difficult nature of her medium remains her pronouncement in "Kindness," she wrote two poems near the end of her life that consider the charged intersection between written and spoken language, between the ideal, imagined communication and its real manifestation. "Words," written just weeks before her death, pictures the tactile actions and persistent effects of dangerous language. "Words heard, by accident, over the phone," on the other hand, which represents one of Plath's first responses to Hughes's affair with Assia Wevill, appears in early drafts as a meditation on the literal clogs in the passages of one's life that undesired words produce. Initially Plath used a conglomeration of phonemes to describe "O Mississippi mud, how fluid / Phone wires, it seems, can carry you homeward— / Thick as Turk coffee, a sluggy impulsion of grounds," but she amended these lines immediately to "O mud; mud, how fluid! / Thick as foreign coffee, and with a sluggy pulse" (Smith Holograph, no. 2). These corrections remove the image's geographic associations; they also move the narrative focus closer to the metaphor's vehicle, infusing it with agency. The apostrophe, as in Johnson's formulation, draws our attention to the sharp impact of the poetic experience, figuring painful words as "mud" and addressing them in the immediate present rather than as an absent object. In keeping with Plath's focus on words' affective function, the next line reveals the real tenor of this metaphor, when the speaker demands, "What are these words, uncoiling from the phone trumpet? / They are plopping like mud. / O god, how shall I clean the phone table?" The only revisions Plath makes to this section of the draft can be seen in the first line, which she changes to "What are these words, these words, these words?" (Smith Holograph, no. 2). This line eventually moves from the first to the second stanza of the poem in the published version, underlining the speaker's concern with the words' intrusion. Their unwelcome presence in the telephone, a bluntly utilitarian object, signifies their potential intrusion into other workspaces as well.

As these drafts evolve, the poem's purpose emerges: to locate a source of blame for the tension disrupting the speaker's domestic life. She expresses both anxiety at the alien words' unlooked-for presence and frustration at being prevented from doing what she wants. The next lines of the poem add personification, suggesting that her partner's actions have caused the speaker to regress to an older mode of expression. Plath amends "They are pressing out of the many-holed earpiece and finding like infants / They are looking for an adulterer, the murderer" to "They are pressing out of the many-holed earpiece, they are looking for a listener / Is he here, is he here?"; the published version remains roughly the same. The shift away from figurative language focuses narrative attention on the guilty actor himself; the disgust that the speaker feels at his actions reflects not only the impossibility of direct communication with him but also her sense of losing control over speech itself. In this early draft, she describes his presence as "The bowel-pulse, loving the open cases of blue food," a phrase which is then corrected to the narratively more detached "The bowel-pulse, lover of all digestibles." In order to illustrate both the nature of the words between them and her partner's identity, the speaker juxtaposes unusual images that reveal his shortcomings and that suggest language itself has been compromised. Plath also tries out and rejects "lover of blue, phantasmagorical lips" in this draft before concluding the stanza with "Speak, speak! Who is it, who is it?" (Smith Holograph, no. 2). While these curt imperatives and repeated phrases are characteristic of Plath's later work overall, here they direct the reader's attention to the linguistic confusion that unwelcome words produce. This disruption to the traditionally meditative space of the lyric voice and her inversion of poetic expectation—from metaphorical to material representation—demonstrates some of the ways in which language functions in Plath's poetry as a tool for radical, not just lyric, communication.

Plath's second draft of "Words heard" appears on the lower half of the same manuscript page, separated from the first only by a single horizontal line. The main differences between the second handwritten draft on this page and the final version can be seen in the order of the lines in the first stanza and the entire third stanza, which has been newly added. Plath attempts several iterations of the third stanza; after "Now the room is ahiss. The instrument / Withdraws its tentacle, its bell,"[9] she tests out "Its little spawn percolate" before crossing out the phrase with three horizontal strokes of the pen. Arriving at the final version, "But the spawn percolate in my heart," she adds "they ravish my heart" and "they whisper and couple" before crossing out both phrases and settling on "They are fertile, they couple" instead. As is the case in many of her other evolving drafts, here Plath eliminates references to the personal—the situation's direct effects upon the speaker—in favor of a more objective, third-person perspective. In a similar vein, she works to delineate the phone's threatening appearance: "It is too big for us, with its spacious articulations / We must kill it. This black bobbly headscrew, this talk-to muck, this funnel of muck" (Smith Holograph, no. 2). None of these lines makes it into the final version as Plath attempts to capture the invasive presence of the telephone as precisely as possible. Instead, as the published poem reveals, she shifts the narrative emphasis away from the phone as instrument to the words that it conveys. The speaker's words replace the actual "words heard" and enable her to reframe the situation in terms that she can understand. This moment in which the speaker achieves control over the nature of her poetic communication, an instance that is repeated in other poems from this period, represents a key dimension of Plath's *ars poetica*.

Plath's later drafts of "Words heard" continue to examine the effects of the speaker's words, expanding the poem's attention to linguistic control. In the first typescript, she presents two more possibilities for stanza 3. The first two lines retain her original concentration on the phone—"Now the room is ahiss. The instrument / Withdraws its tentacles, its bell"—but the final three lines work to highlight the effects of the call on the speaker. All three versions suggest, at the same time, that the speaker struggles to gain control over her language and thus over the circumstances that confront her. "But the spawn percolates in my heart," she notes. "They are fertile. ~~They couple~~. / ~~It is too big, this talk rattle~~. / ~~We must~~ I will kill it." Following these typed lines, Plath adds in three additional handwritten lines: "~~My ear is no place for these spacious articulations~~. / Muck funnel, muck funnel— / You are too big. They must take you back!" (Smith Typescript, revised, no. 2). In spite of these deletions, the last two lines end up as the poem's conclusion. The final metaphor—"muck funnel"—both associates the phone's language with yellow journalism's "muckrakers" and suggests a tornado of painful revelations that the conversations have set into motion. In the end, the poem has little to say about the conversations' actual content; rather, it examines the tactile fallout of misused, misdirected language. Such ill-fated communications, Plath implies, alter the very medium in which the artist works, distorting her chosen mode of creation into something unrecognizable.

"Words heard, by accident, over the phone" was originally titled "Words"; the poem that bears that title in published form was written just ten days before Plath's death, while she was living with the children in the London flat. "Words" was finished on 1 February 1963 and remains one of the most debated pieces in Plath's late work because of its placement in the 1965 version of *Ariel*. Hughes decided to conclude his edited version with this piece, perhaps because of its engagement with notions of writerly craft, or perhaps because it makes reference to the types of astrological insight that he and Plath pursued together during their marriage.[10] As he notes in "Publishing Sylvia Plath," in his version he "added about nine of the last poems [she had written], because they seemed to me too important to leave out" (*WP* 167). The solemn tone of "Words," the speaker's sense of isolation, and the complex metaphors the poem employs to parse out the title concept provide a distinct contrast with "Wintering," the poem that concludes Plath's original arrangement. This latter piece famously ends with an optimistic meditation on the bees' likely fate during the winter months: "The bees are flying. They taste the spring" (*CPP* 219). "Words," in contrast, concludes with, "Words dry and riderless, / The indefatigable hoof-taps. / While / From the bottom of the pool, fixed stars / Govern a life" (*CPP* 270). While "Words" gestures in part toward the isolation that accompanies the act of writing, it also concludes on an optimistic note, by invoking life. As Tim Kendall notes, "Plath's technique [here] is to introduce a subject through simile which later embodies the more physical reality of metaphor" (*Sylvia Plath* 178); its indirect comparisons accumulate into a series of metonyms for the writing process itself. In the end, it becomes "an apology for poetry, or at least for a new style, over which the speaker professes little control" because the device of metaphor itself becomes the poem's subject and controlling force (Kendall, *Sylvia Plath* 205–06). Hughes's "The Bee God," which contains a response to this poem, ends with a much more definitive negation; the speaker posits that his listener's obsession, the "bee god" of her life, remains "Deaf to your pleas as the fixed stars / At the bottom of the well" (*CPH* 1142).[11]

"Words" is useful not just as a site of literary dialogue, however; it also offers insight into Plath's own theory of writing, her sense of the ideal *ars poetica*. The initial drafts of the poem in the Smith collection reveal a process of paring-down, as Plath cut out references to perspectives outside of the speaker's immediate frame of reference. Stanza two, for instance, begins with "Peasants and beggars / Encounter them on the road / Dry and proud, in a lather of sweat" (Smith Holograph, 1963 Feb. 1), lines that are immediately crossed out in favor of the published version: "The sap / Wells like tears, like the / Water striving / To re-establish its mirror / Over the rock" (*CPP* 270). The poem's fourth stanza betrays more evidence of Plath's decision to prioritize objectivity and precision over easy sentimentality. In the draft, she follows "Words proud and riderless," a close approximation of the final version, with "In the still / Pool / Hoof-taps indefatigable. / While from the bottom," then tries out "From the bottom / of the pool, a fixed constellation / Of pebbles governs" before settling on "fixed stars / Govern a life" (Smith Holograph, 1963 Feb. 1). Through these revisions, Plath erases references to other human beings and trims away metaphoric vehicles in order to make the words themselves do the work.[12] As a final statement on the nature of craft, "Words" articulates the pain and isolation that writing can bring with it—the "Axes / After whose stroke the word rings / And the echoes!" as well as "The sap [that] / Wells like tears" and "A white skull, / Eaten by weedy greens" (*CPP* 270). Yet these images also convey the irresistible pull of the medium, its unassailable link to the writer's fortunes. Steven Axelrod has described the poem as an example of "the independent, discontinuous energy of language" and of a "fear of the power language wields" (73). Even if art is as difficult to fix in place as these temporary echoes and the physical signs of nature erasing earlier lives, it continues, "indefatigable" and alive. Plath argues that its power terrifies us but also makes beauty possible.

After brushing the snow off her "Bronze Boy" statue and imagining its metaphoric resonance through journal entry, poem, and story, this was what

Plath discovered: the steep, steady climb toward linguistic meticulousness and the dizzyingly wide span of poetic affect. Her poetry exploits the possibilities of writing against lyric conventions through its sometimes surrealist imagery, its sparse diction, its measured use of repetitions, and its moves to increase narrative agency. The *ars poetica* that she shaped through the last few years of her life becomes increasingly visible through her draft alterations; Tracy Brain notes that the drafts "allow us a more complete picture of Plath's intentions as a writer, and help us to understand her work more fully" (*The Other* 30). In Susan Van Dyne's formulation, Plath's drafts reveal her "subjectivity in process"; her moments of "self-conscious performance" enable her to claim expressive power (7, 63). These transitional writings prepare the ground for *Ariel* through their early excursions into the sequence's "imaginative rhetoric" (Peel 98). Her poetry's challenges to the lyric emerge, then, through these draft strategies, producing a distinctive narrative voice aimed at consolidating a unitary aesthetic self.

NOTES

1. Plath completed English 41b, "special studies in poetry writing," with Fisher during her senior year (*LSP1* 803), which included handing in a group of poems each week for his critique. She notes that his suggestions were so helpful that "I find myself just flying home to rewrite them" (*LSP1* 862); she compiled her first book-length manuscript, the sixty-poem *Circus in Three Rings*, with his assistance (*LSP1* 917).

2. Plath includes the text of "The Dead," along with another sonnet, "Doom of Exiles," in a letter to Aurelia Plath dated 16 April 1954. She notes that the poem now contains "six new lines, and six old revised and rearranged ones," making it "my best so far for both thought content and sound" (*LSP1* 729, 731).

3. Uroff suggests that the poem owes a debt to Archibald MacLeish's sonnet "The End of the World" as well (63–64).

4. Axelrod notes that Plath started using "Marcia Moore" as her pen name after she met Marianne Moore in April 1955. Moore had judged a poetry contest at Smith in which Plath was one of the top prizewinners (Axelrod 134).

5. An unattributed handwritten note at the bottom of this manuscript page says, "P.N. = Peter Norton—boyfriend," in spite of the likelihood that P.N. refers to Perry (Plath mss. II. Writings: Poetry—G-I [Box 7a], Folder 12).

6. Wilbury Crockett also helped Plath to recover from her 1953 breakdown through "language tutoring" while she was a patient at McLean Hospital (Connors 92); he visited her once a week to play a "word game called Anagram," though at the beginning of her convalescence she found it difficult to make any words at all (Wilson 224–25).

7. See, e.g., Axelrod, Clark, Middlebrook, and Uroff.

8. One early piece of writing in which Plath sketches out the expressive possibilities of tulips is a journal entry from August 1950. Here she describes the moon, also

a frequent presence in her writing, as having "undergone a rapid metamorphoses, made possible by the vague imprecise allusions in the first line, and become a tulip or crocus or aster bulb . . . the moon is 'bulbous,' which is an adjective meaning fat, but suggesting 'bulb'" (*UJ* 87).

9. Perloff glosses this line as a "pun on Assia's name" (315).

10. Clark suggests that the poem was likely influenced by Hughes's "Full Moon and Little Frieda" as well (*Grief* 168).

11. Though "The Bee God" is a much more direct response to "Words," it is worth noting that Hughes uses Plath's exact phrase in "A Dream," whose second stanza begins, "Not dreams, I had said, but fixed stars / Govern a life" (*CPH* 1119). In describing the critical debate over whether Plath or Hughes had originated this line, Gillian Groszewski notes that "the phrase, it seems, is indebted to a short poem of Dickinson's which suggests that stars are 'Asterisks / To point a human life?'" (173). Steven Axelrod calls the final lines of "Words" a "disfiguration" of not only "Roethke, Lowell, or Hughes, but William Shakespeare." In *King Lear*, the Earl of Kent describes the difference between faithful daughter Cordelia and her sisters in similar terms: "It is the stars, / The stars above us, govern our conditions" (Axelrod 75–76; *King Lear* 4.4.34–35). Sarah Churchwell concludes that "[w]hat seems far more important than who actually said it first (which we will never know) is Hughes's coupling of their words. . . . Hughes's new line [in "A Dream"] keeps the contest in circulation; he forever entangles their beginnings and endings in publishing and circulating, creating a circuit of baffled intentions and resistant audiences" ("Secrets" 137).

12. Linda Wagner-Martin also reads the poem's final stanza as evidence of Plath's intertextual interests, suggesting that "Words dry and riderless," rather than serving as a "renunciation of her art," offers one element of life for another: "the letter for the resonance (i.e., 'echoes') of spiritual knowledge" (*Literary* 143).

Chapter Three
Silent Partners
Ariel and Crow

Ted Hughes's mature narrative voice emerged in the poetry he produced between the late 1960s and early 1970s. Before the strongly articulated speakers of the *Birthday Letters* poems came to dominate much of the critical and popular conversation about his work, he was known for his portraits of English ecosystems, his animal poems, and his Crow poems. Crow, who appears in more than eighty pieces, evolved during one of the most painful periods of Hughes's life into a contrary and deeply flawed persona with ties to several ancient mythologies. Nearly thirty years after he first created the character, Hughes described Crow in a letter to Keith Sagar as a means of coping with this period using autobiographical, metaphorical, and allegorical methods of representation. Crow became a kind of "oblique symbol" that Hughes worked through between 1965 and 1969, and again after 1970 (*LTH* 718–19).

Crow also likely owes a piece of his origins to Yeats's "Crazy Jane" character, Amiri Baraka's "Crow Jane" (1966), and the Henry figure whose exploits structure John Berryman's *The Dream Songs* (1969). Crazy Jane appears in seven pieces from Yeats's *Words for Music Perhaps* (1933) and in one of his last poems, "Crazy Jane on the Mountain" (1938). The "Crazy Jane" poems incorporate short, trochaic lines, regular rhymes, and refrains that refer both to Yeats's sympathies for nationalist politics and to contemporary marching songs. Crazy Jane herself witnesses the social inequalities of her age, giving public voice to church corruption, for instance, in pieces like "Crazy Jane and the Bishop": "The Bishop has a skin, God knows, / Wrinkled like the foot of a goose, / *(All find safety in the tomb.)* / Nor can he hide in holy black / The heron's hunch upon his back" (Yeats 251). She reproves passersby for their judgmental attitudes and celebrates the strong relationship she had known with her lover Jack throughout the *Words for Music Perhaps* pieces, finally concluding, in her best-known poetic iteration, "Crazy Jane Talks with the Bishop," that both body and soul, the highest and the lowest, are necessary parts of life; after all, "nothing can be sole or whole / That has not been rent" (Yeats 255).

The humorous elements that Yeats uses to delineate Jane's character are present in Baraka's four "Crow Jane" poems as well, as are the sharp critiques of contemporary social conditions. D. H. Melhem has also traced this lineage, noting that "[t]he 'Crow Jane' poems of [Baraka's collection] *The Dead Lecturer*, inspired by the 'Crow Jane' of Mississippi Joe Williams, recall W. B. Yeats's wryly philosophical series on 'Crazy Jane'" (82). As Melhem suggests, however, Baraka draws inspiration for his character from the subversive politics of blues music rather than from Irish political history. Baraka's character is also a person of color, who engages with the history of African-American social and political struggle in the context of the blues. Though no specifically racialized dimensions exist in Yeats's Crazy Jane (who enjoys the privileged, because unacknowledged, properties of whiteness), Crow Jane's implied history of social resistance and her status as an outsider figure lend Hughes's Crow an air of the interloper, one who is not part of the mainstream but speaks truths.

Baraka's epigraph for the "Crow Jane" section of *The Dead Lecturer* (1964), which he takes from the lyrics to Mississippi Joe Williams's song "Crow Jane," focuses on accepting the end of one's life. Crow Jane herself, an openly rebellious figure who also serves as a harbinger of tragedy, bears the title of "Mama Death." Defiance and death, two qualities that seem almost contradictory, frequently coexist in blues music in order to comment on the limited economic opportunities available to artists of color, and to their audiences, in the early twentieth century (Davis 113). Crow Jane articulates the basic injustices that mark the American landscape in "For Crow Jane / Mama Death"; here she bears witness to the ways in which "The wealth / is translated, corrected, a / dark process, like thought, tho / it provide a landscape / with golden domes" (Baraka 66). "Crow Jane in High Society" and "Crow Jane the Crook" also remark upon the paradoxical experiences of someone who voices truth yet is afforded only limited social opportunities. The poetic speaker mourns Crow Jane's enforced absence in "High Society," noting that "She is looking / for alternatives. Openings / where she can lay all / this greasy talk / on somebody. Me, once. Now / I am her teller" (Baraka 67). In "Crook," too, her exploits center the poetic action, yet she is no longer present. The narrator labels her "Wet lady of no image" and "Dark / lady, of constant promise"; his worst fear, repeated three times, is that "we thought you had gone" (Baraka 68). As Crazy Jane's does, Crow Jane's presence signals social resistance, those moments when conventions erode to reveal the real textures of people's lives. Both figures point to painful realities, revel in the ugliness of the everyday, and exist on the margins of society, in the spaces usually reserved for the impoverished, the mentally ill, the homeless, and soothsayers.

John Berryman's Henry, one of the two characters who narrate the *Dream Songs* sequence, possesses many of the same traits that Crazy Jane and Crow Jane do. In his introduction to the 1969 volume, Berryman describes Henry as "a white American in early middle age sometimes in blackface, who has suffered an irreversible loss and talks about himself sometimes in the first-person, sometimes in the third, sometimes even in the second; he has a friend, never named, who addresses him as Mr. Bones and variants thereof" (vi). Though Henry is identifiably male, in contrast to the two Janes, he endures many moments of social censure similar to theirs; his fragmenting psyche also betrays evidence of outside pressures. His performative slippage between real and imagined racial identities bears little resemblance to Crazy Jane's persona, which is assumedly white, yet he sometimes tries to imitate the African-American artists of the blues tradition, the source for Crow Jane's character. Henry's strongest distinguishing traits are his self-doubt and the bad decisions he makes as a result, which inevitably result in his banishment to a self-imposed purgatory. The sequence's first poem describes "Huffy Henry"'s disappointment after "All the world like a woolen lover / once did seem on Henry's side. / Then came a departure" (Berryman 3). This letdown might be due to Henry's unrestrained appetites, as in Song 4, when he admits that "only the fact of her husband & four other people / kept me from springing on her"; aghast at his own temerity, he reflects that "There ought to be a law against Henry" (Berryman 6). His impulses are vast and unpredictable, leading him to doubt the merit of his own existence. The dialectic that his actions establish between self-regulation and complete indulgence engage with some of the broader concerns about social propriety and resistance to norms that preoccupied Berryman's contemporaries.

Like these three predecessors, Hughes's Crow possesses an unusual degree of insight into the social world but finds that his knowledge comes with a cost: personal isolation and self-doubt. He is often self-deprecating, yet he also takes the time to satirize the major issues that shape his world, including the aftermath of war, the atrocities that humans inflict upon nature, and a religion that promises little hope. Because he appears in so many more poems than do Crazy Jane and Crow Jane, his adventures describe a longer narrative scope than theirs; while he does, presumably, give voice to some of Hughes's own preoccupations, his persona gains shape through observation and social commentary rather than through identifiable biographical events, as Berryman's Henry does. Hughes himself saw Crow "as the totem of England," a presence in "early Celtic literature," and the avatar of many other traditions: "Apollo the Crow god. Crow in China. Crow among the Siberian peoples & the North American Indians. Crow in Alchemy" (*LTH*

339). In addition to his mythological origins, which Hughes traces to the Irish goddess of death, Morrigu, and the Welsh mythical crow figure of Morfran (Robinson 170), he has roots in Maori origin myths, Native American trickster tales, and Shakespearean characters like Caliban, among other possibilities (Gifford and Roberts 118–21). Yvonne Reddick interprets his language as a unique discourse comprising "hymns, epiphanic nature poems, the sublimity of the Romantics' nightingales and skylarks, and even some of his own earlier work" (156). She suggests that we might even see Crow's language use and relentlessly pessimistic outlook as contributing to a "poetry of waste" (Reddick 159). He emerges over the course of the sequence's 80 poems as a coherent, if sometimes contradictory, figure who explores the "relationship between language and reality" as well as language's many false premises (Gifford and Roberts 126); Katherine Robinson suggests that he expresses at times an "indifference to language, and, by extension, to the normal human desires it conveys and mediates" (173). His experiences describe a narrative rise and fall that recall the mythic experiences of an epic hero like Odysseus or H.D.'s Helen; yet, in keeping with the "theme of the Western mind exiled from Nature," he participates in an "only partially or provisionally successful quest . . . to overcome this division, in [the] interests of Complete Being" (Bentley 76). Crow experiments with language's structures and functions as one key strategy for resisting conformity to modern social concerns. At the same time, however, these poems center on the ways in which his attempts at conquest will always, inevitably, fall short.

Hughes frames Crow's experiences as a commentary on the inadequacy of human art to represent real-life experience; this extended meditation responds directly to Plath's *Ariel*, which traces the development of her *ars poetica* across a distinctive narrative arc. Heather Clark has gone so far as to call *Crow* "a distorted mirror image of *Ariel*" in which Hughes struggled to hold onto language that was under threat by "'the mother'" (*Grief* 191). In a conversation with Keith Sagar, too, Hughes confessed that "*Crow* had been a way to work through the devastation of Sylvia Plath's suicide" (Clark, *Grief* 187); his post-1963 writings inevitably engage with her final acts in 1962 and 1963, but they also seek a mode of expression beyond and outside the personal realm. Both sequences attempt to delineate the processes by which the writer produces art—specifically, the expressive devices and formal dimensions that define poetic composition as a creative act. The different versions of *Ariel* explore the writer's progression from a mode of questioning and uncertainty through linguistic experiment to a definitive statement on the nature of poetic achievement. Plath pairs this narrative of writerly development with meditations on the personal traumas that help to cohere a unified sense of self. The Crow poems, in contrast, trace Crow's experiences at birth, as a destructive force, and as a kind of deity in order to identify the language in which ontological questions are best expressed. Hughes remarks through each stage of this life story on the creative maturation that a writer experiences.

FROM *ARIEL* TO *CROW*

Much of the critical debate over Plath's *Ariel* centers on the three different orders into which its poems have been placed, since the poems' arrangement signals a particular aesthetic intention and narrative scope. Upon her death, Plath left behind a black binder containing the poems organized in, presumably, the order that seemed correct at that point in time. When Hughes, serving as executor of Plath's literary estate, prepared to publish these poems, he added several poems she had written during early 1963, just before her death. Sparking a controversy that would follow the volume for decades, he "omitted some of the more personally aggressive poems from 1962," and he altered the poems' order with an eye to "introducing her late work more cautiously" to new readers ("Introduction" to *CPP* 15). He also pointed out in a later interview that the collection's U.S. publishers did not want the book in its original form; all of her late work had appeared in collections "within six years of that first publication" (Heinz 79). Plath's *Collected Poems* was not published until 1981; it contains her poems in strict chronological order, without overt reference to their placement in *The Colossus and Other Poems*, *Ariel*, *Crossing the Water: Transitional Poems*, or *Winter Trees*. Critics such as Marjorie Perloff, Tim Kendall, Caroline King Barnard Hall, and Lynda K. Bundtzen, among others, have commented extensively on the omissions, revisions, and personal agendas that may underlie the varying organizations of the poems. Jacqueline Rose suggests that "the poems in *Ariel* have to be read in relationship to each other—not only in terms of the order Plath proposed for her own collection . . . but also in the sense of the way she wrote them" (143). Susan Van Dyne argues that the *Ariel* poems "represented a dialogue between maternity and poetry whose ending was not predictable"; the February poems in particular comprise "a meaningful but perhaps undecidable juxtaposition of figures for motherhood and authorship, counterpointed by their inscribed reverse sides that sometimes may have played a part in the production of the new poems" (165). Gillian Groszewski reads Hughes's edition of *A Choice of Emily Dickinson's Verse* in 1968 as an indication both of the importance he placed on the arrangement of edited collections in general and of "the connections . . . between [Plath's and Dickinson's] poetry" (161). These three perspectives alone demonstrate that a significant number of factors, both aesthetic and personal, contributed to Plath's grouping. In 2004, Frieda Hughes's "restored" edition of *Ariel* reinvigorated the questions of intent and effect that the critics had raised. Such questions, which are stimulated by the poems' illumination of Plath's compositional techniques and aesthetic preferences, provide new insight into the contexts of both *Ariel* and *Crow*. As these and many other scholars have suggested, topics like writerly intention and structural organization will continue to shape our understanding of the three *Ariel* sequences' narrative content and the aesthetic dialogue among them. Meaningful relationships exist among the poems in all three arrangements since, as Neil Fraistat points out, "the individual poems in a contexture are rarely written to fill a specific place in the whole, [and] the continuities between them are more likely to be associative than causal" (8). Additionally, neither the poet nor the book's editor determines the sequence's or the collection's ultimate meaning; no "conscious intentions" can account for the "wealth of unconscious connections and fortuitous circumstances that contribute to the meaning of a contexture" (Fraistat 9). In relation to *Ariel* in particular, how should our knowledge of the three existing versions affect our interpretations of its individual poems? How might the intrinsic meaning and contextual relevance of individual poems change from one version to the next? To what degree should we read the two sequences in relation to Plath and Hughes as artists, Hughes as literary executor and editor, or even Frieda Hughes as potential mediator?

One essential method by which to begin answering these questions is to read each version of *Ariel* as a coherent, organic work—a sequential long poem, rather than a collection of discrete, individual pieces. In an early discussion of the decisions that guided his edition of *Ariel*, Ted Hughes states that he wanted to "point out just how little of [Plath's] poetry is 'occasional,' and how faithfully her separate poems build up into one long poem" ("Notes" 187). Several critical readings illustrate the possible thematic progressions that *Ariel* traces. Marjorie Perloff describes the book's structure in *Ariel 1* as beginning "with the birth of Frieda . . . [then] mov[ing] through the despair Plath evidently experienced when she learned . . . that Hughes was having an affair with another woman, to the period of rage and mysogyny [sic] that followed . . . and then to a ritual death and a move toward rebirth" (313). Lee Upton argues that "the implicit narrative elevates toward renewal through its sequence of bee-keeping poems" (262). Tim Kendall finds that the sequence "record[s] the death of a false or old self and the creation of a new self to replace it" through "poems of becoming rather than being" (*Sylvia Plath* 51). Other analyses, such as Lynda Bundtzen's and Susan Van Dyne's, make note of the darker tone of the 1963 poems added in *Ariel 2*, while Linda Wagner-Martin claims that Hughes's arrangement makes the argument that "Plath's work ran backward, from the point of her suicide" (*Literary* 141). These divergent readings highlight critics' own scholarly agendas, of course, but they also illustrate the collection's identity as a narrative, which Earl Miner defines as containing both "sequentiality and continuousness" (26), though not always a plot; many narratives do contain an identifiable plot, but that element "is not necessary," since "integrated collections," like *Ariel*, "are plotless narratives" (Miner 39). For these reasons, the overall structure and thematic continuity of *Ariel* closely resemble those of *Crow*.

Among other issues, Plath critics have commented extensively on the placement of "Wintering" in the two *Ariel* editions. In Ted Hughes's 1965 edition, as discussed in the previous chapter, it appears about two-thirds of the way through the book, at the chronological end of the bee sequence. In the 2004 restored edition, however, this poem concludes the book. As Erica Wagner points out, by beginning *Ariel* with "Morning Song" and ending with "Wintering," "the first word of the book was 'love' and the last 'spring.' This gives the selection a positive, upward movement that the [first] published collection does not have." In fact, Wagner argues, the final lines of "Words," the poem that Ted Hughes chose to conclude his edition, continue the book's ominous predictions for the future and its "black" end (23). However, the contrast in mood and tone between the two poems may not be as significant as this reading implies. Lynda Bundtzen notes that "Wintering" concludes with a meditation on the images that lead the speaker out of darkness into the spring phase of a new art, with a final line that "ostensibly celebrates rebirth, seasonal renewal, and the resumption of the beehives' honey-making activity in the spring" (*Other Ariel* 133). She also points out, however, that "Plath is seeking mantic power in 'Wintering' by giving herself over to 'possession' by the hive"; the poem's optimistic conclusion is meant to be a "riddle" of sorts that resists easy interpretation (Bundtzen, *Other Ariel* 196). Plath's reference to the "Christmas rose," for instance, resonates with contradictory associations. Bundtzen points out that the plant's root functions as a purgative that, if given in too great a quantity, could serve not just as "a curative medicine" but also as a "deadly poison" (*Other Ariel* 199). "Wintering" contains several of the familiar adjectives and turns of phrase that distinguish Plath's work from this period; the speaker describes her work in a dark interior room, making and saving up food—whether literal or imaginative—for the spring. The poem portrays a process of winnowing; women perform the necessary work for survival now that men, "The blunt, clumsy stumblers, the boors," are gone. The speaker seems to hunch into herself as she works, "Her body a bulb in the cold and too dumb to think" (*CPP* 219). These lines reprise elements of the poetic vocabulary that Plath had worked to develop over the past ten years. Though the poem does end with a positive movement in which the bees fly toward spring's renewal, Plath also includes two questions in the poem's last stanza. Unable, characteristically, to delimit the bees' role, she leaves the possibility of their success open and points toward an unknowable future.

In spite of critics' varying interpretations of the poems' three different sequences, mature compositional techniques cohere each arrangement of the poems. Perloff notes that "both *Ariel 1* and *Ariel 2* . . . have a plot, but the two plots are so different that we cannot help but wonder what it means to reconstruct a poetic sequence after the fact" (311). As analysis of both versions reveals, the two narratives possess intrinsic meaning on formal, thematic, biographical, and aesthetic levels. Tim Kendall points out, for instance, that "reiterated references to colour [function] as an expression of mood throughout *Ariel*" (*Sylvia Plath* 25). Plath created a new set of compositional strategies in this work, innovations that have been acknowledged by critics as diverse as J. D. McClatchy (92) and Christina Britzolakis ("*Ariel*" 110). To unify the poems, she fashioned a series of poetic narrators who analyze the trauma that results from fragmenting personal relationships. This focus on the effects of trauma, usually narrated in a mode of detached lyric observation, heralds a significant ideological shift in Plath's work, away from exploratory visions to statements of the writer's responsibilities to her art.

While Plath's early work had displayed some affiliations with her modernist precedents, the poems she wrote in the 1960s are aligned with Brian McHale's postmodernist mode of ontological questioning (*Postmodernist* 10), just as the *Crow* sequence is. The settings of some of the pre-1960s poems resemble a post-war period which allusions to classical myth and history serve in part to "shore up the ruins" of a damaged society; Plath's careful attention to descriptive details and her poetic narrators' tendency toward introspection help to convey a sense of New Critical self-containment. The postmodernist elements of her 1960s poems, on the other hand, introduce such aesthetic features as a lack of affect, pastiche, and a focus, at times, on rhetoric and formal structures rather than on narrative content (Jameson 6–38). In his interview with Drue Heinz, Hughes observes that Plath was influenced by W. S. Merwin's translations of Pablo Neruda at the time, and that she responded to "the sudden waking up of the world from the ice age of the war" as well as "the shockwave . . . of the lifestyle of the Beat poets" (74, 87). *Ariel*'s formal strategies and unique voice, as well as her responses to these cultural contexts, indicate that Plath conceived of the book as a sequential piece, a long poem of sorts, in which she sought to explore changing notions of art, professional identity, and social responsibility. Though Hughes most likely did not conceive of *Crow* in the same way when he first began writing the poems, he ultimately invented a poetic persona whose life experiences and frequent observations on human shortcomings help to cohere the sequence into a unitary narrative.

Both *Ariel* and *Crow* may thus be productively read as long poems. The long poem, understood either as a single long narrative work or as a book-length (or longer) sequence of short but thematically related pieces, holds a central place in the history of twentieth-century American poetry.

Though many readers associate the genre primarily with such modernist epics as Eliot's *The Waste Land*, Pound's *Cantos*, Williams's *Paterson*, H.D.'s *Helen in Egypt*, and Crane's *The Bridge*, many later works like Charles Olson's *Maximus Poems* (1956), Edward Dorn's *Gunslinger* (1968), Lyn Hejinian's *My Life* (1980, 1987, 2002), and Nathaniel Mackey's *Song of the Andoumboulou* (ongoing) represent essential contributions to the genre. Relatively few critics have examined the contributions of mid-twentieth-century writers to this tradition, although such signature works of the late 1950s and 1960s as W. D. Snodgrass's *Heart's Needle* (1959), Lowell's *Life Studies*, and Berryman's *The Dream Songs* can easily be read as long poems. One exception is Lynn Keller, who identifies long poems and sequences in Projectivist, Black Mountain, postmodernist, Beat, confessional, New York School, feminist, lesbian, African-American, Chicano, Native American, and language poetry. She notes that many of these examples hold in common "a liberating mix of genres, an enlargement beyond the postromantic lyric's focus on a moment of subjective experience, and an accompanying exploration of social and historical materials," along with a frequent "tension between open and closed form" (563). Brian McHale observes that poems from the mid-twentieth century and later often employ a "recycling of earlier narrative modes" as well ("Telling" 256).

Both Hughes and Plath experiment with various formal devices and include pieces in their sequences that engage with historical, social, and political issues. These pieces, as a result, both contribute to their sequences' narrative arcs and illuminate some of the concerns that motivated their compositions. Plath herself famously observed that "personal experience is very important, but certainly it shouldn't be a kind of shut-box and mirror-looking, narcissistic experience. I believe it should be relevant to the larger things, the bigger things such as Hiroshima and Dachau and so on" (qtd. in Bassnett, *Sylvia Plath* 37). Remarks like these suggest that she was interested in linking her meditations on the processes by which the writer creates art, the *ars poetica* with which her later work is profoundly concerned, to larger global tragedies; the traumas that motivate revelation in the poems occur on multiple narrative levels. Sue Vice points out that Plath discusses "the rise of the ecology and disarmament movements, the legacy of the Second World War, . . . the end of the McCarthy era," and "references to popular culture" in the *Ariel* poems (500). Robin Peel argues in turn that the *Ariel* poems could not have been "written as they were without Plath's reading of the interaction of childbirth and the language of conflict and the Cold War" (17). She even wrote to Alfred Young Fisher, several years after her graduation from Smith College, to request that he send her more pink memorandum sheets to use for her drafts: perhaps a kind of lucky charm she thought would ensure the merit of this collection (*LSP2* 781). As Britzolakis has suggested, Plath creates in

Ariel "a mode of argument through metaphor which yokes together historical and psychic events" alternately with "moments of linguistic regression which foreground the material basis of signification" (*Theatre* 159). Her use of multiple expressive modes renders the sequence an appropriate forum in which to explore the possibilities of effective self-representation and writerly legacy. The sequential structures of both *Ariel* and *Crow* contrast with the epic organization familiar to readers from classical, Romantic, and modernist long poems, but they introduce new possibilities for the long form through their engagement with personal history and social concerns.

CONVERSATIONS THROUGH AND ACROSS THE SEQUENCES

The three versions of *Ariel* reflect three different perspectives on the relationship that Plath was constructing between her aesthetic approach and the ontological issues that her poetry examines. In her introduction to the 2004 edition, Frieda Hughes notes that her mother "probably worked on the manuscript's arrangement in mid-November 1962," based on the date of the latest poem included in her black binder (xi). The new tone and formal composition of these poems reinforce the sense that this book exemplifies the culmination of her creative principles. Both versions of *Ariel* begin with "Morning Song," familiar to Plath readers for its images of the baby as "a fat gold watch" with a "mouth [that] opens clean as a cat's." Though the poem's first word is indeed "Love," the comfort that this emotion might offer is undercut by the baby's "bald cry" and the parents who "stand round blankly as walls." The speaker refuses an unquestioningly positive perspective on the parent-child bond by suggesting that "I'm no more your mother / Than the cloud that distills a mirror to reflect its own slow / Effacement." A distant relationship exists between them at this point, as the speaker's attention is more focused on "moth-breath," "flat pink roses" and "A far sea" than it is on the child. Though she rises from her bed as soon as the child cries, she is distracted from her nurturing by "The window square," which "Whitens and swallows its dull stars." However, the child's "handful of notes" ends the poem, suggesting that this "morning song" comes from outside the speaker (*CPP* 156–57). Her initial difficulties seem to disappear when she witnesses the independent acts that she can foster in her child. This moment of transformation establishes the mode of narrative resistance and surprise, both necessary conditions for creation, that Plath sustains throughout the rest of the book.

A similar mode filters through Hughes's *Crow* sequence, which he began just a few years after Plath's death and continued to develop into the 1970s.

Like Plath, in these poems Hughes advances a theory of the *ars poetica* that matures over the course of the sequence. Since he is the sequence's only narrator, Crow gives coherence to the widely varying topics that the poems address while challenging some of Hughes's longtime concerns, such as the evolving properties of the English landscape and the anthropomorphic potential of the animal kingdom. This disruption to the accepted progression of Hughes's poetics enables him to consider some of the same ontological questions that Plath does.

The *Ariel* narrative, whether read through Plath's original arrangement or in Hughes's edited collection, follows a trajectory from meditations on love through the material effects of lived trauma into a complex deliberation on the environment necessary for intellectual creation. For Plath, poetic composition means planning for an artistic legacy while understanding both family experience and personal betrayal as symbols of a developing ethos. Hughes's *Crow* poems take up some of the same concerns but travel through a more focused narrative and philosophical evolution. The metaphors through which Hughes represents Crow's actions often resemble Plath's own figurative language in image and intent, though Hughes's allegories are motivated more often by real historical conditions and sometimes appear in a "stark, unembellished style which can be said to represent a loss of faith in language" (Webb 36). Like Plath, Hughes strives to articulate his poetics through several attempts at the *ars poetica*, many of which revise or rethink the approach he first laid out in "The Thought-Fox." Crow's language and self-presentation also recall "the speakers of Plath's late poems, who never flinch in their attacks" (Uroff 202). These poems assume that one's body and voice both serve as sources of professional ability. Hughes responds to this hypothesis and reflects on Plath's work more generally in the Crow sequences, through "poems that simultaneously address language, writing, and moments of originary 'naming'" (Clark, *Grief* 191). His responses to Plath's *Ariel* poems manifest in his attention to figures that embody stasis or unrealized potential, his comments on the nature of art and its social reception, the ambivalence toward love that Crow often expresses, and the satirical attitude that the poems sometimes assume.

The beginning of Hughes's sequence does not employ the clearly detailed images and strong narrative intent of Plath's "Morning Song." Instead, he establishes the story and argument that the poems trace with an anonymous crow that appears in his 1967 poem "Skylarks": "Cuchulain listened bowed, / Strapped to his pillar (not to die prone) / Hearing the far crow / Guiding the near lark nearer / With its blind song" (*CPH* 176). These lines make reference to Irish mythology and to the role that art plays in determining one's direction in life, both central preoccupations of the work. The specific character named Crow acts first in the uncollected poem "Three Legends," which Hughes wrote sometime between 1967 and 1970. In this piece, the first "legend" originates in a stone that remains impervious to the world's upheavals until it awakes and "open[s] its eyes." As a result of this anthropomorphic transformation, "Crow blinked at the world" (*CPH* 191), and Hughes's signature avatar was born.[1] Hughes himself described Crow as a "Trickster" figure, who possesses an "unkillable, biological optimism that supports a society or individual whose world is not yet fully created, and whose metaphysical beliefs are only just struggling out of the dream stage" (*WP* 239). Crow is a composite character; the "Trickster, the Hero, and the Saint on the Path meet in the Holy Fool . . . on the epic stage, in the draughty arena of 'everything possible'" (*WP* 241). The end of "Three Legends" introduces one of the sequence's major assumptions: that Crow's actions both influence and comment on society's evolution. In the midst of some terrible public conflict, as Hughes narrates, "Among the hurtling spears of the dew / The collision of flowers and blood / The crow's eye widened / Like an emblem on a tattered banner" (*CPH* 192). Crow appears here as a cultural icon as integral to human existence as war or the origins of humankind itself. His presence in this poem and in the pieces collected in *Four Crow Poems* (1970), *A Few Crows* (1970), *Crow: From the Life and Songs of the Crow* (1970), *Crow Wakes* (1971), and *Poems: Ruth Fainlight, Ted Hughes, Alan Sillitoe* (1971) helps to focus the reader's attention on Hughes's concern with the social status of the artist, the cultural aftermath of war, national identities, and the politics of interpersonal relationships. Hughes paints Crow as a mythologically resonant figure who possesses identifiably human traits, including a sometimes alienating sense of amorality. Like the narrators of Yeats's, Baraka's, and Berryman's work, Crow is at times destructive, absurd, and anti-religious. Yet his exploits often hone in on the conventional expectations with which writers are encumbered as well as the difficulty of identifying the true motivation behind one's work. Hughes first described Crow's origin as the intention "just to write his songs, the songs that a Crow would sing. In other words, songs with no music whatsoever, in a super-simple and a super-ugly language which would in a way shed everything except just what he wanted to say without any other consideration" (Faas 208). Reddick glosses this language as comprising "short sentences, stripped-down syntax, repetition, a vocabulary of destruction and ordure" (163). The poems that resulted showcase the grittiest, most brutal experiences that people endure; through these episodes, Crow gives voice to the writer's potential failures.

Plath focuses on a similar possibility of failure from the beginning of her sequence as well. "The Rabbit Catcher," the first poem to be included only in *Ariel 1*, which appears just two pages after "Morning Song," addresses first the speaker's physical experiences within a particular landscape and then her anxiety about the possibility of not achieving her creative goals. This poem offers the first sustained meditation on the fragile nature of artistic legacy in the *Ariel* sequence; this topic is also a major motivation behind the *Crow* poems. In a mode more inwardly focused than the book's opening piece, "The Rabbit Catcher" describes the effects of a personal trauma, which leads to a revelation about the speaker's need to act on her own behalf. Here Plath draws from the body of the surrounding landscape in order to create a metaphor that equates the gradual dissolution of a relationship with the snares a trapper uses to capture his prey. Although the title names the hunter, we read the poem from the perspective of an observer who is invested in the scene; she resists his traps in favor of using her own words. This speaker finds her power undercut when the "wind gag[s] my mouth" and "Tear[s] off my voice." In a suddenly alien landscape, the gorse tastes "malign," with yellow flowers that are "extravagant, like torture" (*CPP* 193). No sensory impression, in other words, can be trusted. When the poem's point of view shifts from the meadow to the home's interior, it admits a series of contradictions: a "still busyness," and the rabbits that wait, "like sweethearts," for the "little deaths" the hunter will bring. Such paradoxes highlight the source of the relationship's deterioration: it was strung on "tight wires" and held by "Pegs too deep to uproot," until the speaker found "The constriction killing me also" (*CPP* 194). Here the speaker's ambivalence toward love, first articulated in "Morning Song," is echoed by a hostile geography. She realizes that, in order to save herself, she needs to look away from the restrictive objects that surround her and concentrate on using her voice to achieve her own goals.

"Thalidomide," the next poem in the *Ariel 1* sequence, signals a transition from the uncertain nature of domestic love, and the constraints it places on one's voice, to a broader consideration of artistic legacy. The poem's importance within the overall sequence can be seen in both its major themes and its form. Rather than composing her usual regularly metered tercets or quintains, Plath creates a series of sparse couplets. Erratic line-lengths mirror the title drug's devastating effects even as they introduce a new form into her oeuvre. The opening line, "O half moon—," suggests the intended sedative effect of thalidomide; however, the following lines narrate the painful results that follow this prescription to ward off morning sickness. Not only do the resulting "dark / Amputations crawl and appal—" in the aftermath of birth, but the very act of being also requires tremendous effort, with "Knuckles at shoulder-blades, the / Faces that / / Shove into being, dragging / The lopped / / Blood-caul of absences" (*CPP* 252). These lines do not fall into the regular, carefully crafted stanzas of Plath's early work; rather, they form a jagged, disjunctive language whose grotesque images are revealed with painful slowness. The words' sounds contribute to the poem's meaning so that "the texture of the poem's language itself presents the experience being offered" (Hall 103). This contiguity between form, language, and meaning contributes to Plath's developing *ars poetica*. The poem concludes with a reference to mercury, another substance harmful to pregnant women, in order to remind readers of the miscarriages, the spontaneous "aborts," that interventions in the natural progression of both motherhood and writerly creation can produce. Plath's decision to position this poem just before "The Applicant," an indictment of traditional marriage roles, intimates that these studies of women's social experiences send similar messages. Both poems' critiques of enforced intrusions into women's narratives suggest that her poetic subjects represent the act of writing itself.

"Barren Woman," which appears after "The Applicant" in *Ariel 1*, includes a number of Plath's signature motifs and terms from her accumulating poetic vocabulary. The poem illustrates the speaker's receptivity to being filled, either with literal progeny or with artistic inspiration. Its title figure initially describes herself as "Empty" and "Nun-hearted," like a "Museum without statues"; however, her work makes her the "Mother of a white Nike and several bald-eyed Apollos." Plath often populates her poems with statues or other inanimate representations of the human, as in "The Disquieting Muses," "The Colossus," and "In Plaster," in order to describe the gap between social and personal perceptions of the self. These references to classical myth suggest the iconic yet impersonal nature of the speaker's aesthetic "children," while their "bald" nature—another recurring term from the Plath lexicon—signals the indifferent reception that her work may receive. Her sense that "nothing can happen" is echoed in the palliative actions of Plath's omnipresent moon, which "lays a hand on my forehead / Blank-faced and mum as a nurse" (*CPP* 157). While this phrasing seems to imply an act of caretaking, in fact it reinforces the theme of disinterest that filters through the rest of the poem. "Barren Woman" serves as a sobering introduction to the satirical tone and conscious detachment from the speaker's audience that characterize "Lady Lazarus," the next poem in *Ariel 1*. Whereas in *Ariel 2* "Lady Lazarus" is introduced by "The Applicant," a similarly sardonic analysis of the speaker's use-value, the presence of "Barren Woman" in *Ariel 1* adds a new dimension to the anxiety about social performance and public reception that "Lazarus" attempts to conceal beneath a satirical tone.[2] Clark identifies the source of this tone in Plath's interest in psychologist R. D. Laing's "techniques of 'impersonation,'" which enabled her both to "disarm the enemy by impersonating him through caricature" and to "wrest control of the dialogue and prove herself the strong poet" (*Grief* 137–38). "Barren Woman" undercuts the notion that the speaker's resurrection was born out of a desire for attention; rather, it reflects another attempt to create an art that will satisfy the "peanut-crunching crowds," who long to see the speaker's body dissected and all of its secrets laid bare.

Similar visions of an impersonal and ineffectual art inflect both "Magi" and "Lesbos," the next poems in the volume that are unique to *Ariel 1*. Here Plath speculates about the effects of independently conceived art on the writer's social relevance. This subject produces one especially significant compositional technique: the unstructured rhetoric of "Lesbos," the book's eighteenth poem. Plath's references to both societal indifference and artistic ambition suggests that the raw anger, pared-down vocabulary, and quick succession of images that comprise "Lesbos" are a natural response to stagnant literary traditions. She invokes the female legacy of Sappho's homeland through a language that relies upon sensory impressions, rapid shifts from one perspective to the next, and short declamatory phrases. This artistic ethos also offers an alternative to the classical epic form's investment in completed quests and restorations to the throne: another contribution that the *Ariel* sequence makes to the history of the American long poem.

"The Other" and "Stopped Dead," the two poems that follow "Lesbos" in *Ariel 1*, provide an alternative to the creative emptiness that Plath's blank statues embody by actively condemning situations beyond the speaker's control. In "The Other," the speaker worries that she might have left "untouched on the doorstep" a "White Nike, / Streaming between my walls" (*CPP* 201). In retribution for her partner's absence and inattention, the speaker takes action: she mounts "your head on my wall" while signs of productivity, "Navel cords, blue-red and lucent, / Shriek from my belly like arrows." Though she possesses "a womb of marble" and feels a cold glass barrier "Between myself and myself," she works to overcome these tactile reminders of the poetic sequence's other featureless forms. In the end, she calmly assesses the stink of "Sulfurous adulteries" and her partner's treacherous smile, which now is "not fatal" (*CPP* 202). These images, which signify, alternately, a dissolving marriage and the speaker's decision to resist betrayal through her work, point the way toward the new reality that she chooses to inhabit. "Stopped Dead" is set in a similarly reimagined world, one that "isn't England . . . isn't France . . . isn't Ireland," but is "violent" instead. The narrator is only "here on a visit, / With a goddam baby screaming off somewhere." This perspective clashes with earlier depictions of the parent-child relationship as metaphor for artistic invention. The baby's cries provoke the speaker to complain that "There's always a bloody baby in the air"; she cannot evoke traditional pastoral imagery because "Whoever heard a sunset yowl like that?" (*CPP* 230). This disruption of Plath's recurrent metaphor illustrates a temporary low point in the overall trajectory of the *Ariel* poems, in which the *ars poetica* that the sequence constructs must acknowledge obstacles to creative progress as well. Finally, the poem's conclusion echoes "Lady Lazarus"'s promise to "rise" "Out of the ash" "with my red hair" and "eat men like air" (*CPP* 247). As "Stopped Dead" ends, the speaker vows to carry her partner's soul off "like a rich pretty girl" and "live in Gibraltar on air, on air" (*CPP* 230). This chronological precursor to "Lady Lazarus" anticipates the anxieties that that poem's speaker articulates but also prepares the ground for her resistance to exploitation: the speaker reshapes the terms of the spectacle that "Stopped Dead" describes, just as "Lady Lazarus" will do.

"The Courage of Shutting-Up," another poem that appears only in *Ariel 1*, is preceded by the vulnerable "red heart" that "blooms" in "Poppies in October" (*CPP* 240) and followed by the ambivalence toward creation and selfhood that characterizes "Nick and the Candlestick." It replaces "Berck-Plage" in the *Ariel 2* order, which appears here after "Nick and the Candlestick." This new arrangement foregrounds a moment of revelation in the work's overall narrative, one in which the mouth is shut and "the tongue, too, has been put by," even as "the discs of the brain revolve." Plath chooses in "Shutting-Up" to focus on the poetic speaker's ability to witness; she uses "the eyes, the eyes, the eyes," which are not the "terrible rooms" of mirrors but "white and shy . . . no stool pigeons" (*CPP* 210). Though the speaker chooses to focus on her physical being rather than her words here, their absence reveals another dimension of Plath's poetics: a blazon-like taxonomy of the elements that comprise a poetic persona. This technique, which breaks a poem's expressive motivation down into its constituent parts, also anticipates the combination of autobiographical detail and writerly observation that defines "Berck-Plage." A unique contribution to Plath's comprehensive *ars poetica*, "Berck-Plage" continues the slow journey that *Ariel* traces toward an existence founded in creativity rather than in pain born of trauma. This transformation reflects the progression in Plath's own poetics from modernist formalism to explorations of postmodernist ontology. The long poem that *Ariel* forms describes a process of artistic discovery and the development of creative strength rather than, as in the classical epic, a consolidation of national identity.

The other two versions of *Ariel* exist, again, as *Ariel 2*, the order into which Hughes placed the poems when he first published the collection in 1965, and the strictly chronological order of the pieces as they appear in Plath's posthumous *Collected Poems*. *Ariel 2* differs from *Ariel 1* in several important ways, which I will discuss here only briefly since they have been covered exhaustively by other critics (see, e.g., Christina Britzolakis, Lynda Bundtzen, Heather Clark, Tim Kendall, Marjorie Perloff, and Sue Vice). Both *1* and *2* begin with "Morning Song" and "The Couriers"; the original continues with "The Rabbit Catcher," which is absent from the 1965 version, while Hughes places "Sheep in Fog" third; it is the only poem unique to this version that does not appear in the book's second half. The two poems capture contrasting views of the English countryside. "Sheep in Fog" maintains a sense of quiet contemplation that is reinforced by its simple adjectives—"slow," "dolorous," "far," "starless," "fatherless," "dark" (*CPP* 262)—but this tone allows the speaker to interpret the sheep as signifiers of her isolation and loneliness. "The Rabbit Catcher," on the other hand, views the land as a backdrop to violence and struggles for autonomy. The thirteen additional poems that Hughes includes in *Ariel 2*—which replace the twelve poems discussed above—appear, with the exception of "Sheep in Fog," as the book's conclusion. Paul Mitchell suggests that this arrangement highlights "a more somber ambiguity and . . . a poetic voice that bears witness . . . to a *jouissance* of a different kind" (38). It also brings forward a series of "circular, non-developmental sounds that Plath weaves in several of her poems that create the effect of stasis within them" (Mitchell 42). Such phonemes draw attention to Plath's familiar poetic vocabulary and confirm the theory of artistic creation that the final few pieces indicate. Hughes keeps the bee poems that Plath chose for *Ariel 2*, including "The Bee Meeting," "The Arrival of the Bee Box," "Stings, and "Wintering," but he also adds in "The Swarm" between these last two. This subsequence appears just before "The Hanging Man,," "Little Fugue," "Years," "The Munich Mannequins," "Totem," "Paralytic," "Balloons," "Poppies in July," "Kindness," "Contusion," "Edge," and "Words."

The contrast between the end of "Words" and the concluding lines of "Wintering" further demonstrates that Plath's *ars poetica* resonates in both *Ariel 1* and *Ariel 2*. While "Wintering" supplies a positive final word, "spring," to pair with the first word of "Morning Song," "Love," the final syllable of "Words" does not cancel out that optimism. Rather, its last word, "life," points to the motivation that underlies the compositional process, while the entire last line alludes to Plath's and Hughes's shared interest in divination, an alternate path to knowledge that assumes insight can be found outside the conventional boundaries of speech and thought. Thus, while *Ariel 1* ends with a subsequence of four bee poems, and *Ariel 2* ends with a series of statements that articulate Plath's poetics, both arrangements consider seriously the writer's progression through acts of composition and the material objects that contribute to poetic metaphor. Tim Kendall glosses this device in Plath's work as a manifestation of the tension between "the desire to control and understand" and "the limitations of language to express the ineffable" (*Sylvia Plath* 129). Motherhood and the aftereffects of painful experiences, a particularly resonant metaphor throughout the book, inflect Plath's idea of what is possible in writing. Her sequence begins by meditating on the speaker's ambivalent feelings about maternal and romantic love, turns away from the social world to an examination of the inner self, explores several perspectives on the potential worth of artistic legacy, acknowledges the many difficulties of pursuing art, tests out satire and parody as methods of distancing the creative self from the spectacle of public reception, challenges the traditional epic form, and imagines the rich possibilities of living an existence defined by confident expressivity. The sequence also marks a conscious shift away from the formal preoccupations of modernism toward ontological contemplation.

In contrast to the evolving narrator of the *Ariel* poems, Crow contributes to Hughes's developing notion of the *ars poetica* through his attempts to achieve unrestricted speech and the obstacles that foreclose it. His battles for a publicly acknowledged voice symbolize the efforts of avant-garde writers to achieve artistic visibility—a struggle that Plath also outlines in "Stopped Dead" and "The Courage of Shutting-Up." Gifford and Roberts describe Crow's experiences as a story in which "God has a nightmare in the form of a voice and a hand, which mocks his creation and which he challenges to do better" (18).[3] As a part of the statements on literary aesthetics that Crow attempts to make, too, Hughes constructs complex metaphors whose vehicles recall some of Plath's recurrent subjects but whose tenors are grounded in the material realities of national history. Crow literally dives into his experiences, using the properties of his physical body, in order to try to understand the "problems of consciousness" (Gifford and Roberts 112), to shed the problems that weigh him down, and to locate strategies through which he can read his social encounters as art. Yvonne Reddick describes the "many plans" that Hughes had made for the character of Crow, including a prose narrative and a final attempt to achieve "world repair" (154–55). Hughes did not realize many of these latter sketches, but Crow's tentative, evolving self reflects two specific periods of his life: the time just after Plath's death, when he labored to find a project that would occupy him, and the years after Assia Wevill's and their daughter Shura's deaths. Though he did not "mourn" Plath in a traditional public sense, he did write back to her in the sequence using a variety of shared techniques (Clark, *Grief* 189). Originally, close friend and visual artist Leonard Baskin "asked Hughes to write poems to accompany a series of sketches" of crows. Though he did not begin writing the sequence until the mid-1960s, Hughes noted that "the poems came quickly and were a shock to write" (Brandes 513). This experience is similar, Clark points out, to Plath's rapid process while composing the later *Ariel* poems (*Grief* 190). As a psychopomp of sorts, Crow helped to pilot Hughes's poetics from the traumas of the 1960s, through the allegorical representations of the natural world that shape *Recklings* (1966) and *Wodwo* (1967), to a new, mythically structured vision of art's potential for social commentary and guidance. Hughes described the project in a 1968 letter to Baskin as "a folk epic which will be the length of a novel—Bushman prose but more poems than prose" (*LTH* 279). In his interview with Drue Heinz, Hughes notes that "Crows are the central bird in many mythologies. The crow is at every extreme, lives on every piece of land on earth, the most intelligent bird" (80). The bird's mythic and material associations both contribute to Crow's persona as narrator of the sequence.

Crow appears in three of Hughes's uncollected poems from the late 1960s, in all of which he consumes vital elements of the world around him in order to fuel his own endeavors. "Crowquill," the most abstract piece of the three, considers the effects when a "crow's feather falls spinning." This seemingly inconsequential event sets into motion countless other actions, including "Rivers [that] peer from its scales" and a "five-coloured leopard [who] / Drops from a tree near the river" (*CPH* 198). From this menagerie, which grows to include rhinos, butterflies, mice, and people, is born poetic inspiration itself, which Hughes characterizes at the end of the poem as "The emptiness through which the feather falls / Like a wand / That has swallowed its wizard" (*CPH* 199). The succession of animals that populates the poem recalls the many earlier pieces, such as "The Thought-Fox," "The Jaguar," or "A Dream of Horses," in which Hughes equates creaturely behavior with the difficult work of artistic creation. He quickly unsettles this vision of Crow/crow as a tool of poetic production, however, in this period's two other uncollected poems, "Crow's Feast" and "A Crow Hymn." With the aside that "'Everything God does not want is mine,'" the protagonist of the former eats a computer programmer's insides (*CPH* 200); in the latter, he hails humans' and animals' inevitable progress toward death. These three poems establish Crow as a key voice in Hughes's post-*Ariel* work. Crow's sometimes passive attitude toward art itself and his recurrent fascination with death and destruction—markers, Jonathan Bate asserts, of the poems' function as "a skeletal autobiography" (290)—also suggest that Hughes saw poetic composition in ambivalent terms during this period. For him, creative efforts seem to have offered neither an ultimate solution to social issues nor a simple way to assess the world around him.

As Plath does in *Ariel*, Hughes draws on anti-epic strategies, elements of satire and parody, recurrent images of blank or empty forms, and thematic ambivalence in the Crow sequence. Though he does include some autobiographical details and recurring images from his larger oeuvre as well, many of the poems are set in environments shaped by contemporary political conflicts. These settings represent his poetics' most significant divergence from Plath's during this period. Crow often interprets his meditations on current political conditions as insights into the status of the artist more generally. Even the autobiographical references that Hughes includes in such pieces as "Crow Improvises" and "Lovesong" (both from *The Life and Songs of the Crow*) illuminate not just his own life after Plath's death but also the English national climate in the mid-twentieth century. Yvonne Reddick identifies three motivations that animate the Crow poems as a group: "a critique of technologized warfare and widespread pollution," the character's "gradual, but fragmentary, move towards a more reverential attitude to the nature-deity," and a "primitive" perspective on ecological conservation (171). "Crow Improvises" includes, for instance, an opposition between "a girl's laugh—all there was of it" and "a seven-year honeymoon—all that he remembered," yet this twinned allusion to Hughes's life with Plath is just one binary positioned among a catalogue of others. While the poem begins with a promise of artistic accomplishment—"There was this man / Who took the sun in one hand, a leaf in the other—/ The spark that jumped burned out his name"—it quickly shifts to images of destruction like "a black orifice," "the battle of the Somme," and a moment in which "he leaned one hand on a gravestone / With his jolly roger in the other." The poetic narrator's investment in his work seems at times secondary to his struggles to deal with the violent threats that surround him. These visions often oppose the natural world to the one that humans imagine—as, for instance, when "he rested a dead vole in one hand / and grasped Relativity in the other" (*CPH* 242)—but neither dimension of existence dominates over the other by the end of the poem. Rather, Hughes seems to conclude that the natural and the artificial, the painful and the pleasurable, the beautiful and the grotesque, are all essential components of the creative process. Crow's purpose here is to dissolve binaries, to identify the material sources of writerly inspiration from among life's myriad experiences.

"Lovesong," a more figurative depiction of a romantic relationship than the one depicted in "Crow Improvises," examines the consequences that follow a troubled liaison, in spite of its potential to generate creative energy. The poem begins with a bald statement of love but also warns readers of the relationship's possible threats; Hughes notes that "His kisses sucked out her whole past and future or tried to," while "She bit him she gnawed him she sucked / She wanted him complete inside her." The poem's second stanza reveals that their mutual obsession is draining their lives, since "He gripped her hard so that life / Should not drag her from that moment / He wanted all future to cease," while "Her embrace was an immense press / To print him into her bones" (*CPH* 255). As in so many of the other Crow poems, the poetic characters' strong emotions manifest in physical reactions; Crow's search for purpose culminates, again, in the figure of a woman, someone who may be a "demon, serpent, or version of the Gravesian White Goddess" (Bate 290). Soon enough, the pair's hunger for one another transmutes into murderous impulses; as "Her smiles were spider bites," so "His looks were bullet daggers of revenge" (*CPH* 255). The poem's simple metaphors and declarative sentences echo the diction in which Plath frames the destructive forces of "The Rabbit Catcher" as well. Hughes also depicts the final stages of this dissolving partnership through a syntactic shift from linking verbs to direct actions; when one partner's "promises took the top off his skull," the other responds with "vows [that] pulled out all her sinews." The poem concludes with a series of violent actions that seem to divide them, but, as Hughes notes, "love is hard to stop"; when their battles ended, "they wore each other's face" (*CPH* 256). Crow's presence here provides insight into the destruction and re-creation that passion enables, though Uroff suggests that the "turbulent energy" of Plath's *Ariel* poems becomes a source of reflection here instead (199). These physical interactions engender the poetic composition but they also underline the real cost that writers pay for their work.

The Crow poems rely upon a series of recurring images that contribute to Hughes's conversations with Plath's work. In "Crow Goes Hunting," for instance, Hughes pairs the emotional impact of war's sudden brutalities with the image of a "bounding hare" (*CPH* 236). This highly resonant metaphor also occurs in one of the uncollected poems from the late 1960s, "Existential Song," in which the protagonist concludes that "he was, in fact, nothing / But a dummy hare on a racetrack / And life was being lived only by the dogs" (*CPH* 203). While this image is a wholly artificial one, evoking the mechanical rabbits that greyhounds chase around tracks, it contributes to Hughes's corpus of rabbit-inspired poems and emphasizes the associations that his work repeatedly draws between rabbits and a lost ideal. The hunt metaphor that recurs across Hughes's work positions the rabbit as the ideal prey—though its literal absence from "Existential Song" and from "The Thought-Fox," the first of Hughes's hunting poems, suggests that the missing rabbit also signifies inspiration. Similarly, Plath's "The Rabbit Catcher" does not contain any references to the animal itself.[4] In another rich example, Crow begins by searching for his work's motivation in "Crow Goes Hunting"; he "Decided to try words" and "imagined some words for the job, a lovely pack—/ Clear-eyed, resounding, well-trained, / With strong teeth." He encounters a quandary that many other writers have faced: "Crow was Crow without fail, but what is a hare?" (*CPH* 236). Crow's every attempt to master his victim, to end the hunt, fails. His words themselves engage in a sort of Moebius action, hunting for meaning from form to form until they finally consume themselves. This version of the hunt recalls Plath's "Tulips," in which the flowers' "red lead sinkers" "eat my oxygen" and "fill up" the air with their "loud noise" (*CPP* 161); their usurpation of the speaker's basic life functions poses a challenge to her creative production, just as Crow's hunt evades a successful conclusion. Here, as Crow tries to control his language, first he "turned the words into a reservoir," then the "water turned into an earthquake," and finally "The earthquake turned into a hare and leaped for the hill / Having eaten Crow's words." Hughes does not paint Crow as dejected at the loss, however; instead, he "gazed after the bounding hare / Speechless with admiration" (*CPH* 236). The hare's materiality is what Crow desires, not its immediate presence. So, too, Hughes suggests that the poem's endurance through time ought to be the writer's goal. Plath's speaker also accepts the tulips' presence once she contains them "behind bars like dangerous animals" (*CPP* 162); she shifts the narrative focus back to her own concerns by offering up images of her heart and her tears. For Hughes, the hare serves as a metonym of the finished work, its tactile presence enforcing the notion that poetic experience manifests through concrete objects and experiences.

In spite of Crow's ongoing search for writerly success and his active participation in a range of life-defining experiences, he remains a figure of uncertainty and self-doubt in Hughes's work. Many of the *Ariel* poems also consider the difficulty of holding onto one's identity in the middle of the creative process. These ontological anxieties remain open and unresolved within the poems' narratives; the poetic speakers voice them anonymously, without making reference to any personal traits. "O my God, what am I," cries the speaker of "Poppies in October," "That these late mouths should cry open / In a forest of frost, in a dawn of cornflowers" (*CPP* 240); "Fever 103°" begins with a question, "Pure? What does it mean?" (*CPP* 231), as does "The Bee Meeting," with "Who are these people at the bridge to meet me?" (*CPP* 211). However, where the *Ariel* speakers pursue answers to these questions, if obliquely, the character of Crow tends to linger on his internal sense of shortcoming, focusing on the sins he believes he has committed rather than seeking out the roots of his current predicament. In "Crow's Nerve Fails," for instance, he interprets his own body as evidence of his wrongdoing: he "Finds his every feather the fossil of a murder." His actions do not motivate him to question the nature of existence itself, as the narrators of "Poppies in October" and "Fever 103°" do; rather, they confirm his sense that he has condemned himself to solitude. "Who murdered all these?" he wonders of his feathers, speculating that he might be "the archive of their accusations" or "their unforgiven prisoner" (*CPH* 232). These dark markers of his pedigree serve a very different function in this piece than they did in the earlier "Crowquill"; he can no longer trace the path of a single feather to its "wizard." This object's transmutation from an agent of composition to an inert signifier of wrongdoing recalls the blind, bald forms that populate "Barren Woman," "Magi," and "The Other." The progress that the metaphorical feather makes from "Crowquill" to "Crow's Nerve Fails" indicates that Crow's efforts do not always produce their desired effect. He doubts his work, and, as a result, he doubts the material that comprises his physical self. In the Crow poems, as in Plath's sequence, a shift in the status of a poetic object away from personhood, a dissolution of human characteristics, connotes a loss of creative strength.

Hughes studies the sources of Crow's self-doubt in "Crowego" as well, which positions his protagonist both as an active participant in centuries of literary history and as a touchstone within Hughes's own collected works.

Though he meets Ulysses, Hercules, Dejanira, and Beowulf, Crow engineers destruction in their company, rather than invention. He consumes the worm left after Ulysses's death, strangles Dejanira, and drinks Beowulf's blood before realizing that "His wings are the stiff back of his only book, / Himself the only page—of solid ink." As the author of his own story, Crow has made no characters that will live on after him, as the writers of the classical epics did; his inward-turned contemplation cultivates only his own ego. Like the twentieth-century modernists who sought to establish their own legacy through long poems modeled on the epic form, Crow looks to the past for source material, but finds obfuscation rather than clarity: "the quag of the past" fails in comparison to "the crystal of the future." His final effort marks out the familiar landscapes of Hughes's work: he looks out "Like a leopard into a fat land" (*CPH* 240). The jaguars, hares, wolves, crabs, and fish that populate so many of the poems usually move the narrative forward, as Crow does not; their actions serve, in contrast to Crow's ambivalent gestures, as vehicles for the poetry's statements on art itself. Crow's refusal of the epic narrative also signals Hughes's turn away from his modernist precedents, however. In this sequence, as Plath had done in *Ariel*, he outlines the search for a theory of art that arises from his own techniques and concerns.

Although "Crowego" tabulates Crow's divergences from his classical precedents, some mythological references in the Crow poems enable Hughes to deploy significant images as a means of interpreting both personal and political crises. "A Disaster," for example, features a graphically delineated portrait of war's physical destruction. A conflict that breaks out across the world ends up "bulldozing / Whole cities to rubble" while "its excreta [is] poisoning seas" and "its breath burning whole lands." As is the case in many of the Crow poems, Hughes uses text itself—a simple "word," in this case—to signify the disaster's origin. Though Crow "saw it sucking the cities / Like the nipples of a sow / Drinking out all the people / Till there were none left, / All digested inside the word," he does not try to forestall its progress. He observes the damage that words can wreak, eats "well" off the resulting carnage, and reflects on the digested civilization that remains (*CPH* 226). Crow does not argue that humans should intervene in such conflicts, but his actions serve to remind readers of the perils that passive observation creates. If we do not take the time to construct and monitor our own words, Hughes suggests, we run the risk of becoming scavengers, like Crow, who profit from the world's ruin without contributing to its beauty. "Glimpse," one of Hughes's shortest Crow poems, also condemns art that lacks a social purpose. Crow begins the piece by voicing an ode to leaves, a valorization of natural beauty that recalls Plath's early experiments with Romantic iconography, but he soon finds that the world itself can hurt: "The touch of a leaf's edge at his throat / Guillotined further comment." When he continues to gaze at the leaves, he must do so "Through the god's head instantly substituted" (*CPH* 256). Seeking material relevance rather than contenting himself with aesthetics brings Crow face-to-face with the divine—though the "god" in this case remains faceless and mute, much like Plath's muses, the magi, and even her earlier "bronze boy." Janne Stigen Drangsholt calls this type of encounter Hughes's "attempt to yield a language that places the human being at a point of vibrant intersection"; Crow's own inability to act on that insight in a poem like "Glimpse" suggests that he is "fundamentally *un*-able to recognize and enunciate the simple 'being-thereness' of sea, stone, wind and tree" (131). Here Crow catches a glimpse of the world's real nature by risking danger, but he must acquiesce to a deity that acts without acknowledging his existence.

In addition to the emphasis he places on poetry's potential for historical and social commentary in the Crow poems, Hughes returns several times across the series to the philosophical insights that myths and legends can provide. Crow operates in some of these poems as a mythic figure whose origin, experiences, and actions help to shape the world itself. "Two Legends," a piece whose thematic focus on birth and darkness harks back to the earlier "Three Legends," looks first at an individual experience of creation and then at the external markers of new life that signal terrestrial evolution. Though Crow is not an active agent in the poem, he appears in generic form as the conclusion to the second "legend": "To hatch a crow, a black rainbow / Bent in emptiness / over emptiness / But flying." Even without color, the crow is born out of a curiously beautiful image. His beginning combines shape, movement, and space, and it contrasts with the "wet otter's head," "rock, plunging in foam," and "earth-globe" that also signal the start of earth's existence (*CPH* 217). Rand Brandes argues that this poem "introduces all that will follow in the [Crow] volume," including "stripped-down language, the use of repetition and parallelism of oral poetry, the predominance of body parts as central images, an informing Primitivism, a mythic infrastructure, and the breakdown of metaphor" (518). The crow is present from the beginning of known life, helping to define both the impossible beauty of what does exist—the "black rainbow"—and what we still lack. This image also echoes the shape, movement, and color that Plath describes in "Ariel": the "Stasis in darkness," the "brown arc / Of the neck I cannot catch," and "the drive / Into the red / Eye, the cauldron of morning" (*CPP* 239–40).

Elements of the natural world also help to articulate new questions about the role of the artist, as Hughes illustrates in "Crow and the Sea" and "Crow and Stone." Crow is an active participant in these two different versions of the world's origin story. Though he tries to contribute to the global narrative, he realizes in both cases that the world's boundaries exceed his imagination, and his words can only begin to sketch the reality he inhabits. In "Crow and the Sea," he finds that the ocean "was bigger than death, just as it was bigger than life." Human modes of communication do not have any impact on its existence; even "just being in the same world as the sea" results in the harsh discovery that "his lungs were not deep enough" (*CPH* 252). Unlike some of the other poems, this piece illustrates Crow as "intelligently curious and wittily playful"; he understands that his being is smaller than "the forces and the mystery of the natural world" (Gifford and Roberts 140). The primal confrontation between a human being and the natural world that Hughes imagines here resonates with Greek, Norse, Irish, and Yoruba origin myths alike. Many Greek stories detail an initial struggle between a god and his parent that leads to the diversification of cultural identities, while Norse mythology begins from the creation of the nine worlds that house various types of beings and the skirmishes that ensue among them. Irish creation mythologies, on the other hand, center on the battles that produced the country's major landmarks and heroes. Finally, Yoruba creation stories describe the process by which the first gods built the continent of Africa from raw materials and fashioned early humans from the land itself.[5] All of these origin mythologies describe not only humans' interactions with the intrinsic properties of the natural world but also the oversight of self-interested rulers or gods. As a mythic figure who possesses human failings, Crow exists within both sides of this narrative structure.

In "Crow and the Sea," Crow acknowledges that his remaining battle, as in so many origin tales, will be with himself. Hughes frames this struggle, in both this poem and "Crow and Stone," as the artist's attempt to create in spite of and beyond his own ego. Crow admits his own unwinnable war against the world when "He turned his back and he marched away from the sea" (*CPH* 252): his act acknowledges that he cannot deny the fundamental nature of the sea, even when it impedes his actions. "Crow and Stone" narrates a similar effort to master the world, using the same symbolic element that appears in "Three Legends": a stone, which Gifford and Roberts have described as a "portent of non-being" in the work overall (97). Hughes labels Crow's far-seeing eyes "two dewdrops," a delicate image that is oddly juxtaposed to the moment when "Stone, champion of the globe, lumbered towards him." The fight's likely outcome shifts quickly, though, as the "stone battered itself featureless / While Crow grew perforce nimbler." By the end of their epic contest, "the stone is a dust—flying in vain," while "Crow has become a monster." Hughes is careful to temper this portrait of Crow's triumph over his adversary, however, by pointing out that even the most powerful figure is vulnerable at the moment of his emergence into the world. To participate in the mythology of creation, to write oneself into being, suggests that one must be born, flourish, and pass away over and over again, in the ongoing cycle of existence. For Hughes, this cycle represents another key metaphor for the work of writerly creation itself. Crow, "*he who has never been killed*," must still start from the beginning, at which point he "*Croaks helplessly / And is only just born*" (*CPH* 253; original italics). Crow engages with iconic cultural myths in this poem; he contributes to the moment of creation, yet reveals his all-too-human traits in his uncertainty about whether and how his contributions matter. This uncertainty mirrors a central theme of the *Ariel* poems as well: the ambivalence about love and creation that Plath articulates in "Morning Song" and "Thalidomide," among other examples.

Hughes wrote one of his earliest Crow poems, "A Lucky Folly," as another exploration of the metaphoric potential of cultural mythologies—which, in this case, imagines a successful quest that takes place in a traditional European fairy tale, but with some anachronistic elements. At the beginning of the poem, Crow encounters a maiden and a dragon but, rather than battle the one and save the other, he "fantasied building a rocket and getting out fast." Unable to escape to "a castle—battlements. A pinnacle prison," he chooses instead to craft an instrument with which to charm the beast. He "cut holes in his nose. He fingered this flute, / Dancing, with an occasional kick at his drum" (*CPH* 203). Here Hughes presents Crow in allegorical terms, participating in a story whose familiar elements of St. George's exploits already communicate a whole history of conflict and romantic triumph to his readers. Hughes himself called this interaction "the classic nightmare of modern English intelligence in particular" (*LTH* 339). Yet Crow's unexpected interventions in the narrative—his insistence upon making the body itself an instrument of distraction, his reluctance to fight physical battles directly—resonate with Hughes's other *ars poetica* and with Plath's reimagination of the artist's tools in, for instance, "Lady Lazarus" and "Magi." In the former, the speaker presents her resurrected body as both a spectacular miracle and evidence of her creative power, while in the latter the faceless "magi" must yield to the baby's potential for independent invention. In order to claim the story, Hughes suggests in "A Lucky Folly," one must use the body in a new way: to create art, rather than war. Crow's efforts gain him adulation; the maiden's and dragon's responses invoke the sublime as a response to art, rather than mere gratitude or admiration. The extreme nature of this reaction borders on the satirical, a tonal echo of Plath's narrative in "The Applicant" and "Lady Lazarus." Satire remains, in fact, a key component of Crow's responses to his environment and to other characters throughout the sequence. In this case, after Crow begins to play, "in horror and awe / The maiden danced with him, incredulous," while the dragon "wept," "licked Crow's foot," and "slobbered Crow's fingers." The dragon is not just tamed by Crow's art but overwhelmed by it: "'More, more,' he cried, and 'Be my god'" (*CPH* 204). The poem employs mythological archetypes in order to suggest that Crow's character can break down the traditional components of a story and then reassemble them into a unique narrative. Hughes argues here that an effective art astonishes its witnesses and shifts their attention to the insights that they can glean from the cosmos. His exploration of this possibility only in the early Crow poems suggests, however, that he does not see his poetic character as capable of sustaining the sublime ideal in the face of the material world's everyday disasters. This concession to Crow's fallibility rests upon the assumption that the writer must address real conditions and experiences rather than focusing on mythological structures alone.

In general, Hughes positions Crow in the sequence as an arbiter of historical and mythical conflict, albeit one who frequently succumbs to human frailties. His psyche betrays evidence of both self-doubt and hubris; he imagines himself a contributor to the cycles of social history but also bemoans his own existence. As a result, he negotiates time and time again between "a desire to trust in language as an effective weapon" and his "realization that the weapon is blunt, inefficient, or aimed at oneself" (Webb 37). In "Crow's Song About England," Hughes explores the contradictory nature of his poetic avatar by linking him to a familiar narrative of desire and censure. This poem appears in the 1971 collection that Hughes published with Ruth Fainlight and Alan Sillitoe; its slightly later position in his work's chronology suggests that Crow now represents a more mature perspective on creation and the world. The poem begins with the traditional fairy tale opening—"Once upon a time there was a girl"—but diverges quickly from its precedents by using a deliberately abrasive diction to narrate bodily trauma. Hughes's first stanza notes that the poem's protagonist tries to give up her "mouth," "eyes," "breasts," and "cunt," yet each of these metaphoric sacrifices produces only violence in return. She is "snatched," "slapped," "knocked to the floor," "crushed," "cut," "canned," and even "produced in open court" before being "sentenced" for some unspecified crime. The next few lines seem to legitimate her position, as she "stole everything back" and "changed sex." As a violent male antagonist, he then stabs "her mouth," "her eyes," "her breasts," and "her cunt." Even after being sentenced for these crimes, he changes sex again, in time to repeat the same treatment. Hughes rewrites his first stanza in the poem's final lines, changing the poetic protagonist's actions from "tried to give" to "tried to keep." This series of actions proves equally impossible for the girl, as she receives the same vicious physical treatment that Hughes depicted in the first stanza and, this second time, "She did life" rather than trying to take back what was hers (*CPH* 269). The poem's vulgar language underlines the violations often enacted upon women's bodies but also ties their experiences to those of the body public; Hughes suggests that both conquerors and citizens have ravaged the country. Yielding its best resources has garnered England pain and public humiliation; the nation's vulnerability persists in spite of its changing identities. Crow appears in this piece as a witness to not only the desecrations that England has suffered but also the horrifying realities of women's physical trauma. Hughes argues, through the figure of Crow, that the poet must expose these painful realities as a source of artistic inspiration. Crow himself feels guilt over the very fact of his existence, yet his "creative and destructive capacities" emerge from the cosmos itself (Gifford and Roberts 145). While this message might sound self-serving, it does resonate with Plath's condemnation of "tight wires" and "constriction" in "The Rabbit Catcher": both poems assess the raw insights that such assaults make possible. Equally important to Hughes, however, is his work's responsibility to tap into the contemporary social and cultural zeitgeist. Crow's recurrent disappointment in his psychological inadequacies and artistic shortcomings is reflected in stories whose outcomes almost always fall short of expectations. In the *Crow* sequence, Hughes describes the inadequate frameworks that structure current narratives about English cultural identities; Crow, in the guise of writer and creator, seeks to correct public visions of historical truth even as he is always aware that he will fail.

MOVING BETWEEN THE SEQUENCES

Hughes's Crow poems draw some inspiration from Robert Graves's *The White Goddess: A Historical Grammar of Poetic Myth* (1948). This book's treatment of metaphorical images of women and the body has been well-documented by writers like Miranda Seymour and Jonathan Bate. Seymour notes that "Ted Hughes and Sylvia Plath were among the young poets who acknowledged the book as a formative influence; Hughes won *The White Goddess* as a school poetry prize and read it when he was in Cambridge in the early fifties. When he met Sylvia Plath, this was one of the first books he wanted her to read" (328). Hughes's pre-Crow work incorporates some archetypal images of women in the three phases of Graves's "moon goddess"; his poetic narrators often express admiration or reverence at a psychic distance from the objects of their affection. In the poems that immediately precede Crow, however, female archetypes take on a more antagonistic aspect as the women that Hughes imagines develop individual shape and agency. Bate notes, as do Gifford and Roberts, that "Hughes sometimes introduced public readings of the *Crow* poems by explaining that Crow's quest was to meet his maker, God. But every time he met Him, it was a Her, a woman, an incarnation of the Goddess. Each time, Crow was unsatisfied and had to move on to another encounter" (459). "This Game of Chess," which he wrote in the late 1960s, employs a familiar chess metaphor in order to interrogate the iconic nature of interactions between the archetypal woman and man. The poetic narrator poses a series of questions—"What hill is this? Is it a hill / Or the crown of a skull? / What is that conflagration? Sun? Moon? / A Supernova? Or a Heavenly bundle?" (*CPH* 204)—that shift the reader's attention from life to death, to the interplay between the earthly domain and the cosmos. Hughes's titular reference to the second section of Eliot's *The Waste Land* evokes the figure of Belladonna, the representative of female identity who recurs throughout Eliot's epic. At the same time, these unanswered questions suggest that Hughes refuses to quantify femininity or female "essence" in the same way that Eliot did. Rather, he examines the role that women play in establishing standards for human morality through scenes recognizable from the collective pool of Western cultural knowledge. They witness "a god and two thieves," "three Kings / Searching on their thrones / In the Nativity snow," and "three Furies / Already on the hill." These groupings point to the trinities that recur throughout Western mythological history and link such familiar representations to the three aspects of Graves's moon goddess. Hughes concludes the poem with a question that works on both literal and metaphorical levels: "*Who shall win this Game of Chess?*" The final answer he offers indicates that these groupings of three are displaced in the ultimate mythos by the goddess herself: "*The Trinity are blinded by / The Triple Face of a Goddess / And a Goddess and a Goddess*" (*CPH* 205). This piece appears in Hughes's *Collected Poems* as the final uncollected work before the Crow poems. Its position both as the conclusion to this earlier period of Hughes's work and as the transition to Crow's narrative illustrates the central influence of archetypal structures on his poetry and highlights the contributions that allegory would make to his *ars poetica*.

"Her Husband," one of the poems that explores the politics of interpersonal relationships in *Wodwo* (1967), provides another source of insight into Hughes's perspectives on archetypal identity prior to his composition of the Crow poems. This piece is conventionally organized, comprising five four-line stanzas whose erratically recurring spondees give the poetic narrative an unpredictable meter and a harsh expressive mode. Hughes syncs his subject-matter with this form by portraying a domestic environment in which husband and wife air their disagreements only through awkward physical actions, rather than speaking them aloud. The husband appears first in the narrative, "dull with coal-dust deliberately / To grime the sink and foul towels." He feels justified in these actions by the bodily cost he has already paid, the "dust" and "sweat" that produce "the blood-weight of money." In response, the wife provides "fried, woody chips, kept warm two hours in the oven." Their mutual dissatisfaction registers in his "voice / Of resounding corrugated iron" and her careworn back, which has "bunched into a hump as an insult." These rough and unwelcoming images, which collide with one another both aurally and semantically, demonstrate the husband's and wife's ability to register their unhappiness without making a substantive difference in the quality of their day-to-day lives. Their silent acts of aggression toward one another gain them some autonomy without shifting the balance of power noticeably toward either side. The poem's title also decenters its subject, suggesting that the man might be the piece's true focus even as the woman emerges as the definer of their relationship. Their unhappy coexistence is contained neatly within Hughes's regular stanzas and recurring spondaic feet; their attempts to change the situation finally come to nothing, as "Their brief / Goes straight up to heaven and nothing more is heard of it" (*CPH* 148). This pattern of interactions, reflected in the poem's formal qualities, establishes the ground on which Crow himself would emerge into existence, encounter humanity's familiar problems, and flounder in his attempts to salvage creative energy from disaster.

"Magi," the seventeenth poem in *Ariel 1*, continues Plath's exploration of parenthood as a metaphor for intellectual expectations and establishes allegory and archetype as central concerns in the volume. As in "This Game of Chess" and "Her Husband," this poem centers on allegorical figures who communicate both artistic potential and a lack of affect. These anonymous but material forms include "dull angels" wearing only "the ethereal blanks of their face-ovals." At first, the speaker anticipates that the magi will bring personal accomplishment and ensure her legacy, yet she finds her art overwhelmed by the inertia of social expectations: she feels pressured by "the Good, the True" (*CPP* 148). Magi, traditionally the heralds of Christ's birth, here represent, according to Plath's commentary in a BBC recording, "'the great absolutes of the philosophers gathered around the crib of a newborn baby girl who is nothing *but* life'" (qtd. in Hughes, "Notes on Poems" 290). The poem's baby understands "Evil" in terms only of temporary personal discomfort and "Love" as the fulfilled promise of food. If on the one hand this perspective simplifies art's major preoccupations, on the other it gives the poetic speaker a reason to resist. She notes that the magi, "these papery godfolk," "want the crib of some lamp-headed Plato," yet she dismisses their advances in order to protect her offspring. "What girl," she asks, "ever flourished in such company?" In the end, the speaker seeks a different fate for her daughter, a new purpose for the work she will produce. Here Plath's *ars poetica* imagines that writing within the traditions established by "magi" and other "lamp-headed Platos" will result in empty and purposeless work; she argues instead for a "merit" that will "astound his heart" (*CPP* 148): writing so distinctive that it will sway readers' emotions.

Many of the other poems that Hughes wrote in the period just preceding the Crow pieces focus on the same questions of artistic purpose and social relevance that Plath ponders in "Magi." These contributions to his *ars poetica* form a bridge between Hughes's earliest collections and *Crow*; they also highlight his investment in some of the same issues that Plath had first raised in *Ariel*. Like Plath, too, Hughes's works from this period include several images that have accrued special resonance across his oeuvre. In "Dog Days on the Black Sea," for instance, Hughes describes the everyday labors of an author, whose "world hangs like a bead of perspiration / In [his] eyebrow." The weight of his need to write his text is suspended like humidity over a beach; he hears a "Voice struggling away ahead for relief / From the ache of its body." The poem's protagonist endures tension strung out through the slow passage of time: "The writer's sweat drops. He stares hopelessly" (*CPH* 197). The questions that conclude the poem—"Why should Time be a road? / Why should tomorrow be a destination? / Why should yesterday be another country?"—are powerful enough to alter its perspective from third-to first-person. As the narrator observes, "Everything is in the scales / And every second weighs / Exactly everything—as I can see / With my see-saw brains" (*CPH* 198). This shift in viewpoint reflects, again, the writer's anxiety about the act and products of composition. He finds that even his physical body is compromised by his work, but he still chooses to accept the encumbrances of creation.

Both "Purdah" and "Amnesiac," the final two poems unique to the *Ariel 1* sequence, also focus on questions of artistic relevance even as they explore images and cultural discourses that recur across Plath's body of work. Unlike the looser organization of "Dog Days," however, these poems are carefully structured in tercets: a nod to Plath's formalist roots but also a means by which to emphasize her increasingly sparse syntax and surrealist successions of discrete images. Read as self-contained narratives, each poem culminates in resistance to the title concept. As do several of the other poems in her sequence, both of these pieces examine the effects that social censure has on writerly production. They refer to fields in which women face public restrictions but position these images as metonyms of the obstacles that obstruct artistic innovation. In "Purdah," a name for the Islamic practice of maintaining a personal and physical distance between men and women, the speaker reveals forbidden sights as a direct challenge to this segregation.[6] She characterizes herself as "Jade," "The agonized / / Side of green Adam," but, rather than allowing the moon to "My visibilities hide," she "gleam[s] like a mirror" (*CPP* 242). Even when the speaker is properly attired, in a socially sanctioned head-covering, "the mouth / / Veil stirs its curtain"; she "Revolve[s] in my / Sheath of impossibles," promising to "unloose / One note / / Shattering / The chandelier / Of air" (*CPP* 243). These acts suggest only a minor rebellion, but the poem's conclusion unleashes the vengeful spirit that has been concealed behind such obedience all along: "I shall unloose— / From the small jeweled / Doll he guards like a heart— / / The lioness, / The shriek in the bath, / The cloak of holes" (*CPP* 243–44). The images here recall Agamemnon, stabbed in the bath by the wronged Clytemnestra, as well as the avenging possibilities of a lioness or a wrathful angel. The speaker's surface beauty, concealed beneath veils and a pretense of submission, transforms into an instrument of argument, one that crafts and utilizes dangerous stories.

The anger that the speaker expresses in "Purdah" metamorphoses in "Amnesiac," however, to another rhetorical tool: parody. She mocks "The little toy wife / Erased, sigh, sigh," and proclaims, "Down the drain with all of it!" This strategy enables Plath to both reimagine traditional social roles and redefine public spaces as valid arenas for creative expression: two compositional tactics that Hughes also makes use of in the *Crow* sequence. Moving from contemplation to action, the speaker concludes with a tercet whose nursery-rhyme structure both recalls Eliot's "Sweet Thames, run softly, till I end my song," from *The Waste Land* (l. 183), and cuts off the possibility of reconciliation: "O sister, mother, wife, / Sweet Lethe is my life. / I am never, never, never coming home!" (*CPP* 233). This poem precedes the intense emotionality of "Daddy," "Fever 103°," and the final four bee poems in *Ariel 1*. Plath could not have created the terse diction, jarring images, and explosive rhetoric of these last pieces without having worked out in the earlier poems a path toward the writer's ideological and creative emancipation.

Drawing on an interrogative mode and sudden shifts in emotional tone similar to Plath's, Hughes examines dialectics resonating between art and self-doubt in "Wodwo" and "Second Glance at a Jaguar." Rather than alluding to classical mythology and modernist precedents as Plath does, though, Hughes chooses to generate philosophical reflection through richly evocative animal imagery. "Wodwo," whose title refers to a traditional "wild man" figure in the mythology of medieval Europe, traces the movements of an undefined creature that treks through the woods in an effort to answer one key question: "What am I?" Unlike most of Hughes's other work from the late 1960s and early 1970s, this piece employs long run-on sentences enjambed across several lines, erratic punctuation, and an associative rather than linear narrative. It also serves as the concluding poem in the eponymous collection, suggesting that in this book Hughes traced problems similar to those articulated through Crow: the search for a coherent self-identity, the purpose of existence, and the possibility of making meaningful contributions to the world. Hughes himself described this book's aesthetic achievement as a shift from a "'closed' [to an] 'open' Universe" (*LTH* 272). The poem combines Hughes's characteristically precise focus on the special properties of natural beauty with an unusual series of repeated actions. The poetic narrator wonders, for instance, "What am I to split / The glassy grain of water looking upward I see the bed / Of the river above me upside down very clear." The unexpected transition here from an interrogative mode to a descriptive one, held together by the linchpin phrase "glassy grain of water," demonstrates the speaker's uncertain position in the world, one in which "I seem / separate from the ground and not rooted but dropped / out of nothing casually I've no threads / fastening me to anything I can go anywhere." Like Crow himself, this protagonist notes that "me and doing that have coincided very queerly," yet he continues to assess his surroundings and attempts to make sense of the quest he has set himself. In a manner similar to Crow, too, he fancies himself the source and beginning of all things—"I suppose I am the exact centre"—but also finds himself repeatedly distracted by other elements of the world: "but there's all this what is it roots / roots roots roots and here's the water / again very queer but I'll go on looking" (*CPH* 183). As the finale to *Wodwo* itself, this last line points the reader toward the investigatory nature of Hughes's later work, its thematic tendency toward doubt and the pleasure of discovery.

"Second Glance at a Jaguar," a poem that appears near the beginning of *Wodwo*, centers on another familiar group of poetic images: an animal moving confidently through its habitat as the poetic speaker analyzes its physical and narrative power. While this portrait of an isolated predator does not seem an obvious analogue to the writer's process, as in "The Thought-Fox" or even "The Jaguar," its careful delineation of the animal's outward appearance and instinctual movement demonstrates the precision that poetic craft demands. In "Second Glance at a Jaguar," Hughes compares the cat's head first to "a brazier of spilling embers" (*CPH* 151) and then to "the worn down stump of another whole jaguar" (*CPH* 152); these similes evoke danger, productivity, and metonym, all tools that a writer uses. Hughes employs similes in these lines in order to approach the jaguar's being obliquely; in this compositional strategy, authors "refuse to take total possession of things even as they make a claim for thinking about them." His depiction of the jaguar is meant to fail, to argue that it can never be fully and accurately represented in a text, yet the many images that seek to capture it "also prevent the jaguar from going entirely free" (Castell 96–97). Though the poem does not conclude by revealing his immediate target, the jaguar moves in active pursuit, "Muttering some mantra, some drum-song of murder / To keep his rage brightening" even as he is "Hurrying through the underworld, soundless" (*CPH* 152). This relentless emotion, and the unnamed goals that provoke it, also define Crow's existence.

Many of the thematic, tonal, and didactic elements of the *Crow* poems resonate with Plath's work in both versions of *Ariel*. *Ariel 1* in particular reveals an increasingly precise concentration on the act of writing and the resulting artistic legacy. Though the *Ariel* narrators do not struggle with constant self-doubt and a desire to mock the world's capacity for dissolution, as Crow often does, they do engage a similar dialectic between creation and temporary stasis in the course of realizing Plath's final vision of the *ars poetica*. She includes moments of anger in the poems that may originate in her personal life, but these moments serve primarily to illustrate her particular vision of art's potential for social and self-expression. Rather than producing work that relies upon modernism's formal structures and classical allusions, Plath fashions a poetics of anticipation and declaration. Her work's many exclamation points and question marks emphasize "moments of excitement or discovery" as well as hope (Kendall, "From the Bottom" 27). She does not contribute another chapter to the history of the classic epic form, as so many modernists did, nor does she construct a series of correlations between her own past and the overall poetic narrative. Instead, she carefully organizes *Ariel* into a progression from uncertainty over creative production to a purging of past hindrances—which in turn reveals new possibilities for innovative art. The collection's title itself refers not only to the horse that Plath rode during her lessons and Shakespeare's spirit from *The Tempest* but also to the sacrificial position of ancient Jerusalem (Gjurgjan 138). Etymologically, the word designates "altar or, more specifically, fire-hearth of God" (Kendall, *Sylvia Plath* 127), while its Hebrew translation is "God's lioness" (Wagner-Martin, *Biography* 220), suggesting that Plath acknowledges her historical precedents even as she creates a new poetics based in material experience and the didactic potential of art.

In turn, Hughes's work in *Wodwo*, the uncollected poems, and even *The Hawk in the Rain* prepares the ground for Crow's emergence in the late 1960s as the voice and arbiter of the author's complex perspective on his craft. Although many of the Crow poems engage more directly with the processes of creation, the writer's position in history, and literature's mythological precedents, they also underline Hughes's sense that the poet is responsible for recording the atrocities that he witnesses, not just the aesthetic pleasures of the natural world. "T.V. On," one of the uncollected poems from the late 1960s, points to the violence that scars every continent; Reddick calls it "an important early ecopoem" that "foreshadows Hughes's Crow poems about nuclear conflagration" (162). Here the speaker expresses his disgust with the voyeuristic techniques of visual journalism: "All chewed up with chat, / The camera's salivations." At the same time, he recognizes that his own art contributes to the global chaos—"And I keep on stoking it with myself – / There go my guts and nerves, too"—but cannot find a different way to act. He is weighed down by all that he has produced and owns: "Trousers, shirt, coat, all too heavy, / My body too inaccessibly heavy" (*CPH* 193). Just as Crow does, this poetic narrator blames himself for the horrors that crowd the world. This fundamental conundrum—the speaker's awareness of the negative forces to which he has contributed coupled with his inability to imagine an alternative—centers the Crow poems as well.

Hughes always wrote with a strong sense of his poetic precedents, contemporaries, and influences. As a result, Crow contributes to a poetic lineage that includes Yeats's Crazy Jane, Baraka's Crow Jane, and Berryman's Henry. Like these antecedents, Crow identifies social inequalities, condemns evidence of public corruption, and readily admits to his own frailties. Hughes forms Crow, as these writers fashioned their own characters, as a participant in contemporary historical events who describes both large-scale and more subtle patterns of social injustice. Crow's unique qualities exist, however, in his attention to the ecological properties of his geographies and his overwhelming anxiety about the consequences of creative work.

When read alongside Plath's *Ariel* sequence, the Crow poems engender a dialogue about the compositional process and the insights that writing makes possible. The figure of Crow enables Hughes both to assess the issues that he and Plath explored in their 1960s poetry and to look for the obstacles to their resolution. Crow, as poetic avatar and icon, points to the scavenging that poets do and the apprehensions that plague them. In turn, Plath's poetic speakers in *Ariel* explore ambivalence, self-contemplation, various strategies for public self-presentation, and the possibility of a new existence in the course of a narrative that outlines the evolution of the writer's craft. Perhaps Hughes also pokes some fun at that craft through Crow, in an attempt to lighten the inescapable burden of personal and professional representation that followed him after Plath's death. Diane Middlebrook describes Hughes's position during this period as a "double bind" because "he could neither avoid his responsibilities to her writing, nor . . . fulfill them in a way that satisfied anybody, least of all himself" (*Her Husband* 235). The conversation between Plath and Hughes that began in the years after *Ariel*'s publication and lasted through the *Crow* poems remained unfinished for many years. Not until the publication of *Birthday Letters* and *Howls and Whispers* did Hughes seek a final conclusion to the formal and thematic exchanges between their work—in part because, as Heather Clark has noted, the dialogue between them "consistently resists a reading in which one always refashions or revises the other's work in the same way" (*Grief* 10). Plath drew on material from Hughes's work even during their separation, and Hughes continued the pattern of poetic sampling, quotation, revision, and response that had long existed between them through the publication of his two 1998 volumes. *Birthday Letters* in particular became a study in the struggles for recognition, acclaim, and literary accomplishment that Plath and Hughes had both sought; as Sarah Churchwell puts it, this volume's "invocation of experiential authority and personal memory is constantly undermined by doubts about truth and accuracy" ("Secrets" 122). Hughes drew this tension directly from Plath's exploitations of her own trauma as metaphors for the writer's path toward success and self-realization in *Ariel*.

NOTES

1. One of the final appearances that Crow makes is in *Cave Birds* (1978), which includes a poem entitled "A Flayed Crow in the Hall of Judgment."

2. Tracy Brain reminds us that "it is less important to see Hughes's work as 'his side of the story' than as part of a continuing conversation between his poems and Plath's"; "The Applicant" responds to his 1962 radio poem "The Wound" (*The Other* 200).

3. They summarize the narrative of *Crow* after having heard Hughes explain the story at two different readings, at Ilkley and Cambridge, in 1975: "After having created the world God has a nightmare in the form of a Voice and a Hand which ridicules the creation and particularly God's masterpiece, Man. God claims that his creation has been a complete success and a debate ensues which is interrupted by a message from the world that Man wants God to take life back. God challenges the Nightmare to do better and the Nightmare's response is to create Crow. God, who regards Crow as a poor competitor for his creation, shows him round the universe and sets him various challenges and ordeals, in the course of which Crow becomes more intelligent and resourceful. This universe is one in which all history is happening simultaneously, so Crow is able to move freely from one era to another, from the beginning of the world to the end. He observes and is occasionally implicated in various aspects of the Creation. During his adventures he begins to wonder who his own creator is and he encounters various female figures who are avatars of his creator, but he never recognizes her and always bungles the situation" (116). Hughes used similar phrasing in his letter to Baskin: "God has a nightmare—a Voice attacks him. He cannot understand what is wrong. Man comes to heaven and asks to be permitted to cease to exist since life is too awful. God is flabbergasted hearing these words from his prime creation. The Voice scorns man and God his creator. God finally challenges the Voice to do better. The voice creates Crow. Crow goes into the world and God tries to do everything to destroy him, pervert him, educate him out of himself etc—an epic of ordeals. This style of prolonged forging gradually transforms Crow into a superbeing who gets sacrificed" (*LTH* 279–80).

4. Clark describes imagistic and rhetorical connections between Plath's "Ariel" and two of the Crow poems as well: "Crowcolour" and "Bones" (*Grief* 197).

5. See, e.g., Ingri and Edgar Parin D'Aulaire's *Book of Greek Myths* and *Book of Norse Myths*, Daragh Smyth's *A Guide to Irish Mythology*, and Cristina Boscolo's *Odún: Discourses, Strategies, and Power in the Yorùbá Play of Transformation*.

6. Tim Kendall notes that Plath recorded the word's etymology on the poem's first draft: "'Hind. & Per. pardah—veil curtain or screen India to seclude women'" (*Sylvia Plath* 68).

Chapter Four

"This is the last"

Words Between Them

Hughes's and Plath's drafts reveal each writer's characteristic compositional techniques and the evolution of their individual approaches to the *ars poetica* over time. The two major sequences that they wrote in the 1960s, *Ariel* and *Crow*, illuminate the themes and formal elements on which both writers drew as well as the moments when their work diverges in style and argument. The third major point of contact between their work exists in the dialogues generated between pieces that they published outside of these sequences. Employing some compositional strategies common to Hughes's work as well, including a focus on the materiality of the poetic object and speculations on the nature of writing itself, Plath's middle-period poetry is often set in familiar locations in which its protagonists find themselves existing at odds with the surrounding landscape.

As Diane Middlebrook has suggested, "Pursuit" (1956) may be the poem in Plath's pre-*Ariel* writings that is most directly inspired by Hughes's work in *Hawk in the Rain* and *Lupercal* ("The Poetry" 158). Its opening image of a panther immediately recalls Hughes's "The Jaguar"; Plath's speaker responds to his cat "hurrying enraged / Through prison darkness after the drills of his eyes" (*CPH* 19) with the promise that "One day I'll have my death of him" (*CPP* 22). Her piece emerges from a disjunction between her vision and Hughes's; his jaguar prowls within a cage, safely barred from curious visitors, while hers "prowls more lordly than the sun" and "ransacks the land." Like Hughes, she creates a landscape whose inhabitants become increasingly recognizable as poetic characters in her other work; "From gaunt hemlock, rooks croak havoc" echoes the physical details of "Black Rook in Rainy Weather" (as well as the villanelle "Doomsday" and the story "Stone Boy with Dolphin"), for instance, while the "Charred and ravening women" who "Become his starving body's bait" might anticipate "All the Dead Dears." Plath is careful in "Pursuit" to describe her panther's environment in broad strokes as he searches for "meat [that] must glut his mouth's raw wound." He prowls, and the "hills hatch menace, spawning shade," while "Midnight cloaks the sultry grove" (*CPP* 22).

The end of the poem's second stanza marks, however, the point at which Plath's narrative turns decisively away from Hughes's. Rather than maintain an uninterrupted image of the stalking animal, Plath chooses to reveal her metaphor's motivating tenor. The women are "bait" for his appetite; the speaker fears him as she anticipates his movement "in dreams' ambush." The panther demands her blood as "sacrifice"; he awakens a "secret want" in her through an "assault of radiance." Finally, though the speaker tries to hide from the revelation, she knows that "The panther's tread is on the stairs, / Coming up and up the stairs" (*CPP* 23). Hughes's jaguar embodies a caged power; Plath's panther stands in for an uncontained passion both feared and desired. Lynda Bundtzen asserts that Plath specifically imagined the panther as Hughes (*Other Ariel* 83). The poem's concluding image is echoed in a March 10, 1956 passage from her journal: "The panther wakes and stalks again, and every sound in the house is his tread on the stair" (*UJ* 233). In a letter to Aurelia Plath dated one day earlier, her daughter annotated the image as "a symbol of the terrible beauty of death, and the paradox that the more intensely one lives, the more one burns and consumes oneself; death, here, includes the concept of love, and is larger and richer than mere love, which is part of it" (*LSP1* 1133). This explication of the symbolic resonance of "Pursuit" both speaks to the intensity of Plath's and Hughes's relationship during this period and illustrates the close attention that they paid to the details of each other's work. Yet Plath does not reiterate Hughes's familiar images unaltered; she examines the cat from a new angle in order to frame the hunter's chase in different terms.

Plath's 1957 poem "The Lady and the Earthenware Head" provides another key example of the shared source material, here interpreted through an allegorical lens, that began the dialogue between her work and Hughes's. This piece was inspired by a red-clay model of her head that Mary Bailey Derr, a friend of Plath's from Smith, had made (*LSP2* 65). Plath both feared throwing it away and longed to be rid of it; while they were still living in Cambridge, Hughes suggested that they take it out to Grantchester Meadows and leave it in a willow tree. Here they could see it each time they went for their favorite walk. Anne Stevenson suggests that Plath could also ensure in this way that it would not be drowned, another of her fears (105), though Plath herself noted in a letter to Aurelia that "I didn't have the heart to throw it away, because I'd developed a strange fondness for the old thing with passing years" (*LSP2* 65). Hughes's response to both the model and Plath's poem was "The Earthenware Head," which juxtaposes their shared anxiety about the head to the blissful serenity of the country landscape. Both poetic elements function in his piece as metonyms of the writer's efforts to create. Written in second-person, like most of the poems in *Birthday Letters*, it begins with a question: "Who modelled your head of terracotta?" Though that query is answered in the very next line, it establishes the mysterious nature of this artifact from the beginning. The head seems to embody an unnamed threat, yet the speaker finds himself unable to turn away from it. He notes that "You did not like it. / I did not like it" but feels compelled to assess its symbolic potential. In spite of his unease, he finds a "twiggy crotch" and makes it into "a mythic shrine for your double," leaving the head "To live the world's life and weather for ever." These actions suggest that the speaker identifies the head as a witness whose observations he can plunder in spite of the fact that his partner wants to distance herself from it by investigating its origins. In reimagining this scene from their shared life, Hughes refers directly to Plath's own writing about the sculpture: "You ransacked thesaurus in your poem about it, / Veiling its mirror, rhyming yourself into safety / From its orphaned fate" (*CPH* 1079). Though Plath took pride in her poem at first, she later decided it was overdone; this passage comments on her "change of heart" (Wagner 129). As a result of this shift in perspective, perhaps, Hughes sets a scene in the middle of his poem that describes her dealing with the head on paper, from a distance, in contrast to the direct physical confrontation that his poetic narrator attempts in the first stanza. Underlining an ambivalence about creation that filters through much of the *Crow* sequence as well as through *Birthday Letters*—Hughes's "uncertainty as to the authority of [his] writing—who is right and who is writing?" (Churchwell, "Secrets" 135), in other words—the poem witnesses both its originating scene and the process of composition itself.

The setting of Hughes's poem describes an unwelcoming landscape in which the clay head's conspicuous appearance connotes a threat. The trees' "comfortless antlers" and the autumn day's "fen-damp haze" suggest a general uneasiness with the head's presence that Hughes tries to dispel by invoking the river's cleansing properties. The head's fate remains uncertain; Hughes asks another question—"What happened? / Maybe nothing happened" (*CPH* 1079)—that reaffirms its hold on the imagination. "Perhaps," the speaker ventures, "It is still there, representing you / To the sunrise, and happy / In its cold pastoral" (*CPH* 1079–80). Yet Hughes's speaker persists in wishing for its destruction, asking "Or did boys find it—and shatter it?," as though the speaker longs for an action that he cannot bring himself to perform. The poem's second half imagines the head's likely fate, which now exists outside the boundaries of the text itself:

> Surely the river got it. Surely
> The river is its chapel. And keeps it. Surely
> Your deathless head, fired in a furnace,

> Face to face at last, kisses the Father
> Mudded at the bottom of the Cam,
> Beyond recognition or rescue,
> All our fears washed from it, and perfect. (*CPH* 1080)

Hughes's use of anaphora here signifies a mantra that can keep such mythic threats at bay, yet this formal device conflicts with the poem's ambivalent tone, which threads between reassurance and a veiled threat. The poem concludes with a final breath of warning: "Evil. / That was what you called the head. Evil" (*CPH* 1080). The speaker gives up narrative control to the lyric subject in the end, allowing her assessment to serve as the head's ultimate indictment. The river's cleansing is only temporary and symbolic; human judgment is the poem's final arbiter. Through this engagement with one of Plath's earlier pieces, Hughes examines her analytical perspective and her developing approach to composition; he responds to her physical representation, the material head itself, and to the mindset she assumed while processing it in order to acknowledge her work's aesthetic differences.

In "The Lady and the Earthenware Head," in contrast, Plath establishes her subject through a singularly focused interrogation of the object, as both creative inspiration and personal threat, with no reference to its origins or to its interactions with the social world. Her description of the same head Hughes witnessed comments on its "sanguine clay," its "brickdust-complected" appearance with an "eye under a dense lid." She characterizes its strangely captivating gaze as a "spite-set / Ape of [a] look" with a "sullen and pompous" expression; she imagines the head, if thrown away, "Glowering sullen and pompous from an ash-heap" and tempting passersby to rescue it. Similarly, if thrown into the water, the head might "leer" and "Lewdly beckon" the unsuspecting. In the only passage that the tone and setting of Hughes's poem echo, the poetic speaker decides "more ceremoniously to lodge / The mimic head—in a crotched willow, green- / Vaulted by foliage." This indecision about which option to pursue is not represented in Hughes's piece. Instead, his response pictures the head's impact on its observers and its potential for imaginative engagement. Plath not only renders the head itself but also imagines the as-yet unknown conclusion to its narrative trajectory in order to focus on its receptivity and open symbolic capacity. She imagines the head as emerging organically from whatever landscape it touches, whether it is a bookshelf, an ash-heap, or a "dark tarn" that is "thick-silted, with weeds obscured" (*CPP* 69). The poem ends, however, before the head can be transported; rather, "shrined on her shelf," it "endure[s]," "Steadfast and evil-starred," "ogl[ing]" its possessor with an "antique hag-head," always directing toward her an ominous "basilisk-look of love" (*CPP* 70). Plath's earlier visions of the head's possible destination dissolve at the end of the poem, superseded by the speaker's compulsion to define this entity more precisely. It is the poetic object itself that endures, its presence illustrating one of the elements—the concrete icon—that spurred both Plath's and Hughes's compositions.

On the one hand, "The Lady and the Earthenware Head" offers a version of a real sculpted head's fate that Hughes's "The Earthenware Head" disputes. Yet, on the other, Plath's piece proposes that the head is most evocative, most productive of symbolic resonance, when it remains right where it is. Thus we can read the poem as an early version of Plath's own theory of composition. The poetic speaker explores her own terror at the head's unyielding gaze by recursively articulating several possibilities for its disposal; these possibilities practice the device of accretive repetition in order to approximate an experience that cannot be fully captured in words. The head also evokes literary myth, a common element in Plath's work, through its "evil-starred" "hag-head" and "basilisk-look." As Uroff asserts, the head functions as a kind of double for Plath herself: "she must keep the head safe in order to be safe herself" (80). In contrast, Hughes's poem ends with a definitive moment of farewell; having slotted the head into the crotch of a likely tree, the speaker resolves to move on even as he is haunted by its apparently "evil" essence. Given Plath's engagement with the processes of creation in her piece, this narrative move away from the head in Hughes's poem suggests that he means to respond to their shared experience rather than to her outline of the *ars poetica*. Plath's poem also represents the "lady" in its title and story; the speaker's third-person narration makes her an active participant in the story, rather than cutting her perspective out, as Hughes's second-person address does.

"Lady Lazarus" and "The Shot" offer another opportunity to investigate the shared elements and the philosophies of writing that underlie both Plath's mid-career work and Hughes's later poems. The two pieces examine the theatrical nature of Plath's rhetoric and the techniques through which she tested out textual innovation. "Lady Lazarus" remains one of Plath's most famous works and a distinctive example of the "October poems"; its form and content exemplify the sparser lines and intense narrative energy of these later pieces. Hughes's "The Shot" initially seems to resemble "Daddy" more closely, in its opening claim that "Your worship needed a god" because "It was a god-seeker. A god-finder. / Your Daddy had been aiming you at God / When his death touched the trigger" (*CPH* 1052). Some critics assert that Plath refers not only to Otto Plath but also to Hughes himself in the angry indictment of father figures that "Daddy" makes (Bundtzen, *Other Ariel* 30–31; Wagner 73); the poem invokes her father directly through the images of a "Ghastly statue with one gray toe" and "a head in the freakish Atlantic" (*CPP* 222). However, the dominant imagery and diction of Hughes's "The Shot" imitate the formal elements of "Lazarus" precisely in order to critique

Plath's extended metaphors for self-expression. Hughes answers her proud contention in "Lazarus" that "I have done it again. / One year in every ten / I manage it—" (*CPP* 244) with a description of the potential suicide as "undeflected. / . . . gold-jacketed, solid silver. / Nickel-tipped. Trajectory perfect" (*CPH* 1053). As these phrases imply, the subject's attempts at self-destruction endow her with an impervious exterior that protects her from real danger. The public attention she has gained, he suggests, shields her from critique while enabling her to perform whatever kind of identity she likes. The self-conscious melodrama with which Plath's speaker delivers her lines, her claims to a fame that the "peanut-crunching crowd / Shoves in to see" (*CPP* 245), is undermined in turn by Hughes's bald statement that "your real target / Hid behind me. Your Daddy, / The god with the smoking gun" (*CPH* 1053). The first-person perspective of Plath's piece enables her to frame the poetic narrator's dramatic self-presentation as a necessary condition of survival; Hughes's second-person address, on the other hand, diminishes the sense of precarious, contingent existence that dominates the earlier poem. His speaker argues instead that he has been the target of her performances, that he has suffered the ill effects of her self-presentation in a way that her absent father never could. In addition to renegotiating the perspective of Plath's poem, too, Hughes employs some of her trusted compositional devices in order to claim a different sort of authority. To Plath's "cake of soap," "wedding ring," and "gold filling" (*CPP* 246), a list that suggests both what might remain after the men in her life are gone and the heartbreaking traces of gas-chamber victims, Hughes poses "A wisp of your hair, your ring, your watch, your nightgown" (*CPH* 1053). One catalogue's form echoes the other, yet Hughes's list centers on items that point directly to a lyric subject. Both the watch and the nightgown also recall Plath's "Morning Song," which begins with a simile describing the beauty of the baby at birth and ends with the mother's feelings of confusion and entrapment in the muddiness of postpartum life. In "Morning Song," the images of the watch and the nightgown bookend Plath's encomium for young parenthood; Hughes adds them to his own catalogue in order to acknowledge, perhaps, the creative debt he has to their partnership. This second catalogue also redirects the dramatic tension of Plath's piece, centering it in a space of private contemplation rather than in the context of other public spectacles.

Borrowed phrases and images like these echo between several works from the later periods of Plath's and Hughes's work. These textual reverberations illustrate the creative purposes that they share as well as the insights into compositional processes that new poetic contexts can produce. Hughes's "Remission," which makes reference to such poems about Plath's illnesses as "In Plaster" and "Tulips," labels her a "fragile cutting, tamped into earth" (*CPH* 1113); this image points to the vulnerability of the cast body in the first poem and the "dozen red lead sinkers" of the tulips in the second (*CPP* 161). At the same time, readers of the period's work will recall Theodore Roethke's "Cuttings" poems; Plath alludes to some of his recurring themes and tries out a similarly experimental diction in pieces such as "Poem for a Birthday" (Middlebrook, *Her Husband* 109–10). In contrast to Roethke's precise investigation of the natural world, here Hughes employs a delicate metaphor for productivity to describe someone who "flourished only / In becoming fruitful—in getting pregnant" (*CPH* 1113). "Remission" foregoes, therefore, the resistance to social conformity that the speakers of both "In Plaster" and "Tulips" express and focuses instead on birth's potential for keeping the mother alive. "Remission" addresses Plath's frequent use of motherhood as a representation of creative work, as in "Thalidomide" and "Poems, Potatoes," and identifies her poetry's powerful capacity for extratextual signification. These examples, just a few among many, indicate that Plath's work both before and during the period of *Ariel*'s composition gave Hughes inspiration for his own writing and prompted him to extend his own philosophy of the poem as *ars poetica*.

THE BEE POEMS: FINALIZING THE *ARS POETICA*

Plath's five-poem bee subsequence, "The Bee Meeting," "The Arrival of the Bee Box," "Stings," "The Swarm," and "Wintering," all of which she composed in late 1962, has received a significant amount of the critical attention generated by the composition, publication history, and reception of the *Ariel* poems.[1] Hughes chose to engage in dialogue with this portion of Plath's work in one poem from *Birthday Letters*, "The Bee God," which contains both a direct quote from her work and several moments that reflect on the subsequence as a whole. These points of interaction between Hughes's piece and the bee poems, the largest group of topically linked poems that Plath ever composed, provide a detailed illustration of the two poets' compositional styles, the aesthetic divergences between them, and the theories of poetry's functions that each developed. The broad topical scope of "The Bee God" also suits it as an introduction to the extended dialogue that *Birthday Letters* sustains between Hughes's late work and Plath's, in part as his direct response to the philosophy of creation she advances in these poems.

Hughes's poem begins by musing on the Electra-esque elements of Plath's imagined relationship with her entomologist father: "When you wanted bees I never dreamed / It meant your Daddy had come up out of the well / . . . / But when you put on your white regalia, / Your veil, your gloves, I never guessed a wedding" (*CPH* 1140–41). In "The Bee Meeting," Plath's narrator contrasts her "sleeveless summery dress" with the "white shop smock" that the villagers give her, complete with "cuffs at my wrists and the slit from my neck to my knees" (*CPP* 211). Rather than serving as "regalia" or a "wedding" dress, this garb is both protective and confining, transforming her into "the magician's girl who does not flinch," even when used as a sacrifice (*CPP* 212). She wears a "moon suit and funeral veil" in "The Arrival of the Bee Box" as well (*CPP* 213); this time her protective clothing shields her not from the bees' physical violence but from the power of their voices. Adding another dimension to the *ars poetica* that Plath had begun to articulate in earlier poems like "The Lady and the Earthenware Head," this speaker comments that "It is the noise that appalls me most of all, / the unintelligible syllables"; when she tries to discern any kind of meaning, she hears only "furious Latin" coming from "a box of maniacs." This view of the bees' behavior, which may refer both to Otto Plath's absence and to his facility with the languages that frustrated her, establishes a contrast between the speaker's struggle to be understood and an oblivious auditor. Yet, as the poem concludes, "Tomorrow I will be sweet God, I will set them free. / The box is only temporary" (*CPP* 213). The speaker reasserts authority over the bee box, indicating that she controls the means both of communication and of interpretation. For the moment, the bees—her art's source and inspiration—are unintelligible, but her evolving tools for expression will enable her to assume command of the language once more.

Hughes makes reference to this fight for control over creative expression about a third of the way through "The Bee God," when his speaker describes "Your page a dark swarm / Clinging under the lit blossom." Though the poem's addressee has apparently tamed the bees, making them into an instrument of creation rather a menace, their status remains precarious and unknown. It is not clear who "the bee god" is, since the speaker claims that "I had given you something / That had carried you off in a cloud of gutturals" (*CPH* 1141). Is the one gifting the bees their master, or the subject who writes with and about them? Hughes's image of "gutturals," which evokes the German language Plath struggled to acquire, here suggests that the language has mastered the writer, rather than the other way around, a notion that runs contrary to the speaker's conclusion in "The Arrival of the Bee Box" that "The box is only temporary" (*CPP* 213). Plath's speaker regulates her own speech and controls its dissemination; Hughes's implies that communication is always partial and contingent. This divergence indicates that Plath's concept of the *ars poetica* emerges in part from evocative metaphors that reimagine a personally significant symbol (i.e., the bees that formed the centerpiece of Otto Plath's academic studies) as creative impetus. These symbols function differently in Hughes's work, as the ambiguous rhetoric of "The Bee God" suggests, but his piece also narrates a search for the sources of imaginative power, finally locating them in the artist's ability to cast off the materials of the past when they threaten work in progress.

Both "Stings" and "The Swarm" also illustrate Plath's perspective on the influence—personal, social, even cultural—that one can exercise through the act of writing itself. Hughes alludes to this force through the recurring struggle in "The Bee God" between the poem's lyric subject and her "Daddy." He does not credit his subject with a pure desire to create; rather, he explains her interest in apiculture as lingering regret over an absent father. In contrast, however, in "Stings" the speaker is "Bare-handed," handing off honeycombs to a man with "The throats of our wrists brave lilies." She displays a confident stance toward the bees and, as a result, gains the rewards of physical and intellectual labor. Resisting the difficulties of her past, she affirms the struggle she has endured and its likely outcome: "It is almost over. / I am in control" (*CPP* 214). Because she remains curious about the sources of her creativity, the speaker seeks the hive's queen, yet she must evade "a great scapegoat" along the way. Her summary of this process—"They thought death was worth it, but I / Have a self to recover, a queen"—refuses the familiar readings of Plath's late work as evidence of her approaching suicide. Instead, the speaker identifies the work of writing itself as her strength and her reason for continued existence. Combining images of fragility and nobility, she describes the queen's body as "lion-red," with "wings of glass." The queen defies the threatened loss of self, instead "flying / More terrible than she ever was, red / Scar in the sky, red comet / Over the engine that killed her." The presence of some of Plath's frequently used words in this passage—including "red," "terrible," and "scar"—suggests a gathering of her poetic arsenal in preparation for an attack or defense. The queen's flight defies "the engine that killed her— / The mausoleum, the wax house" (*CPP* 215), posing her movement forward in response to the stagnant images that populate these final lines. This portrait of accomplishment and vengeance differs from the passive depiction of the poetic subject that Hughes advances in the second half of "The Bee God": "Your face wanted to save me / From what had been decided. / You rushed to me, your dream-time veil off, / Your ghost-proof gloves off" (*CPH* 1141–42). Here the speaker observes the attempt at salvation, yet notes that the lyric subject leaves herself vulnerable, through her absent clothing, to the concrete threat of stings instead. She is not a queen in Hughes's formulation but a lone figure covered in "Sticky, disemboweled bees." These creatures, in their turn, appear not out of love but because they are "Fanatics for their God, the God of the Bees" (*CPH* 1142). While Hughes's second-person addressee manifests an irresistible attraction for the bees, drawing them to her through an inherent magnetism, the poem interprets the person as the source of this allure, rather than art itself. "Stings" is the central bee poem in *Ariel 2*, which adds to its rhetorical and thematic impact within the subsequence overall—and underlines its likely influence on Hughes's responses to Plath in "The Bee God."

In *Ariel 1*, Plath followed "Stings" with "The Swarm," a poem that was written one day later, on 7 October 1962. This piece enlarges the bees' symbolic resonance beyond the scope of their signification in "The Bee Meeting," "The Arrival of the Bee Box," and "Stings." Here bees do not denote personal preoccupations, gathering strength, or even latent artistic promise. Instead, they stage what appears to be a full-scale war on the repositories of memory itself. Plath employs, again, examples of her characteristic rhetoric and diction in this piece; the bees' engagement with enemy fire is signified by the repeated "Pom! Pom!" (*CPP* 217), while she chooses to underscore moments of particular drama through apostrophes and short exclamatory phrases. Her references to "Waterloo, Waterloo, Napoleon," "French bootsoles," and "Russia, Poland, and Germany" (*CPP* 216) also give the reader a sense of looking beyond the boundaries of the personal to the broader consequences of misused power.

Though Plath composed "The Swarm" during the period of her separation from Hughes, the presence of familiar tropes from the rest of her oeuvre expands the poem's relevance beyond the personal. The speaker points out that "These are chess people you play with, / Still figures of ivory"; their actions occur within a vast landscape, in which "The gilt and pink domes of Russia melt and float off / In the furnace of greed." The movement of the bees here is both vertical—"Seventy feet high!"—and philosophical; they "argue, in their black ball, / A flying hedgehog, all prickles" (*CPP* 216). This poem, second-to-last in the subsequence, represents the series' strongest indictment of both personal betrayal and social conflict, two themes that Plath often identifies as motivations for art in the October poems. She recognizes the potentially malignant presence of "The man with gray hands," whose silent passivity contrasts with the bees' activity, and warns of the fate that he forces "The dumb, banded bodies" to face. The poem's references to Napoleon suggest that the gray man is a tyrant, but a rather inept one; the bees' "Stings big as drawing pins!" offer an effective resistance in their embodiment of words' representational power (*CPP* 217). Though Hughes may make reference to "Stings" in his poem's statement that "the bees' orders were geometric— / Your Daddy's plans were Prussian" (*CPH* 1141), which suggests the carefully ordered processes that Plath followed while writing, in contrast to her father's sudden disappearance from her life, the imagery in her earlier piece remains, deliberately, indeterminate. The "man with gray hands" could be an image of Hughes, grayed out with forgotten love, or it could refer to any number of European leaders whose despotism led to modern wars—or it could be Otto Plath, already described in "Daddy" as a "Ghastly statue with one gray toe." Here the bees help Plath's speaker to reimagine and transform her painful memories. Their stings combat the gray man's passive inaction, while their triumph over these adversaries prepares the ground for the oft-noted optimism of the final bee poem, "Wintering."

Hughes concludes his comments on Plath's bee poems in "The Bee God" with an allusion that comes not from the bee sequence, however, but from "Words." As discussed in chapter 2, Plath ends this poem with an *ars poetica* of sorts that invokes both the isolated nature of creative work and its life-giving properties through the image of "fixed stars [that] / Govern a life" (*CPP* 270). Though Bundzten calls this piece "a farewell to life and to writing" (*Other Ariel* 133), while Wagner labels it "foreboding" and ties it to the threatening image of the "drowned head" in "All the Dead Dears" (130), its series of discrete images sketches a landscape populated by sounds and sights that inspire invention. In "The Bee God," Hughes responds to Plath's sense of astrological determination at the end of "Words" with an image of bees swarming the speaker, as "Deaf to your pleas as the fixed stars / At the bottom of the well" (*CPH* 1142). Most obviously, both images of "fixed stars" shimmering up from beneath the water recall the interest in astrology that Plath and Hughes pursued during their marriage (Stevenson 112; Middlebrook, *Her Husband* 55–56).[2] Hughes's lines here might also serve as a challenge to the many critics who attacked his editorial decisions and his position as the executor of Plath's estate; he quotes from one of her late poems to acknowledge the significance of this period in both his and her work and to comment on the creative intensity that her writing retains.

In addition, if we read both "Wintering" and "The Bee God" in part as a commentary on Plath's relationship with her father, the former leaves readers with an unexpectedly positive signifier for Otto Plath as a creative and professional model: "The bees are flying. They taste the spring" (*CPP* 219). When Hughes recasts the final statement of "Words" as the conclusion to his own poetic perspective on the two Plaths, he asserts that as the bees' symbolic impact diminished, her art demanded new material. His poem argues that, by returning to the bees throughout this sequence, her art remains tied to the "fixed stars" and the "bottom of the well," images that signify potential without completion. From this perspective, "Wintering" would represent yet another rehearsal of familiar themes rather than the new outlook on her craft that "Words" suggests. Hughes, too, seems to undermine his own lifelong interest in astrology and the occult in "The Bee God," casting doubt on such practices' efficacy. Instead, he suggests, the bees—signifiers of the past—defy any attempts to redirect their paths. This assessment of Plath's dominant symbolic object contrasts with the *ars poetica* she defines in the subsequence, which includes an interest in establishing rhetorical control over one's language, regulating the effects of that language, employing metaphors that signify in both immediate and symbolic contexts, and incorporating the poetic vocabulary that has accumulated throughout her career. The dialogue in which Plath and Hughes engage through these bee poems illustrates some of their beliefs about poetry's aesthetic functions and anticipates Hughes's conclusions about their shared material in *Birthday Letters*.

DIALOGUE AND DISPUTE

The 1998 publication of Hughes's *Birthday Letters* was greeted with the kind of widespread public interest that has accompanied few other modern books of poetry—except, perhaps, for the 2004 publication of Plath's *Ariel: The Restored Edition*. As Katha Pollitt pointed out in *The New York Times* on 1 March 1998, "[i]t isn't often that the publication of a book of poems is announced on the front page of newspapers on two continents." She denounces what she sees as Hughes's tendency to forsake an "intimate" tone for "ranting, self-justifying, rambling, flaccid, bombastic" portraits of their life together (BR4), describing Plath's work, in contrast, as "complex and ambiguous" where Hughes's is "lax and digressive" (BR6). In a 5 March 1998 review published in *The New York Review of Books*, James Fenton observes that "[t]he idea that Hughes has only just come around to recognizing Plath's talents is to an extreme degree improbable. . . . But the Plath myth is a story that insists on being told (with all its variants) whether it fits the facts or not" (n. p.). A 14 February 1998 review in the Toronto *Globe and Mail*, on the other hand, calls Plath Hughes's "sounding board" and "spectral muse," citing his use of autobiographical and mythic elements as well as references to Plath's own literary influences in structuring the collection (D16). Katherine Viner, in a now-famous review published in the *Guardian* on 30 October 1998, just two days after Hughes died, describes his actions after Plath's death as "censorious," even as his "association with Plath made him into something other than just a great poet." She calls *Birthday Letters* "his last and greatest poetic achievement," created at what he felt was the best time to write about Plath: in the moments before death (4).

These reviews, just a few among the many critical and popular responses to the book, reflect some of the widely varying perspectives on Hughes's work and its relationship to Plath's. Though the reviews rely too heavily in some cases on biographical interpretation, and, as Anne Whitehead has observed, they "almost unanimously located Hughes in a fixed position with regard to the past and to memory" (227), they acknowledge both the significance of this publication at the end of Hughes's career and the fact that its poems take up the formal, rhetorical, and thematic challenges posed by Plath's best-known works. Sarah Churchwell describes *Birthday Letters* as, in fact, "a public response to disputes over the politics of publication, representation, and literary authority" ("Secrets" 103). While it purports to offer new insight into Hughes's relationship with Plath, it became, through the contexts of its composition, publication, and reception, "a volume hesitating uneasily between disclosure and encryption" (Churchwell, "Secrets" 104). The book in many ways offers an exploratory, contemplative approach to its subjects in place of Hughes's formerly guarded perspective on his life during the 1960s. As he himself noted in a letter to Seamus Heaney, "publication came to seem not altogether a literary matter, more a physical operation that just might change the psychic odds crucially for me, and clear a route" (*LTH* 703). In these poems, he couches his interpretations of several experiences that he shared with Plath in relation to his ongoing love for nation and nature; he also acknowledges the writer's body as the seat of creativity by "revisit[ing] his younger self" (Wootten 189). The specific geographic locales that Hughes evokes in the poems indicate that he locates memory and experience in real places. At the same time, he creates a mythological vision of English identity as a means of coming to terms with a key element of the work, Plath's own ambivalence toward her adopted country. Paul Bentley notes that, in Hughes's dialogue with Plath about England, she "serves to demystify [his] sense of a mystical, mythical England," situating the poems instead within material geographies and refusing to entertain his self-created roles of "the alchemist, the mythologist" (129, 131). For Hughes, his poems are an instrument by which to recoup and reimagine the past. As Heather Clark has speculated, the collection represents "verse more confessional than anything Plath ever penned" (*Grief* 13); William Wootten identifies in it Hughes's admissions of guilt and an "evasive" approach to both form and theme (191).[3] The pieces' visions of England and of several key moments in their marriage help him understand the material that bound him and Plath together, the sources that they shared and often transformed into very different creative statements.

The British Library holds the bulk of Hughes's early drafts and manuscript revisions of *Birthday Letters*. These drafts illuminate his composition and revision processes, which bear striking similarities to Plath's in some instances. Each folder contains a collection of poems in approximately chronological order; five of the folders contain typed or handwritten drafts of the book's table of contents that reflect significant changes to the poems' order before final publication. As previously discussed, Hughes's ordering of the *Ariel* poems has been one of the central controversies in Plath scholarship since 1965; that furor revived after *Ariel: The Restored Edition* appeared. The meticulous plotting of *Ariel* through its two editions suggests that Hughes placed significant weight on individual poems' contextual resonance and narrative position. The repeated reorganization of the poems in the British Library papers provides further evidence that Hughes, like Plath, agonized over the poems' ability to speak to and against one another: their ability to produce, in other words, what Neil Fraistat calls "purposeful thematic iteration among the poems" in order to "establish an overall narrative pattern" (7). The earlier folders in the British Library papers contain groupings of the *Birthday Letters* poems beginning with "Caryatids" (folder 2), "A Pink Wool Knitted Dress" (folder 4), "The Dogs Are Eating Your Mother" (folder 5), and "Fulbright Scholars" (folder 12), for instance. Though "Fulbright Scholars" became the first poem in the published work, its position was not assured from the beginning, as these re-orderings indicate; Hughes struggled with the question of whether to begin with his assessment of Plath's early work in "Caryatids,"[4] or with a vision of their wedding day, as represented in "A Pink Wool Dress," or with critics' exploitative attitudes toward her work. "The Dogs Are Eating Your Mother," as one distinctive example of the book's changing narrative, ultimately appears near the end, but its shifting position within the draft manuscripts unsettles readers' assumptions about its relation to the collection as a whole.

Jo Gill assesses *Birthday Letters* as a "complex, mutable, and intense transatlantic exchange" between Hughes and Plath on both personal and aesthetic levels ("Exaggerated American" 163). Because Hughes continued to participate in the processes of revising and borrowing material from Plath even after her death, the collection's forms and themes articulate this decades-long collaboration across national borders, compositional divergences, and interpersonal difficulties. More than just a series of responses that Hughes made to the poems that Plath wrote during the short period between their decision to separate and her death, the *Birthday Letters* poems stake out the themes and experiences that informed both poets' writings and identify the compositional techniques that they held in common. Clark suggests that, in the book, "[h]is decision to abandon his 'high-minded' aesthetic principles in favor of a raw style shows that Plath still exerted a powerful influence years after her death" (*Grief* 185); Tracy Brain, on the other hand, calls the poems' lyric subject "a poetic character who is no more stable or real as 'Plath' than the object of any intensely felt love poem—or love letter" (*The Other* 181). Hughes himself notes in an unpublished diary entry from 23 January 1998 that he experienced a "renewed sense of how that withholding has blocked my real work since 1970 at least. . . . I did not understand what had happened—as I do now. Belatedly. Then I was 41. Now I am 67. . . . Too late to regret. But what a price." This entry suggests that Plath's death, as well as Assia and Shura Wevill's, not only "interrupted" his writerly career but also influenced it to an immeasurable degree. He concludes at the end of the entry that life's greatest challenge may be learning how to do productive work. As he defines it, "That difficulty: how to take the path that maintained the centre of gravity of a talent—how to find the cause of behavior that activates it, optimizes possibilities, and does not—as is the case of almost every poet, if not every artist of other kinds—leave the life's work as a series of hasty campfires rather than a solid city. The first necessity, I'm sure, is to live alone, or as if alone" (BL Add MS 88918/1/2). These speculations, voiced just as *Birthday Letters* was appearing in British bookstores, illustrate Hughes's concern for maintaining an equilibrium between the personal and the aesthetic, for continuing to improve upon the formal methods that enabled him to articulate the challenges that writers face. In this collection, indeed, he succeeds in achieving the balance between metaphorical representation and writerly speculation that characterizes his strongest work.

SOURCES OF THE VOICE IN *BIRTHDAY LETTERS*

Several critics have documented the central role that Leonard Baskin's crow sketches played in the genesis of the *Crow* poems. Most readers are less familiar, however, with the visual representations of his subjects that Hughes created while working on *Birthday Letters*. The British Library papers include a diagram that he had sketched as, presumably, a means of making sense of the themes and images to which these poems repeatedly return. Shaped like a large asterisk or clock-face, the diagram contains nine subjects, each written at one of the asterisk's stems (beginning at 11:00): "Electric Shock," "Fairy Godmother," "Critics," "Lives of the Saint," "Biographies," "You as traitor and all-teller," "The Bell Jar," "Being Christlike," and "Jealousy." Hughes further annotated most of these subjects with a list of subpoints. Under "Electric Shock," for instance, he notes, "(a) Close up of it / (b) What it destroyed / (c) What it revealed / (d) What it left." "Critics," on the other hand, serves as the header to "(a) hyena-work / (b) you as icon, as genius / (c) your poems as release drug / (d) their madness." Under "Lives of the Saint," Hughes lists "(a) Father death / (b) Mother-fears / (c) Academic pressure-cooker / (d) The Outer Life / (e) Electric Shock / (f) Lovers." "Biographies" is followed by "(a) Their varieties / (b) Their affect and motive / (c) Their audience / (d) Your many lives in their words." "The Bell Jar" is annotated with "(a) You as insect / (b) Who kept the BJ? / (c) Smashing the BJ (writing the book) / (d) So who then was smashed." The heading "Being Christlike," with some notable differences from the poem by the same name, is followed by "(a) Throws away Mother and Father / (b) Throws away family / (c) Throws away body—burn it in cook oven / (d) Go out on—a naked soul." Finally, "Jealousy" is followed by "(a) Your hatred of women? / (b) What did you hate about them? / (c) What did you want from them?" (BL Add MS 88918/1/6, ff. 139). Each of these headings introduces subjects familiar to Plath and Hughes scholars; their subpoints tie these topics to the book's shifting perspectives on them. Through this diagram, Hughes assesses some of the popular viewpoints on Plath's writing—such as "Critics," "Lives of the Saint," and "Biographies"—and condenses the poems' recurring themes into highly resonant symbols and motifs, as in "Electric Shock," "The Bell Jar," "Being Christlike," and "Jealousy."

This web of interrelated ideas motivates the poems of *Birthday Letters*. Sarah Churchwell, investigating the book's potential responses to Hughes's longtime critics, speculates that its poems reward readings through multiple critical lenses ("'Your Sentence'" 260). At least one of these lenses illustrates Hughes's attempts to reconcile his perceptions of their shared life with the ones Plath explored in her work. The *Birthday Letters* poems consider Plath as writer, lover, mother, public martyr, and critical subject—but they also expose Hughes's own frailties at this late point in his creative life, allowing readers to see the vulnerability of his professional persona as a part of the book's meditations on self-presentation. He represents not only familiar objects and moments from his life with Plath across the book's often doubly-voiced poems but also the specific locales in which these objects and moments resonate. The composition of *Birthday Letters* arose from both these physical geographies and the textual geographies of his manuscript revisions. An archaeology of the two landscapes reveals the patterns of their shared life: experiences written across Britain, England, and Spain, and articulated through the shifting diction, rhetoric, repetitions, themes, and recursive motifs that both poets employed.

Hughes's drafts of "A Pink Wool Knitted Dress" illustrate some of the compositional strategies that he had adapted from Plath's work. As is the case in several of her October poems, this piece centers on a single concrete image, one tied to a richly emotional moment in their lives. In one prominent example of their shared techniques, Hughes arrives at this image through a catalog similar to those Plath often used; for her, this device served as a means by which to come to terms with an ambiguous or painful experience. Here he wrote in and then crossed out several lines whose images attempt to fill in the sketch of Plath's famous wedding dress. After describing his own attire on that day, for instance, as "the used-up symbol of a tie," he adds and then excises "Sandals—one repaired with a drawing pin." He also describes the scene in terms that recall their mutual pursuit of astrology as both predictive device and compositional aid: "Cold as an absent giant's fireless / fireplace. / I was watching you wrestling your flames / In your pink wool knitted dress / And in your eye-pupils—great cut jewels / Jostling their tear-flames, truly like big jewels, / Shaken in a dice-cup, held up to me" (BL Add MS 88918/1/4). These lines, first written in, crossed out, and then restored in the final published version, serve as the poem's conclusion and its final statement on the nature of their early relationship in life and in print. The instances of recursion that Hughes tries out here—the "fireless / fireplace" and "great cut jewels . . . truly like big jewels"—closely resemble some of Plath's own compositional strategies, the near stutters that she employs in poems like "The Applicant" and "Stopped Dead" in order to signal heightened emotionality controlled by writerly precision. David Sergeant has also noted that *Birthday Letters* in general contains "a surprising late florescence of end-rhyme" not present in Hughes's other books; this type of aural repetition, while also suggesting emotional saturation, "gives the volume its weird, fixed and transfixed quality" (53). This device stands in contrast to the "lines which are . . . indistinctly stressed, and approach the rhythms of everyday speech," as seen in much of Hughes's earlier work (Sergeant 58). In this draft of "A Pink Wool Knitted Dress," the "tear-flames" of these lines are precious to the poem's speaker yet also, in the context of the "dice-cup," prophetic of the couple's later difficulties. In spite of this sign of discord, however, the image suggests that the two are playing a game in which they participate willingly. As in so many of Plath's signature poems, too, the "eye-pupils" draw readers' attention to the metaphorical functioning of the body's individual parts. Hughes may have included this image here not only to indicate his struggle to make sense of Plath's enduring poetic persona, but also to illustrate one of his mature compositional techniques: to fit together some of her formal elements to make a different kind of sense in his own work. The published poem's second-to-last stanza contains a similar catalog of signifiers for Plath's wedding-day self, including a vision of her as "A nodding spray of wet lilac" and a description of her happy tears as "ocean depth / Brimming with God" (*CPH* 1065). Hughes's manuscript revisions suggest that he considered, rejected, and finally incorporated compositional strategies that Plath had employed. His letter to her, in this case, meant that he inherited knowledge from the lines and stanzas she left behind. As is the case in some of the other poems from *Birthday Letters*, "A Pink Wool Knitted Dress" demonstrates the methodologies that Hughes sometimes shared, if reluctantly, with Plath—but also his determination to recast the lived experience in an idiom of his own.

The fourth poem in *Birthday Letters* is "Visit," which underlines this negotiation between shared compositional techniques and individual perspectives on life-events and poetic themes. This piece, which depicts the time when Hughes first met Plath, is set not in 1956, during their time at Cambridge, but in 1973: "Ten years after your death" (*CPH* 1048). Structured by a series of related memories, the poem describes a night outside Plath's Newnham College window, the discovery of her journal after her death, and their daughter's desire to see her mother on a cold, quiet evening. Hughes narrates each of these events in its own stanza, separating them both temporally and spatially as if to underline their unique signification and the varying rhetorics in which he captures each one. In reference to their earliest interactions, Hughes observes that his then-girlfriend

> fed snapshots
> Of you and she did not know what
> inflammable celluloid into my silent
> Insatiable future, my blind-man's-bluff
> Internal torch of search. (*CPH* 1047)

These images of static portraiture juxtaposed to dynamic fire point to the gap between Hughes's early idea of Plath and the desires he hoped to fulfill, one fueling the other. The interaction between these two divergent forces is what motivates his poetic self to keep "Aiming to find you, and missing, and again missing. / Flinging earth at a glass that could not protect you / Because you were not there" (*CPH* 1048). Although the poem takes place seventeen years later, he refers here to a night in March 1956, before they had begun dating, when "he went with Lucas Myers around to the house where Sylvia Plath lived with other female students from abroad. Throwing clods at what he thought was her window, he called out her name, but she was out with another man, and anyway he was calling at the wrong window" (Middlebrook, *Her Husband* 23). The earliest interaction in "Visit," is framed, therefore, in terms of memory's tenuous logic; their relationship, now far in the past, reemerges through reflection and transparency—the celluloid, the fire, the glass.

In contrast to this narration of the objects that guided him through their relationship's early moments, when Hughes describes Plath's perspective on their first meeting in the third stanza of "Visit," he focuses on the moment when

> I meet on a page of your journal, as never before,
> The shock of your joy
> When you heard of that. Then the shock
> Of your prayers. And under those prayers your panic
> That prayers might not create the miracle. (*CPH* 1048)

Here, instead of imagining inanimate surfaces that serve to capture and refract their exchanges, Hughes depicts the materiality of her words and her fierce internal desires. After hearing of his visit to her room, she had hoped for the miracle of a relationship coalescing between them, yet in the poem her determination produces a web of conflicting emotions—what he labels "the unthinkable / Old despair and the new agony / Melting into one familiar hell" (*CPH* 1048). Hughes offers readers this insight into Plath's private writings, which he reframes in a new diction and from a different perspective, one stanza before the poem's final vision of their relationship, seen this time through their daughter's eyes. Frieda, a common subject in both of their poetry from the early 1960s, here anchors the words that Hughes chooses for their first meeting to the style and rhetoric that Plath herself used. He describes the way in which Plath's writing shaped the family's life after her death:

> Your actual words, as they floated
> Out through your throat and tongue and onto your page—
> Just as when your daughter, years ago now,
> Drifting in, gazing up into my face,
> Mystified,
> Where I worked alone
> In the silent house, asked, suddenly:
> "Daddy, where's Mummy?" (*CPH* 1048)

Hughes frames this final image of his personal and professional collaborations with Plath in their daughter's words, as well as through her father's missing answer. This emphasis upon the language that circulates among the three of them sets up the poem's conclusion as a veiled answer to the decades of critical questions that have followed him.

This conversation with his daughter is the section of "Visit" to which Hughes paid the most attention in his manuscript revisions. In one of the early typewritten drafts, he tries out a version of the poem's final six lines that attempts to reconcile his account of these meetings with Plath's own: "I look up—as if there were still time / To synchronise myself with the voice / That has found me / And burst in on me. Then look down / at the book of your printed words, / And you are ten years dead. It is only a story. / Your story. My story" (British Library Add MS 88918/1/5). In comparing this draft with the published version—

> I look up—as if to meet your voice
> With all its urgent future
> That has burst in on me. Then look back
> At the book of the printed words.
> You are ten years dead. It is only a story.
> Your story. My story (*CPH* 1049)

—the revisions may seem minor at first. Yet Hughes's adjustments of possessive pronouns, conjunctions, and prepositions change the passage's rhetoric. He relocates "the voice" to Plath herself and identifies the "urgent future" that it is meant to reveal; in the published version, her voice carries a more powerful resonance than does "the book of the printed words," perhaps belying the importance that so many readers have attached to her October poems as the final word on their relationship. Hughes's poem suggests, instead, that she can still speak for herself—even through his words—and that the mythologies that have arisen to define them are, in the end, only that. Churchwell interprets this conclusion as one in which "[r]eading is imagined as an act of introduction: he 'meets' Plath's words on the page just as he 'meets' Plath herself"; his description of the visit ends by both "emphasiz[ing] Hughes's ambiguous, painful position" and "finalizing his version" of events ("Secrets" 123). The poem's two final lines are essentially the same in both versions, reminding his readers that they are both known for their versions of these events—which are just "Your story. My story." As a commentary on his notion of the *ars poetica*, too, these lines point to a contrast between the control that the writer exercises over his or her language and the multiple interpretations of that language that readers create.

Hughes employs some of Plath's most familiar compositional strategies more explicitly in "The Afterbirth," which he initially titled "The Hare" in his *Birthday Letters* drafts. These formal similarities are all the more interesting because of the critical controversy to which the poem seems to contribute: its central imagery and narrative recall both the interactions, discussed in chapter 1, between "The Thought-Fox" and "Burning the Letters" and the opposing stances that Plath's and Hughes's "The Rabbit Catcher" represent. The description that begins "The Afterbirth" recalls the blood-soaked vision of a ripped fox that anchors the final stanza of "Burning the Letters." In revisions to the manuscript draft written in red pen, Hughes notes that his poetic subject "ripped her face off / And threw it to the floor" (BL Add MS 88918/1/3), while in the published version of "The Afterbirth," which repeats those lines, he describes it as "already offal," "a tangled / Puddle of dawn reds and evening purples, / To be rubbished." Bold colors appear in many of Plath's poems; the violent dismemberment and vivid colors of this passage resonate with several of the *Ariel* pieces. Hughes emphasizes these abrupt movements in the precisely drawn images of "The Afterbirth":

> A tear-splitting dazzle
> Like the noon sun finally stared at
> Had burst into the bedroom when the Gorgon
> Arrived and ripped her face off
> And threw it to the floor. (*CPH* 1127)

Like Plath, he draws upon a rich reserve of Greek and Norse mythological references in constructing his metaphors. In this case, however, the Gorgon is linked to the hare's dismembered body, a reminder that hunting is a practice rooted in the nation's sense of identity and survival. The "dazzle" of these lines recurs in the next stanza in connection with the speaker's auditor, whose "eyes [are] dazzling tears" and who lifts the now-dead "dazzler" in sorrow at the hare's death (*CPH* 1127). Some of Plath's boldest poems also introduce unique representations of physical violation—as in the "little poppies" of "Poppies in July," which she describes as "little hell flames" and "Little bloody skirts" (*CPP* 203), or the "Little pilgrim," "turkey wattle," and "million soldiers" of "Cut" (*CPP* 235)—by reconfiguring ordinary objects as sources of destruction and horror.

In "Fever," Hughes achieves another distinctive variety of formal and rhetorical correspondence between his work and Plath's. The poem is not an obvious response to her "Fever 103°," nor does it rely upon the vivid colors and incongruent images that define many of her contemporary pieces, but it does echo her tendency to reimagine the familiar elements of an everyday situation. In this case, instead of framing a cut finger or a flower as an embodiment of physical violence, though, Hughes comments upon the power that words in and of themselves can exercise. "Fever" depicts a painful period early in the Plath-Hughes marriage through references to well-known biographical details, but it also contributes to Hughes's *ars poetica* by considering the particular dilemmas that writers face. In contrast to Plath's poem, which laments the way "Lemon water, chicken / Water, water make me retch" during the protracted bout of flu she suffered along with the children in the fall of 1962 (*CPP* 232), Hughes's speaker looks outward at a once comfortable domestic scene, part of a honeymoon, that has been transformed by a partner's illness. As in more directly critical pieces like "You Hated Spain," the poetic subject rejects her immediate surroundings because she longs for another clime; her sufferings both cement her certainty that the place itself has rejected her and give the poetic speaker an opportunity to become the moment's savior. Plath describes in her 1962 poem "My head a moon / Of Japanese paper, my gold beaten skin / Infinitely delicate and infinitely expensive" (*CPP* 232), a portrait of the martyred subject's self as it has been refined by the extremities of illness. Hughes describes 35 years later, albeit in reference to a scene from a different point in time, "your helpless, baby-bird gape," "your tear-ruined face," a response to disease that "jammed so hard / Over into the red of catastrophe / [that it] Left no space for worse" (*CPH* 1072–73). With a clarity born of later knowledge, the speaker begins to suspect that his partner might be exaggerating her distress. His "chilly, familiar thoughts" warn that if she does not "'Stop crying wolf,'" he will not "'know, I shall not hear / When things get really bad'" (*CPH* 1073). Already, he suggests, their interactions follow habitual patterns; the speaker records this conversation in order to observe its distinctive elements and remember them for later use.

Aside from the almost perfect echo between the two poems' titles, the most convincing evidence of the dialogue that they generate can be seen in their conclusions. In keeping with her poem's focus on the effects that bodily illness has wrought upon the speaker's psychic self, Plath suggests in the last few lines an outcome that recalls the condemnatory end of "Lady Lazarus": "I think I am going up, / I think I may rise—" toward some perfect but unknown destination. The speaker notes that she may be "Attended by roses, / By kisses, by cherubim," but "Not him, nor him / (My selves dissolving, old whore petticoats)— / To Paradise" (*CPP* 232). Hughes's final lines, in contrast, focus on the fact that "You were overloaded," presumably by the possible threat of bodily harm. The speaker responds tersely to this concern: "I said nothing. / I said nothing. The stone man made soup. / The burning woman drank it" (*CPH* 1073). In order to elucidate the tensions between the speaker and the poetic subject, Hughes erases the agency he had assigned to the speaker earlier in the poem, inserting faceless icons into the narrative situation instead.

In early drafts of "Fever," however, Hughes imagined the poetic speaker making an attempt to communicate more frankly with his partner. Rather than stepping away from his struggle to reason out the poetic subject's motivations, a move recorded in the published version, the British Library drafts reflect a return to the ongoing conflict in which the pair has been engaged. The typed draft ends with "I'm losing you," which is amended in handwriting to "I shall lose you / You were too overwhelmed to find words for me" (BL Add MS 88918/1/3). Though both of these lines are absent from the final publication, their presence here points to Hughes's perspective on the correlations between Plath's work and his own. The two lines can be read as simple ruminations on a failing relationship, but their potential as more pointed commentary on the work that the two exchanged cannot be discounted. Reading the poem with these lines as an end goal casts the narrated illness in a new light. While it may have historical roots in the events of Plath's and Hughes's 1956 honeymoon, its presence in this 1998 piece reflects not only their marital conflicts but also the compositional approaches they learned from one another. In this context, the line "You were too overwhelmed to find words for me" points to the creative obstacles that Hughes faced after Plath's death, in particular the grief and sense of dislocation that he sought to work through in the *Crow* sequence. Her legacy, her own pages of poems, had been so besieged by readings from critics and fans that Hughes could no longer locate his own inspiration there. At the same time, the line presses the poetic speaker away, urging him to find his own voice and story. This type of dual narration, which produces both the poem's surface-level meaning and its function as a metaphor for the challenges that the writer faces, echoes a compositional method that Plath herself often employed, particularly in 1962 poems like "The Applicant," "Medusa," and "Cut."

Hughes also draws upon rhetorical techniques that Plath cultivated when shaping the *ars poetica* of "The Afterbirth." The butchered rabbit at the center of this poem, a "curled-up, chopped-up corpse," threatens to "come hobbling down from under the elms / Into our yard, crying: 'Mother! Mother! / They are going to eat me.'" The twinned exclamations that Hughes includes here embody a heightened emotional intensity that resembles similarly demonstrative moments in "Daddy" and "Lady Lazarus," among others. In the poem's second half, Hughes's speaker suggests that the hare might have "Died silent, a black jolt, / Under my offside rear wheel / On the dawn A30" before moving to one of the book's most striking moments. The speaker claims that his auditor "heard nothing," yet the hare's death "bled out of my pen. And re-formed / On my page. The hieroglyph of the hare" (*CPH* 1128). These lines recall the moment of creation that concludes "The Thought-Fox," yet the key difference between the two poems, published more than forty years apart, lies in each animal's fate. The first statement of Hughes's creative process embraces the fox's material existence, while "The Afterbirth" picks up some of Plath's compositional tools—a repurposed diction, repetitions, exclamations, moments of concentrated expressivity—in order to examine death's potential for creative inspiration. The poem's lyric subject interacts directly with the text that the hare inspired: in a clear reference to "Words heard, by accident, over the phone," Hughes notes that she hears "the hieroglyph of the hare" scream "in your ear like a telephone." The poem ends on just this note of terror and pain, "The hare in the bowl screamed—" (*CPH* 1128), as if to suggest that the combination of Hughes's and Plath's compositional techniques in these lines strains the image without bringing the narrative to a conclusion.

Two significant drafts of "The Afterbirth" appear in the British Library papers, both of which are labeled "The Hare" (Add MS 88918/1/2 and Add MS 88918/1/3). Hughes's decision to title the published poem "The Afterbirth" indicates that its metaphorical scope extends beyond the animal alone; the imagery of hunting, birth, and death represents not just the life shared between two people but also the deeply personal act of poetic composition. Incorporating Plath's writing strategies alongside his own enables Hughes to expand the work's expressive and figurative possibilities. The poem also reimagines the violent images conventionally associated with childbirth—blood, ripped flesh, screaming—as a means of exploring the limits of one's literal flesh and one's writerly productivity alike.

Another of the pieces in which Hughes explores a metaphor tying the writer's body to the text it produces, "Being Christlike," is represented in the British Library *Birthday Letters* papers as a highly resonant signifier of Plath's and Hughes's relationship. Of the subjects outlined in the asterisk diagram described above, "Being Christlike" is the only to also appear, using the identical phrasing, in a Hughes poem. The diagram itself outlines the ways in which Plath rejected domestic concerns and her own self in order to maintain detachment from her problems. Hughes deduces from this list of censures—of parents, family, and the body—that a "naked soul" is the final goal (British Library Add MS 88918/1/6, ff. 139). The published poem argues, however, that Plath did not seek out this state of being intentionally. Hughes structures the poem using four iterations of the same statement: "You did not want to be Christlike. Though your father / Was your God and there was no other, you did not / Want to be Christlike" is followed nine lines later by "You did not / Want to be Christlike" and then another seven lines later, in the piece's conclusion, by "But you did not / Want to be Christlike." The poem initially represents its title concept as a burden imposed upon its subject, yet the three enjambed repetitions of the sentence position the verb at the beginning of the line, emphasizing the desire rather than its denial. Hughes does not mention Plath's "peanut-crunching crowd" explicitly, but its invisible presence informs every line; he labels her father "your God" and her mother "the stranger" with "great hooded eyes" whose threat Plath can only dispel by invoking an ancient ward against the evil eye, crying *"Get thee behind me"* (original italics). The poem's argument assumes that both her closest family members and the outside world chose to see her as a martyr, a role that was imposed without her consent. Unlike the metaphoric use to which Hughes puts a dead hare in "The Afterbirth," this poem's imagery focuses on the real dimensions of physical experience: "your body / Barred your passage. And your family / Who were your flesh and blood / Burdened it" (*CPH* 1142). Hughes attempts here to locate the posthumous associations with divinity that Plath's readers created and her tendency toward self-destruction in outside pressures and genetic predestination rather than in her internal ambition for fame. Her life, he suggests, centered on an ongoing search for her dead father, while her immediate family further exacerbated the personal difficulties that she endured.

The perspective on Plath that this poem offers appears quite different from that of "The Afterbirth," yet it too is concerned with her reactions to external stressors and the kind of work she produced. One of the British Library folders contains a manuscript table of contents to *Birthday Letters* with a note from a copyeditor: "I think this is very aptly, succinctly and courageously put, but it does allow critics to say that, under pretence of telling SP either what she knows already, or what she does not know and might actually dispute, you are really, blatantly, delivering a rebuke to the idolators. If anyone wants to pick holes in the general enterprise, this is where they might begin. Which is not to say that I'm against it—poem or enterprise. Quite the reverse" (British Library Add MS 88918/1/15). This statement underscores the thematic importance of the poem to the book as a whole, and its inclusion here suggests that Hughes felt that it deserved a central place in the collection. Like "A Pink Wool Knitted Dress," "Fever," "The Afterbirth," and "The Bee God," "Being Christlike" illuminates key elements of Hughes's established *ars poetica*, particularly those techniques that he shared with Plath's later work: the writer's struggles to control his language, his attempts to capture an object's precise significance through multiple variations, his interest in the metaphorical potential of ordinary events, and the strong analogy he pursued between bodily experience and textual production.

LETTERS AT THE END OF A LIFE: THE FINAL METHODOLOGY

Hughes experiments in *Birthday Letters* with unique rhetorical, semantic, and syntactic devices, as well as with traditional poetic modes like the pastoral and the elegiac. Reddick identifies consistent statements made in an elegiac mode in his work, which includes "mournful animal poems," "family elegies," and "ecological elegies" in *Remains of Elmet, Moortown Diary*, and *Wolfwatching* (273); Clark sees traces of Plath's influence in *Wodwo* and *Gaudete* as well, through Hughes's use of revisions, elegiac turns, and direct quotations (*Grief* 203). Poems written to memorialize not just Plath but also specific moments in time and personally cherished locations fill *Birthday Letters*. Iain Twiddy locates "emotional simplification, withdrawal from previous attachments, the voicing of aspirations and the establishment of a legacy" in modern pastoral elegies by Hughes, Michael Longley, and Paul Muldoon. The form has remained flexible over time, focusing on "mediation, to negotiate between inside and outside, past and future, and between loss and consolation"; more recently, it has sought to engage with the irrational nature of historical trauma and a general loss of consolation (Twiddy 1, 13). Twiddy suggests that in *Birthday Letters* in particular, Hughes's work participates in "the communal" by "achieving dissociation from the dead"; here, as Plath does in *Ariel*, he "create[s] myths which make experience explicable, and which allow [him] to move away from traumatic and inhibiting personal events" (79–80, 92). Clark agrees with Twiddy that Hughes's elegies "frequently subvert the traditional consolatory and conciliatory functions," resulting in "nearly as many instances of self-elegy as elegy in the collection" (*Grief* 224), while Laura Webb points out that these pieces honor "loss by creating a permanent 'space,' albeit textual and two-dimensional, which stands in honour of the dead" (38–39).[5] Like Plath in some respects, he relies upon catalogs of symbolically resonant objects, moments of focused emotionality, recursive statements, and exclamatory apostrophe in constructing these commemorative portraits of their shared life and work. In Hughes's work, these elements illuminate his investigations of the writer's failings and his strategies for resistance.

"The Table," one of the poems in the British Library holdings that displays evidence of significant revision, contains refined versions of these elements that illustrate a mature stage in Hughes's craft. As I note in the introduction, this poem draws its central image from Plath's work: the elm of which the table is built, the subject of her 1962 poem "Elm." The poem's speaker turns the elm to multiple uses: upon witnessing his subject's dead father dragging her into the earth through the "Coffin elm," "Down through the elm door" (*CPH* 1132–33), he finds himself alone on the stage from Plath's "Lady Lazarus." Absent the curious onlookers and the performer herself, the speaker awakes "on the empty stage with the props, / The paltry painted masks. And the script / Ripped up and scattered." At this point in time, more than 30 years after Plath's death, Hughes's speaker notes that "now your peanut-crunchers can stare / At the ink-stains, the sigils / Where you engraved your letters to him / Cursing and imploring" (*CPH* 1133). In "Lady Lazarus," Plath styled herself the object of their gazes; Hughes reimagines the scene in his piece as a tourist destination at which the site of her creation, a table that he helped to make, draws the endless fascination that now influences critics' and fans' views of Plath.

In "The Table," more broadly speaking, Hughes attempts to dispel some of the direct associations that critics have made between Plath's life and her work by focusing on a single poetic object with extensive metaphorical resonance. Most importantly, the table serves as a touchstone for Plath's and Hughes's compositional strategies. In its published version, the poem begins with a straightforward description. As a "coffin elm," though, the table immediately takes on metaphoric and even mythological connotations. Hughes employs the same vocabulary of divination and prophecy that informs "A Pink Wool Knitted Dress" and "The Bee God" to suggest that while the new table might be "a perfect landing pad / For your inspiration" (*CPH* 1132), it also helps the determined writer to "divine in the elm, following your pen, / The words that would open it." He borrows imagery from Plath's "Daddy" to sketch "Your Daddy resurrected, / Blue-eyed, that German cuckoo" who "limped up through it / Into our house." The table, initially framed as gift and creative inspiration, becomes a device for augury whose "ink-stains, the sigils / Where you engraved your letters to him" attract not just tourists' gazes but also artistic inspiration (*CPH* 1133). In one of the early British Library drafts, Hughes expands the prophetic overtones of the poem's first stanza as well. The final published version relies upon a simple pun: "With a plane / I revealed a perfect landing pad" (*CPH* 1132). In this draft, however, Hughes alludes to the mythological possibilities that this object could reveal: "And elm—somehow elm / Has become the solemn concierge / To the underworld. With a plane" (BL Add MS 88918/1/3). Though this phrasing did not survive in the poem's final version, its presence here indicates that Hughes understood the table's materiality as a central dimension of its poetic denotation. The object enables the writer's act.

In Western literature, elm trees often signify mythic prowess and accomplishment. In ancient Greek rhetorician Athenaeus's third-century study of mythology, the *Deipnosophistae*, he names one of the eight Greek hamadryads, or nymphs of the forest, Ptelea, which means "elm." After Achilles kills Andromache's father Eetion during the Trojan War, as depicted in *The Iliad*, "round the tomb / Grew elm-trees planted by the mountain-nymphs" (Book 6, l. 269). Elms also appear in several examples of pastoral poetry, such as Greek poet Theocritus's first *Idyll*, as places that offer coolness and peace to passersby; in this poem, the Goatherd invites Thyrsis to "come and sit yonder, beneath the elm, this way, over against Priapus and the fountain-goddesses." These references link elm trees to such concepts as oversight, memorialization, and solace, and they lend a pastoral element to the dialogue between "The Table" and "Elm." In order to maximize his poem's contribution to an *ars poetica*, Hughes focuses on the concrete object rather than on its intangible associations. His decision to excise the passage cited above reflects the book's general concentration on the objects that shape memory rather than on Western literature's mythological roots. The poem evokes the interests in soothsaying and folklore that Hughes pursued with Plath, yet its compositional devices reflect the divergences between them. Plath's "Elm" employs personification and several images already present in her poetic vocabulary to articulate the speaker's private sense of danger. The speaker describes herself as possessing "red filaments" and moving under a "merciless" moon; she feels "terrified by this dark thing / That sleeps in me" (*CPP* 192–93). As Plath glossed the poem in a letter to Howard Moss of *The New Yorker*, "the whole poem is the elm talking & might be in quotes. The elm is talking to the woman who contemplates her—they are intimately related in mood, and the various moods, I think, of anguish, are explored in the poem" (*LSP2* 815). In contrast, Hughes's elm signifies in literal terms. His speaker acknowledges the familiar images that populate Plath's poem, but he identifies the table as a manmade object specifically destined for artistic production. He does not draw on Plath's devices of repetition, exclamation, and catalog, as in some of the book's other poems. Instead, the table's biographical resonance and physical properties combine to describe the *ars poetica* inspired by Plath's work; Hughes's advocacy of concrete representation and direct statement add to the perspective on compositional process that he describes in "The Thought-Fox" and "The Afterbirth."

Hughes's drafts of and revisions to the *Birthday Letters* poems illustrate his late-career interest in the writing body itself as well as the role that national identity plays in determining the subjects of one's writing. The book opens with "Fulbright Scholars," which already positions Plath in a liminal space between American and English identity; poems like "Sam," "Trophies," "Fate Playing," "Your Paris," "You Hated Spain," "The Chipmunk," and "The Badlands," among others, extend Hughes's investigation of her sense of nationhood to encompass not just London but also France, Spain, the English countryside, and the American Southwest. In keeping with his use of Plath's signature compositional techniques, he shifts narrative perspective in these pieces away from the encomia for England that fill *The Hawk in the Rain, Lupercal, Wodwo, Season Songs, Gaudete, Cave Birds, Remains of Elmet, Moortown Diary, A Primer of Birds, River, Flowers and Insects,* and *Wolfwatching*. Rather, in *Birthday Letters*, he investigates human perspectives on nation and national identity by reconstructing specific moments from the time that he and Plath shared. Hughes's decision to draw upon her style and rhetoric and to challenge his own sense of England's dominant presence in the book anticipate in some ways the massive international response that the poems would generate. The poems also link human frailties—including the mind's susceptibility to misremembering and the body's gradual deterioration—to the role that real, material bodies play in creative production. Hughes explores this dimension of the *ars poetica* through pastoral and elegiac modes that center on direct rather than metaphorical representations.

THE CONTEXTS OF PUBLICATION

Unpublished letters that Hughes wrote at the time of *Birthday Letters*' release in the UK attest to the book's unique status within his oeuvre. These letters confirm that its earliest readers understood that Hughes had tested out some new compositional devices in this collection. As Brain asserts, the book deploys a "constant questioning" and "refusal of any one meaning or privileged viewpoint" that contributed to its impact on readers (*The Other* 182). The letters also suggest that these aesthetic departures helped to produce some of his finest work—and that the public was eager to participate in conversations about the collection's historical and literary implications. The *Times*'s Peter Stothard wrote to Joanna Mackle at Faber and Faber on 2 December 1997 to describe, for instance, the cultural moment that the book helped to define: "The experience of being an early reader of this book is not one that I will ever forget. Please be assured that I will put my very best effort into making sure that *Times* readers gain some of that sense of verbal excitement and physical closeness that I felt myself. We would aim to reveal the book's existence in a prominent front page story on Saturday 17 January. On the same day we would print an article from an understanding critic and a *Times* leading article in which the significance of the *Letters* is made clear. We would also select several poems to publish on the Saturday and would probably want to publish others throughout the following week. I look forward to discussing with you the choice of those poems and the way in which we introduce them to readers" (BL Add MS 88918/1/13). This statement indicates that the *Times* decided to emphasize the individual poems' literary value over their biographical revelations. Stothard also underlines here the emotional impact that the work is likely to exercise upon its readers.

Stothard's excitement about the collection and his vow to publicize it extensively are echoed in Hughes's February 1998 correspondence with Faber and Faber publisher Matthew Evans and BBC arts producer David Kerr, who hoped to produce a documentary film about Hughes and Plath to accompany the publication of *Birthday Letters*. In a fax from 5 February, Kerr argues that even gaining permission to quote from the poems "would be dependent on convincing Ted that ours will be an 'even-handed' programme." The public's intense desire for such a program is demonstrated, he asserts, by the fact that "the near-unanimous praise of these poems has been resounding; even those commentators who have in the past cast Ted Hughes in an unfavourable light have been forced to reassess their assumptions. Our film would be made in this 'revisionist' context, with the ambition of giving a balanced account" (BL Add MS 88918/1/13). Along similar lines, Evans notes in a letter dated 10 February that "if you're not reading the papers yet I can tell you that the comments from editorials continue to be extremely positive and sympathetic toward you, and although the firefighters will no doubt arrive shortly, things still look very good indeed." He tempers his enthusiasm, however, by urging Hughes to rethink his earlier decision to block the BBC documentary. Evans points out that "you have now published the book and the book is the subject of public debate. As you said it's the nearest thing you will ever write to an autobiography and it is absolutely inevitable that radio and television are going to make programmes. . . . I'm not suggesting for a moment that any floodgates are opened but the guy who phoned me from the BBC sounded like an extremely sensible person and rather than simply reject everything if we responded sympathetically to one television programme and one radio programme . . . it would enable us to turn everything else down. . . . This is not advice I would have given you pre-*Birthday Letters* but now that the book has been published perhaps things have changed" (BL Add MS 88918/1/13). Hughes had long possessed a reputation as one of the most highly respected and award-winning poets in England; these letters reveal, however, that the book's reception generated feelings of ambivalence in the author himself. The poems shed light on specific aspects of Hughes's and Plath's life together, and their ideas about the work of the writer, but they also prescribe, to a certain degree, readers' insight into these moments. As Sarah Churchwell points out, the book carries with it a significant economic implication as well: "Both Plath's and Hughes's poetry 'about' each other commodifies their 'private' story and sells it to the public" ("Secrets" 113). The intense desire of Hughes's correspondents to produce the documentary testifies to their lives' significant financial value. Hughes seems to have been satisfied with allowing his audience to examine the properties of their craft that the two poets shared, but he refused in the end to yield a full disclosure of their private experiences to the public, no matter what personal gain he might have accrued.

Although Hughes remained reluctant to share personal details with a public television or radio audience, his responses to Matthew Evans's inquiries acknowledge the timeliness of the book's publication and its weight within his career as a whole. In a letter dated 8 February 1998, he had already dismissed the possibility of appearing in a documentary, suggesting that "maybe the best line to take at the moment is: 1) No appearance or interview from me. 2) No programme [illeg.] S.P. and me. Not even one that promises to be 'even-handed.' The 'even-handed' clause would merely hand them a licence for recycling all the malign rubbish, dramatized and sensationalized further in a court-style controversy. . . . No reason why I should facilitate that kind of thing, where I can block it. 3) No dramatizations. 4) Just straight readings (by others than me) and commentary, or nothing." On 10 February, however, he writes back to Evans, admitting that "I see your point. Maybe, if any initial enquiry about a programme etc. combining SP and me can be met with a clear proviso: that 'I am not interested in making material available for a programme which then proceeds to recycle the sensational falsehoods that have at various times been used against me.' . . . That will probably sound like outrageous censorship but maybe applicants could be asked to consider the special circumstances and the lessons of history" (BL Add MS 88918/1/13). Hughes sent these two letters in such close succession that it is clear he had reconsidered the possibility of a documentary. Such a production would publicly recognize the book's disclosures and underscore the innovative work that Hughes had produced.

Hughes's contributions to this exchange seem to envision a documentary that would focus on the technical aspects of his and Plath's work, with little biographical commentary. Ultimately, the project would not be made during his lifetime. In 2015, the BBC released *Ted Hughes: Stronger Than Death*, a ninety-minute film that features commentary from A. Alvarez, Simon Armitage, Jill Barber, Jonathan Bate, Ehor Boyanowsky, Melvyn Bragg, Ruth Fainlight, Elaine Feinstein, Daniel Huws, Frances McCullough, Robin Morgan, Elizabeth Sigmund, Vicky Watling, and, in her first public appearance in connection with her father, Frieda Hughes. Matthew Evans conceded in a letter to Hughes dated 26 February 1998 that "It's clear [the BBC] can't do the programme and that's fine." However, Faber and Faber wanted him to consider an alternative instead: "The current season of Start [the] Week finishes at the end of March. What [Melvyn Bragg] would like to do is to devote the last programme in the series to you. What this would mean is that he would come down to Devon, talk to you about **Ovid, Birthday Letters**, and your work generally and this would go out at 905 on the last Monday in March. . . . It's an idea worth considering for two reasons. First of all, you can absolutely trust Melvyn and he would only talk about things you were prepared to talk about. Secondly—and this is very important for me—you will have done something after the publication of **Birthday Letters** so that we can say when we get other requests that you've said everything you're going to say" (original bold type). However, this program was never made. David Kerr also chimed in on the canceled BBC project, noting in a letter to Evans dated 24 February that "There seem to me to be so many areas in which the facts are difficult to ascertain, and interpretation such an invitation to controversy, that I cannot devise an approach which might be satisfactory without involving Ted in the more active role I was hoping, at the outset, he might adopt. Part of my difficulty is also practical; even assuming that our synopsis might be acceptable to Ted, subject to minor alterations, I am not convinced that our project might be feasible in the timescale available to us. Regrettably, therefore, I feel we have no choice but to abandon our intention of making this film" (BL Add MS 88919/1/13). Hughes's proven literary status, his role as national poet laureate, and his strong concern about the invasion of privacy that such a project would entail proved to be more than enough to shutter the BBC's plans for the time being.

The inclusion of this BBC correspondence with the *Birthday Letters* manuscripts underlines the importance of the book not only for Hughes's readers but also for scholars of Plath's life and work. Hughes clearly saw the collection's purpose, at least in part, as a corrective to longtime popular readings of their relationship. His desire to avoid participating in an accompanying documentary suggests that, despite the book's obvious biographical content, he wanted to discourage largely personal readings of the work—or that he wanted to control the nature of those readings himself. Both the organization of *Birthday Letters* and the individual poems' manuscript drafts make the argument that readers should apply their critical focus to its formal and structural innovations; Hughes employs some of the same compositional strategies that Plath had developed in several of the book's most rhetorically assertive pieces. The collection's investigations of the writing body and, by extension, the body of the nation also underline Hughes's decision to concentrate his poetic narrative on the larger factors that motivate the act of writing itself.

AFTER *BIRTHDAY LETTERS*: *HOWLS AND WHISPERS*

While *Birthday Letters* received the bulk of the critical and popular attention associated with Hughes's work at the end of his life, *Howls and Whispers* was his last published book and his final collaboration with lifelong friend Leonard Baskin. Jonathan Bate describes it as "an opportunity to release, but avoid excessive public examination of, some of the most intimate poems that he had stepped back from including in *Birthday Letters*." Hughes and Baskin created one hundred copies of the book, then an additional ten copies that included "a unique leaf of Ted's manuscript" plus "colour-printed etchings and additional watercolour drawings" by Baskin (Bate 509). This brief collection returns to some of the themes and images that filter through *Birthday Letters*, reflecting the fact that, for Hughes, "there was more to come" in his revelations about Plath and about the evolution of his own art: "he had been gestating the project for more than a quarter of a century" (Bate 510).

Several of the pieces that fill *Howls and Whispers* employ a recursive approach to composition consistent with the drafts that Hughes obsessively rewrote throughout his lifetime; Brain also describes its "novelistic" approach to telling "the long story of a relationship over time" (*The Other* 183). The book's second poem, "Religion," for instance, begins with a direct reference to the penultimate piece in *Birthday Letters*, "The Dogs Are Eating Your Mother," which Henry Hart has glossed as an example of Hughes's "antagonism toward urbane literary critics," described here as "bloodthirsty animals" (154). In the latter poem, the speaker cautions that

> That is not your mother but her body,
> She leapt from our window
> And fell there. Those are not dogs
> That seem to be dogs
> Pulling at her. (*CPH* 1168)

"Religion," in contrast, reassigns the agency to the poem's auditor, as the speaker claims "You wanted to eat your mother" because "Murder is of a piece / With the mouth." The poem suggests that the speaker possesses a control over the situation that did not exist in "The Dogs." Here, he informs the listener that capitalizing on others' painful experiences means that critics' work can only ever be partially complete: "A mother was killed but not eaten," because she exists in memory even after her death. Hughes implies, further, that the process of poetic composition itself serves to inoculate its subject against total annihilation. Because he had been recreated—and preserved—in some of Plath's most famous later poems, "Your father also died / And could not be eaten" (*CPH* 1174). Thus the act of writing, the art that makes possible her enduring life after death, is also the act that condemned her, and their shared critics, to commit "inexorable murder" and to function as "your own Church." Wresting control over the parents' legacies away from their readers, a situation that Hughes first describes in "The Dogs Are Eating

Your Mother," means that they must reimagine the literary landscape their works occupy. Though Hughes concludes "Religion" by asserting that "your kiss, your real lips, / And your words / Were the blessing" (*CPH* 1175), the piece's ultimate argument supersedes a simple analogy between writing and the faith in oneself that motivates it. Rather, the "religion" that it outlines contributes to Hughes's late notion of the *ars poetica*: a final attempt to understand the tools with which the writer creates her work and the effects of its reception.

Hughes completes the story of another *Birthday Letters* poem in "The Minotaur 2," one of the shortest poems in *Howls and Whispers*. Its precursor, "The Minotaur," appears about two-thirds of the way through *Birthday Letters*: a one-page portrait of a dissolving marriage that evokes the table imagery already familiar to readers of both Plath and Hughes. Iain Twiddy labels this piece an illustration of "Plath's entry into the irresistible mythological pattern, as one of the human sacrifices to the Minotaur" (83). Hughes's tendency to forestall the possibility of consolation comes into play here: Plath "plays out an old story, as she is pulled back into history and the underworld, rather than actively climbing away from it" (Twiddy 84). As he does in so many of the volume's other pieces, Hughes frames their relationship in material terms; his poetic subject destroys first a "mahogany table-top" and then a "high stool" out of rage at their inability to communicate. The poem follows a recursive structure, alternating between the speaker's furious reaction to this violence—"'Marvellous!' I shouted, 'Go on, / Smash it into kindling. / That's the stuff you're keeping out of your poems!'"—and the archetypal mythologies that help him to make sense of their shared chaos. In spite of the poem's heavy investment in the stuff of myth, including a "goblin" and "tunnels in a labyrinth," its narration keeps returning to the anger at the center of the marriage. This focus on the realm of the everyday enables Hughes to reinterpret the poetic narrative as a metaphor for a fundamental dilemma that writers face: whether to represent one's experiences directly or to frame them as creative inspiration. Hughes reimagines the thread Ariadne bestows on Theseus as "the bloody end of the skein / That unravelled your marriage"; the patriarch who overshadows their union is the "horned, bellowing / Grave of your risen father." This reading of the myth reveals the steep cost that the speaker and his partner have paid for their work. At the same time, however, he implores her to "'Get that shoulder under your stanzas / And we'll be away'" (*CPH* 1120): if nothing else, they can salvage their work from the wreck of their relationship. The broken furniture and the lonely children that the speaker's partner leaves behind blur the easy analogy between her father and the minotaur; he suggests, rather, that her ruthless tendency to plunder her life for poetic material left a series of tangled stories in her wake. The writing that we do, Hughes's *ars poetica* implies here, always levies a fee on our lives.

In "The Minotaur 2," which is exactly half the length of "The Minotaur," Hughes bestows the poem's animus on its subject rather than on its speaker. The violence of the relationship's earlier incarnation is gone; instead, its two participants "touch . . . like cripples" and reframe their problems as a "surreal mystery" that "Opened your performance quietly" (*CPH* 1178). Here he quotes directly from Plath's "Event," which she wrote three days after David and Assia Wevill visited Court Green in late May 1962, at which point Plath already feared that Hughes was interested in Assia (Clark, *Grief* 232). Plath concludes her poem, a meditation on the alien landscape that appears to a lover who fears she has been betrayed, with "The dark is melting. We touch like cripples" (*CPP* 195). In the second of the three stanzas comprising "The Minotaur 2," in contrast, Hughes returns to his earlier poem's central image: "You had picked up the skein of blood / That twitched and led you, ignoring me." This time he positions the skein not as a thread that pulls apart a marriage but as a tool leading to a goal. As a result, the poem speaks directly to the Minotaur myth, harkening back to both Hughes's and Plath's habitual reliance on Greek and Norse mythologies. Where the original myth features Theseus slaying King Minos's hidden son, though, this version renders the monster the victor instead. The poetic subject arrives not at the exit to the labyrinth, as had been Theseus's goal, but at "the very centre"; as a result, "the Minotaur, which was waiting to kill you, / Killed you" (*CPH* 1178). Because of its conclusion, this poem reads like a revision of the first rather than just another variation on the Minotaur theme. The relationship between poetic subject and speaker dissolves into the myth itself, rather than resolving into the expected and familiar tension between two partners in a marriage. Using the myth as the poem's organizing principle allows Hughes to present the conflict at its center as a result of uncontrollable external forces rather than profoundly intimate ones. Unlike the relationship in "The Minotaur," which portrays interpersonal hostility as a deliberate inspiration for art, the marriage ends in "The Minotaur 2" because the stories surrounding the poetic subject, the myths that define her, have finally consumed her as well. Through this gesture of narrative distancing, Hughes not only deflects the anger and blame associated with so many other depictions of his marriage but also identifies the writerly acts that motivate the poem itself.

The titular poem of *Howls and Whispers*, which immediately follows "The Minotaur 2," also uses an intertextual lens, this time as a means of illuminating an analogy between personal retribution and writerly production. Rather than delving into classical mythology, Hughes turns in this case to English Renaissance drama—namely, two of Shakespeare's most famous tragedies, *Hamlet* and *Othello*. "Howls and Whispers" begins by speculating about "What was poured in your ears / While you argued with death" (*CPH* 1178), in a likely reference to the poison poured in the sleeping king's ear before the events of *Hamlet* begin. The Ghost describes his end in similar terms: "Sleeping within my orchard, / My custom always of the afternoon, / Upon my secure hour thy uncle stole, / With juice of cursed hebenon in a vial, / And in the porches of my ears did pour / The leperous distilment" (*Hamlet* 1.2.802). In the next lines of his poem, Hughes revises Iago's famous insistence that Rodrigo "put money in thy purse" (*Othello* 1.3.382) when the poetic speaker claims that his mother-in-law advised his wife repeatedly to "'Hit him in the purse'" (*CPH* 1178). Both of these well-known passages, taken from monologues delivered in the first act of each play, accumulate dramatic weight through unexpected revelation. The Ghost's listener, who is the king's son Hamlet, learns of his uncle's treasonous act early on and spends the rest of the play trying to avenge his father. Rodrigo, on the other hand, who believes himself to be Iago's friend, is as yet unaware of Iago's plan: to use the money not to help Rodrigo win Desdemona's heart but to further his own ends. The "howls and whispers" that shape Hughes's poem also emerge from shocking narrative twists, which demonstrate the motivations underlying the creation of art itself.

Rather than imagining a story that includes such Shakespearean plot elements, Hughes assembles a second group of outside texts to explain the sources of the betrayal he outlines in the poem. These documents update Shakespeare's iconic portraits of duplicity to reference both romantic conflict and literal war, expanding the metaphors for artistic production that the poem employs. "After the event," the speaker notes, "I found her letters"; he describes these missives as, alternately, "war-banners," "your Intelligence Corps," "our only Marriage Guidance Council," and "Thunderheads of static experience / Unloading into your ear" (*CPH* 1178–79). The speaker's partner turns away from him after writing her letters and joins forces with a double agent instead, a "double spy, / The manquée journalist, the professional dopester," who uses guile to reframe the marital situation to her own advantage. Like the mother-in-law, she is a "Pretty, innocent-eyed, gleeful Iago" whose words change the wife's perceptions of the marriage. In spite of its reliance upon Shakespearean tropes and its references to wife's changing self, however, the argument of "Howls and Whispers" bears a close resemblance to that of "The Minotaur 2." Hughes identifies the medical technologies that his poetic subject endured—"the step-up transformers" and "the masks that measured out the voltage / That they wired so tenderly / With placebo anesthetic / Into your ear"—as the marriage's true death-knell. Again, the poetic speaker locates the cause of their dissension in forces external to their relationship; electroshock treatments generated her pain and anger, which in turn shaped the texts she could produce. As the poem's closing lines note, "that killed you / Even as you screamed it at me" (*CPH* 1179): their final artistic collaboration arose from the pain they endured together, which the speaker now lays bare for the world to see.

"Howls and Whispers" extends the dialogue between Hughes and Plath by engaging with the key themes Hughes identifies in the aforementioned notebook diagram. The poem considers, for instance, the experiences listed in the diagram under the topics "Electric Shock," "Lives of the Saint," and "The Bell Jar." Yet Hughes refuses to contribute to the existing biographical interpretations of his and Plath's work. Instead, he creates a distance between his poetic speaker and the poem's likely inspiration by posing questions, rather than making direct statements, and by identifying the sources of his subject's pain as external to their relationship. The poem's opening lines—"What was poured in your ears / While you argued with death?"—make reference both to the ambiguity that defines many poetic texts and to the ways in which betrayal manifests on the physical body. Hughes makes no attempt to clarify the sources of this particular disagreement. The poem looks, as an alternative, at the outside forces that constrained its subject: her mother's letters, a deceitful friend, and even the treatment she sought for her illnesses. While one of the items Hughes includes on his diagram seems to assign blame to Plath for revealing their shared secrets—"You as traitor and all-teller"—he did not choose to make any references in his poem to the annotations that many of the others (including "Biographies," "Being Christlike," and "Jealousy") contain. Perhaps the detached perspective that "Howls and Whispers" offers— articulated through its queries, the documents it reimagines, and the unnamed friend whose malice influenced the marriage's end—is meant to suggest that this "traitor and all-teller" simply did not exist. Rather, Hughes's subject dies in the course of a final, therapeutic attempt to ease her pain, a process that also leads to her last texts. As an extension of the many complex personal and aesthetic statements of *Birthday Letters*, the poems of *Howls and Whispers* attempt to redirect decades of criticism, animosity, and debate over Plath's final days. Hughes suggests in the title poem itself that the clamor surrounding his and Plath's personal life and work is nothing but that: noise, which increases or dies away according to the listener's particular investment in the situation, but is not subject to others' wills.

"The Offers," which at 118 lines is the longest poem in *Howls and Whispers*, represents a fitting conclusion to Hughes's commentary on his professional relationship with Plath. Diane Middlebrook refers to it, in fact, as "the definitive poem" about their marriage (*Her Husband* 81). Tracy Brain emphasizes its reliance upon "Hughes's rhetorical tendency to indicate (or inadvertently reveal) doubt"; his repeated use of the word "seemed," in Brain's estimation, "signals Hughes's awareness of his imperfect ability to perceive, to make sense of what he sees and trust it" (*The Other* 188). At the same time, as Anne Whitehead asserts, it centers on a "question of ethical responsibility" that grows out of both the speaker's guilt over having survived and his desire for empirical knowledge of the situation (238). The poem employs a series of references rooted in the idiosyncratic vocabularies that Hughes and Plath shared: the languages of publishing, astrology, travel, and romance. In broad terms, the poem imagines a series of encounters between a recently bereaved person and his departed lover, who appears repeatedly when he is in transit between one place and another. Her intent is not merely to visit him but to guide him toward an as-of-yet unknown destination. Specifically, the poem "describes a dream in which Sylvia Plath returns from the underworld three times, offering herself to [Hughes's] understanding. He first encounters her on the Northern Line of the London Underground, two months after her death. . . . The date is mid-April 1963" (Middlebrook, *Her Husband* 281). According to the narrative that the poem traces, the couple's first encounter takes place on the train after the speaker boards at Leicester Square; though he gets off at Chalk Farm, she does not follow, and so he misses a rare post-death opportunity to "follow you home" and "make some effort to seize / This offer, this saddened substitute" (*CPH* 1181). The next time they meet, it is at home—though not in a house they shared, but "you . . . sitting in your own home. / Young as before, untouched by death. Like / A hallucination—not to be blinked away." This time, though they speak, Hughes includes no dialogue. His poetic subject lives in a home he never occupied but retains her original relationship to him; he describes "The dream of your romantic life, that had lasted / Throughout our marriage, there in Paris—as if / You had never returned until now" (*CPH* 1182). The poem's speaker interprets the subject of their silent conversation as a revised version of their real life; he finds himself inhabiting a "doubled alive and dead existence" (*CPH* 1183). The twinning that this phrase implies reflects Plath's lifelong interest in doubling, what Steven Axelrod sees as her belief that she and Hughes had inhabited in their marriage "the myth of the double." She had already explored this idea in literary studies on Joyce and Dostoevsky, and it would continue to inform her poetry's major themes and images throughout her career (Axelrod 196–97). The motif of twinning or doubling also resonates with readers'—and Hughes's—knowledge of the poems that speak to one another. Its presence in this poem suggests a palimpsestic approach to describing their shared life; his decision to create a text by layering different representations of the same events upon one another adds another dimension to Hughes's final view of the *ars poetica*.

"The Offers" concludes with a third encounter between the poetic speaker and his subject: a number that stands out because of its mythic associations with Jesus Christ's resurrection on the third day after his death, the three stars in Orion's belt, the three Wise Men who greeted Jesus's birth, the three Great Pyramids at Giza, the three Greek Fates, and the three times Peter denied Jesus before his crucifixion, among many other examples. Perhaps the most relevant cultural references are the many different goddesses who possess three aspects that Robert Graves identifies in *The White Goddess*. Graves describes, for instance, "the Triple Goddess in her three characters as Goddess of the Sky, Earth and Underworld." In these three guises, the Triple Goddess is associated with "Birth, Procreation and Death," with "the three seasons of Spring, Summer and Winter," and with "her three phases of New Moon, Full Moon and Waning Moon." Yet, as Graves points out, "it must never be forgotten that the Triple Goddess . . . was a personification of primitive woman—woman the creatress and destructress" (386). These traits inform the meetings described in "The Offers," which take place in three discrete settings, include interactions with the poetic subject at three different ages, and illuminate three different intentions. Hughes suggests that his poetic characters' final encounter might signal either the true resurrection of their union or a reincarnation of sorts. The speaker's late wife appears unexpectedly: "You came behind me / (At my helpless moment, as I lowered / A testing foot into the running bath)." Vulnerable, he receives her final directive without a chance to ask questions or make an offering of his own. Her "familiar voice" is "urgent, / Close," as it asserts that "'This is the last. This one. This time / Don't fail me'" (*CPH* 1183). The sparse, repetitive phrasing of this request lends the poem's final lines a recursive tone; the conclusion articulates patterns of narrative return and reprisal, incorporates direct statement, makes efforts to assert linguistic control in the face of an ambiguously defined situation, and exploits the symbolic potential of everyday events. These techniques compose an appropriate end to one of Hughes's last public statements on aesthetics. While the last two volumes of his career both include several pieces that address well-known dimensions of his life with Plath, only this poem conveys the implied mandate that might have motivated a conclusion to his writing days. The poem makes no argument for closure—personal, poetic, or otherwise—but leaves this command hanging in the metaphoric air to suggest that the work between them remains unfinished.

These lines are not the book's final word, however; Hughes includes one more poem after "The Offers," the aptly titled "Superstitions." After a series of references to mythological beliefs ("Friday the thirteenth" and "the cold / Epicanthic fold lifted in the bride's / Mirror"), the poem ends with a startling revelation. Perhaps in a final gesture toward the last few lines of Plath's "Kindness," the poetic speaker answers the blithe suggestion that one should "Let them laugh / At your superstition" with a chilling reality: "(Remembering it will make your palms sweat, / The skin lift blistering, both your lifelines bleed)" (*CPH* 1184). The divination strategies that recur in Hughes's work here portend a final moment of insight that requires a physical cost. As in the "blood-jet" that famously signifies Plath's own creative approach, these bleeding lifelines serve as the poetic speaker's admission into the creative world, the price he pays to craft his art. As Plath occasionally does, too, in pieces like "Fever 103°," Hughes chooses to offer his final lines in parentheses, as a sort of afterthought or addendum. This methodology gives the poem's conclusion a prophetic tone: the extra information promises that truth-tellers pay a physical cost for expressing their beliefs. As the ultimate conclusion to Hughes's collected oeuvre, the lines seem particularly fitting. Without making reference to any English environments in this case, he gestures toward the physical act of writing, the toll it takes on the writer, and the nearly magical insight that such self-sacrifice to one's art enables. References to these three aspects of the writer's professional life recur throughout his work, but it is not until this final volume that these ideas receive closure. The gift of prophecy that interested both poets here enables Hughes to state what such insight will cost and to suggest, obliquely, that the knowledge their writing produces comes from both of them at once: "Remembering it will make / . . . both your lifelines bleed." These final words resonate both with the conclusion to "The Bee God," the most fervent anthem to his and Plath's shared creative life in all of *Birthday Letters*, and with "A Dream." Whether the "God of the Bees" that the former poem invokes is meant to be Otto Plath or Hughes himself or some other imagined patriarch of compositional effort, it ultimately ignores the poetic subject's entreaties by appealing to a sense of predetermined fate. The end of "Superstitions" offers a similar warning against relying upon familiar patterns of action and belief. Only through rejecting old gods and the superstitions that accompany them, Hughes suggests, can one produce truly innovative work. As Iain Twiddy describes the poet's goals for the collection, the book attempts a "re-germination of the forces that make up Hughes's creative and psychological self, with the poet regaining pastoral control" (99). This poem's apparent rejection of divination strategies might represent a surprising conclusion to his poetry, given his longtime curiosity about astrology as a source of knowledge, but it in fact points to the artist as the final arbiter of insight. All readings and interpretations originate, at last, in the self.

WRITING THROUGH THE MAELSTROM

In a set of unpublished journal entries headed "January 22 98" and "23rd Jan 98," Hughes speculates about the probable impact of *Birthday Letters* on the literary world. His remarks illustrate the anxieties that such a personally revelatory collection would naturally produce; he also draws repeated connections between the book's reception and his ongoing treatment for colon cancer, both of which he seemed to view as obstacles that he would battle through. He notes in the first entry, for instance, that he will undergo "Treatment next Thursday. Healer Wednesday. So by then back into maelstrom of B.L., etc. Still for the time being I feel steady. After treatment, I shall be back on the high seas, on which I've just spent a good month of more or less manning the pumps. . . . I am before the Birthday Letters started coming out in The Times—in other words, last Friday, I became apprehensive, briefly. . . . Wondered if in general I wasn't doing an imprudent thing." These musings move seamlessly between worries about the book and concern about his health; his emotions run the gamut from calm acceptance and anticipation of the future to doubt about his work. The second entry in this journal conveys, in contrast, a consistent sense of resolve: "Now the Times exposure of BL is complete and the book is in the shops. The usual will now do their usual with it, I expect. So no point taking account of what they say. Renewed sense of how that withholding has blocked my real work since 1970 at least. Since I started trying to live a life <u>in spite</u> of it I should have been warned by that strange phase of 71–72 when I had to go back to A.B.C.—as if everything I had attained up to that point had become overnight obsolete, useless, wrong.[6] A calamitous moment. I did not understand what had happened—as I do now. Belatedly. Then I was 41. Now I am 67. The first moment in which I began to touch the older curses was in the pieces about Assia—written just before the [illeg.] book—then to a degree in the BL pieces written after. . . . Too late to regret. But what a price. Best I can do is first walk away and see if anything at all can be salvaged and redeemed. . . . An interesting life instead, maybe" (BL Add MS 88918/1/2). In this second reaction to the book's public appearance, Hughes takes stock of the intersections between his creative and personal experiences; he meditates on the ways in which private calamity redirected the development of his career while imagining what might happen in the next stage of his life.

In the latter half of this entry, Hughes expresses anger at the illness that is eroding his abilities in spite of his best efforts to work and wonders what form his next writing project ought to take: "Then why I am so wrecked, physically—a fact not to be denied, at the moment. I play with the possibility of being bitter as I imagine those Japanese chefs play with that poisonous fish—which with care can be turned into the delicacy. The puffer fish? Bitter about? Letting myself be hijacked? But the alternative? After all, what happened to the creature that wrote 'Soup' in 1948 and never another word. Then to the creature that wrote Thought-Fox, Jaguar, and Wind—that met S.P.? Curious to speculate on the roads not taken and why not. Easy answer—my fault, very clearly" (BL Add MS 88918/1/2). This rather pessimistic assessment of his career suggests that Hughes viewed his books' various subjects as the products of different phases in his creative psyche, which rendered him a series of continually evolving "creatures." The entry also demonstrates that his struggle to reconcile his body's physical needs with the demands of a successful writing career recurred throughout his life. Both journal entries, which lie in the archives amidst drafts of hundreds of individual poems as well as several hand-corrected manuscripts, draw readers' attention for both their frank assessment of the physical cost that his work exacts and their conjectures about what creative choices remained to him. In keeping with his lifelong fixation on principles of divination, he approaches this conundrum in abstract terms inspired by past choices and experiences. Yet the distrust of astrological prophecy that seemed to emerge in "Superstitions" also plays a role here: Hughes identifies his own actions as the concrete source of not only his current weakness but also his indecision about what else he wants to write. The *ars poetica* that he spent so many years compiling now exists as a set of principles to guide the progress of his art and as an aesthetic key for the readers who study his work. With retrospective knowledge of his rapidly approaching death, however, we recognize that the instructive dimensions of his work function less to fix his oeuvre in a specific place in time than to gesture toward the limitless possibilities of his poetry's future.

NOTES

1. See, e.g., Tracy Brain, *The Other Sylvia Plath*; Christina Britzolakis, "*Ariel* and Other Poems"; Marjorie Perloff, "The Two *Ariels*"; and Erica Wagner, *Ariel's Gift*.

2. In a letter to poet Ruth Fainlight, Plath notes that she opened a book of Yeats's plays for cosmic guidance after applying to live in a flat he had previously occupied: "I shut my eyes & pointed, then read from 'The Unicorn from the Stars': 'Get wine & food to give you strength & courage & I will get the house ready.' I was scared to death, but very excited. I felt oddly in touch with the old boy, who believed in spirits too" (*LSP2* 914).

3. Lynda Bundtzen identifies the confessional dimensions of *Capriccio* as well, calling it "an allegory of melancholy, the poems persistently evoking memories of [Assia] Wevill that dramatize Hughes as a suffering melancholic who refuses to surrender the lost object of his desire, even while repeatedly stressing her absence and permanent loss." Though she appears in only one *Birthday Letters* poem, "Dreamers," her presence informs Hughes's depictions of women ("Traumatic" 130, 132).

4. See Diane Middlebrook's skilled reading of the contexts and composition of Plath's unpublished and uncollected "'Three Caryatids without a Portico,' by Hugo Robus. A Study in Sculptural Dimensions," in her article "Plath, Hughes, and Three Caryatids."

5. Webb identifies three means by which Hughes employs an elegiac mode in his animal poems, for instance: in "conjuring and commemorating the absent subject," through "animals . . . as metaphors for an endurance that transcends animality and extends towards the human," and as memorials intended for the animals themselves (45).

6. Though this sentence suggests, of course, that Hughes contemplated returning to the basic elements of his life and work (i.e., back to A, B, C), Bate quotes from an

unpublished journal entry in which Hughes refers to Assia Wevill, Brenda Hedden, and Carol (Orchard) Hughes using these initials: "In his journal he castigated himself for his dishonesty in relation to the two women, then wrote that he was convinced that the choice of C as opposed to B was the correct one. So 'full tangle with B' was to be 'suspended and pushed into a cupboard'" (Bate 299).

Conclusion

WRITING ACROSS TWO LIFETIMES

Ted Hughes and Sylvia Plath wrote material in concert for nearly seven years. Their collaborations continued long after Plath's death, however, in the form of critics', fans', and reviewers' assessments of their work's shared influences and sources. The various lenses through which we read their poetry—including biography, cultural theory, formalism, visual aesthetics, gender politics, and historical context, among many others—each illuminate their contributions to the history of Western poetry and make arguments about the unique traits that distinguish them. In *Turning the Table*, I argue that we can most effectively understand both writers' positions in that history and their poetry's innovative elements by analyzing their compositional techniques, from early drafts through their latest published works. Drafts of their first publications as well as the books that concluded their careers reveal the evolution of writerly strategies influenced by predecessors, contemporaries, and each other; the final versions of these pieces often reflect the techniques that they developed together or borrowed from one another as well. The organization of this book demonstrates the four major stages of artistic co-development through which Hughes and Plath traveled: Hughes's early sources of inspiration and formative influences, Plath's inspirations and influences, the overlapping sequences that they wrote in the 1960s, and Hughes's responses to Plath's life and career in *Birthday Letters* and *Howls and Whispers*. Each of these stages also discloses dimensions of the *ars poetica* that both poets devoted a significant amount of time to developing.

Both Plath's and Hughes's drafts uncover formal elements and rhetorical concerns that they pursued throughout their professional lives. In the drafts of her juvenilia, Plath focused on subtle shifts in punctuation and rhythm that affected individual poems' delivery and tone. Her later poetry's sparse lines emerged over time from the long, dense lines and extended stanzas of her post-Smith work. In every stage of her development as a writer, she worked to foreground precisely limned images and material objects, even as her poetic narratives exploited the expressive possibilities of ambiguity. As is common for any writer performing revisions, she eliminated extra details and baroque phrasing from her first attempts, often creating images that carry symbolic rather than literal resonance. These images shift narrative focus away from the personal to a sense of detachment communicated via a third-person perspective. Where she does include more elaborate phrasing, it appears in the form of repetitions-with-a-difference that approximate speech patterns, highlight moments of emotional intensity, or disrupt narrative continuity. Such techniques help her to pose challenges to the lyric tradition; her poems' voices assert control over the nature of the story being told and over language itself.

Hughes, in contrast, employs various forms of repetition in his drafts, from *The Hawk in the Rain* through *Birthday Letters*. Like Plath, he tried out multiple versions of central images and phrases in his handwritten manuscripts, making small changes in each iteration until he arrived at the piece's final form. Subtle shifts in punctuation, capitalization, and stylistic elements like enjambment allowed him to emphasize central ideas and to reshape narrative progressions. Hughes developed these draft strategies in the course of investigating the expressive possibilities of English natural and national landscapes, exploiting the metaphoric potential of animal metaphors, and outlining the ontological questions on which much of his post-1963 poetry centers. In particular, he tends to create blazon-like portraits of animals, whose individual parts and overall corpus enable critiques of human attributes. The distinctive metaphors that he shapes using animal and other imagery give him a consistent means by which to represent allegorically the issues that motivate his writing. In a few cases, too, Hughes includes pictorial representations alongside his drafts that clarify individual poems' narrative focuses or illustrate the thought processes that culminated in thematically related sequences.

Both the compositional techniques that Plath and Hughes developed through their drafts and the preoccupations of their later works help to illustrate their shared theory of the *ars poetica*, or the art of writing poetry as a means of self-reflection and instruction. The principles that their poetry advances are not didactic; rather, they advocate a focus on formal craft, linguistic innovation, and social responsibility. Specifically, the philosophies of writing that Hughes and Plath espouse center on the writer's need to assert control over her language, negotiations between regulated speech and contingent forms of communication, an accretive poetic vocabulary, the central importance of metaphor and metonymy, the possibilities of dual narration, writing within various modes in the same text, sparse and recursive phrasing, direct statements, narratives that emerge from concrete objects, and an assumption that the artist serves as the ultimate source of creative knowledge. The *ars poetica* signifies on literal and metatextual levels. As Plath and Hughes developed more focused ideas about these techniques in their work, they both tended to create poetic speakers with inward-turned perspectives on their subjects who explore their struggles with the creative process as much as—if not more than—their successes. Over time, their perceptions of art evolved in independent directions that allowed them to imagine the new realities that the writer could produce, or to argue that existence itself is founded in acts of public creative expression. While many of Plath's and Hughes's antecedents and contemporaries also focus on such compositional priorities, this particular conjunction of formal techniques with writerly obligation marks out their shared aesthetic: one that Hughes continued to explore for the thirty-five years that followed Plath's death.

Hughes and Plath chronicled more explicit thoughts on their individual approaches to the *ars poetica* in their essays; though we have the benefit of many fewer such reflections from Plath, elements of their philosophies about the act and purposes of writing often coincide. In her 1962 essay "A Comparison," which documents her ongoing struggle to produce well-crafted prose, Plath describes the necessary brevity and the compact nature of the non-epic poem: "a door opens, a door shuts. In between, you have had a glimpse: a garden, a person, a rainstorm, a dragonfly, a heart, a city" (*JP* 62). These discrete, self-contained, but endlessly evocative images illustrate her notion of the literary text's densely allusive nature. The poem also, she argues, occupies an extremely short span of time: "And there is really so little room! So little time! The poet becomes an expert packer of suitcases" (*JP* 63). Though it is easy to measure a poem's duration differently, in terms of the emotional and connotative resonances that continue to expand after it has been read, here Plath underlines the literal space it occupies in the reader's mouth or eyes rather than the work that she does with it afterward. In one sense, Plath turns the poem over to her audience, telling them to make of it what they will, after her own labor of observation, construction, and craft has ended. She suggests, in another 1962 essay entitled "Context," that many of her poems are "deflections" but not "escapes"; her work examines "the issues of every time—the hurt and wonder of loving; making in all its forms" in order to create art that reflects real, organic life (*JP* 65). This assessment demonstrates Plath's commitment to overlaying social relevance with aesthetic concerns in her art, a tendency that often resulted in compactly allusive phrasing. In a letter she wrote to Fr. Michael Carey at Oxford's Assumption College, Plath recommends studying as much poetry as possible, in particular the "tense & special lyrics" of Thomas Wyatt, Gerard Manley Hopkins, Eliot, and Pound, and the "assonances and consonances in Emily Dickinson" (*LSP2* 916): a wide-ranging and difficult list whose traits contribute to but also diverge from her own. As Hughes also observes in his introduction to *Johnny Panic*, Plath's tendency to memorize and record detailed descriptions of the people she met and the scenarios she encountered provide "good evidence to prove that poems which seem often to be constructed of arbitrary surreal symbols are really impassioned reorganizations of relevant fact" (2). He also highlighted the unique qualities that *Ariel* possesses in other publications, including an issue of the *Poetry Book Society Bulletin*: "It is not much like any other poetry. It is her. Everything she did was just like this, and this is just like her—but permanent" (*WP* 162). In a letter to Hungarian poet János Csokits, Hughes noted that *Ariel* "is in a class apart. . . . In English, there is nothing quite so direct & naked & radiant—yet complicated & mysterious at the same time" (*LTH* 272).

In his own "Context" essay, Hughes suggests one approach to understanding the function of creative work: by allowing his poetic "gift" to develop and progress naturally (*WP* 1), readers give the writer space to become the kind of poet he must be. Hughes describes the poet's evolution in general terms, as someone whose "gift is an unobliging thing"; he is allowed to "study his art, experiment, and apply his mind and live as he pleases," as long as he accepts the fact that "the moment of writing is too late for further improvements or adjustments." The material that he will pursue is already set because "[c]ertain memories, images, sounds, feelings, thoughts, and relationships between these, have for some reason become luminous at the core of his mind" and "it is in his attempt to bring them out, without impairment, into a comparatively dark world, that he makes poems" (*WP* 2). While shaping this material, Hughes speculates, in an essay entitled "Myth and Education," the poet employs a mode of true imagination, which he calls a "large, flexible grasp, an inner vision which holds wide open, like a great theatre . . . and which pays equal respects to both sides"—in other words, to "the world of things and the world of spirits equally" (*WP* 150). To capture or to articulate both sides is, according to Hughes, nearly impossible. That struggle to do so constitutes the writer's work. As he notes in "Words and Experience," an essay from *Poetry in the Making*, "[i]t is one thing to get the information, and quite another to become conscious of it, to know that we have got it" (*WP* 21). Art itself—which Hughes describes as "music, painting, dancing, sculpture, and the activity that includes all these, which is poetry"—is motivated by a "struggle truly to possess his own experience, in other words to regain his genuine self" (*WP* 24). For both Plath and Hughes, successful composition produces concise expression, plumbs imaginative depths, and contemplates the nature of the self. The principles that their shared *ars poetica* outlines reflect the artist's efforts to accomplish these goals and to communicate them to others.

Much of Hughes's and Plath's poetry, from *The Hawk in the Rain* and *The Colossus* to *Ariel* and *Birthday Letters*, originated in personal experience and emotional response. However, each writer's use of specific formal elements and revision strategies produced consistencies in organization, argument, and compositional techniques that resonate between their works. In many instances, they take up similar themes from distinctive perspectives because of their diverging approaches to collecting source-material: Plath's obsessive collation of experiences in her journals and letters stands in direct contrast to the largely singular focus that Hughes pursued through such interests as animals, English landscapes, mythologies, ecological concerns, and life studies. They evidenced a strong interest in collaboration and co-study from the beginning of their relationship, nevertheless, which manifested in their tendencies to recycle, revise, and borrow material from one another. Some of Plath's central compositional techniques include fragmentation, sparse phrasing, an imperative mode of address, a vocabulary that accumulates through repetition across the body of her work, sharply focused imagery, a detached sense of lyric observation, and thematic considerations of trauma, often as metaphors for the writer's labor to produce meaningful work. Hughes, in contrast, uses a short list of concentrated interests as a means by which to consider the types of ontological questions that preoccupy artists.

This study began by investigating the imagery, compositional strategies, and narrative situations of Plath's "Elm" and Hughes's "The Table," which illustrate some of the continuities and divergences that exist between their work in general. The living tree and its constructed product, or the natural environments that surround us and the pragmatic uses that we make of them, represent major concerns for both writers. The *ars poetica* that Hughes and Plath imagined, articulated through their poetry, and continually worked to emulate arises from such seemingly contradictory sources. Neither could set his or her writing in motion without an inspiration rooted in personal, natural, or national meaning; both needed to create, in the end, "a solid writing-table / That would last a lifetime" (*CPH* 1132). As readers, we scrutinize the texts written at that table for insight into their compositional processes, even as we receive the always surprising gift of their work's beauty.

Bibliography

Alexander, Paul. *Rough Magic: A Biography of Sylvia Plath*. Viking, 1991.
Alvarez, A. *The Savage God: A Study of Suicide*. W. W. Norton & Company, 1990.
Athenaeus. *Deipnosophistae*. C. 3 A.D. Trans. Charles Burton Gulick. Loeb Classical Library Vol. 204, Harvard UP, 1969.
Axelrod, Steven Gould. *Sylvia Plath: The Wound and the Cure of Words*. Johns Hopkins UP, 1992.
Badia, Janet. *Sylvia Plath and the Mythology of Women Readers*. U of Massachusetts P, 2011.
Baraka, Amiri. *The Leroi Jones / Amiri Baraka Reader*. Edited by William J. Harris, Thunder's Mouth Press, 1995.
Bassnett, Susan. *Sylvia Plath: An Introduction to the Poetry*. Palgrave MacMillan, 2005.
———. *Ted Hughes*. Northcote House Publishers, Ltd., 2009.
Bate, Jonathan. *Ted Hughes: The Unauthorised Life*. Harper, 2015.
Bentley, Paul. *Ted Hughes, Class, and Violence*. Bloomsbury, 2014.
Berryman, John. *The Dream Songs*. Farrar, Straus, and Giroux, 1969.
Boscolo, Cristina. *Odún: Discourses, Strategies, and Power in the Yorùbá Play of Transformation*. Brill, 2009.
Bradstreet, Anne. *The Works*. Edited by Jeannine Hensley. The Belknap Press of Harvard UP, 1967.
Brain, Tracy. "Hughes and Feminism." *The Cambridge Companion to Ted Hughes*, edited by Terry Gifford, Cambridge UP, 2011, pp. 94–106.
———. *The Other Sylvia Plath*. Longman/Pearson Education Ltd., 2001.
———. "Unstable Manuscripts: The Indeterminacy of the Plath Canon." *The Unraveling Archive: Essays on Sylvia Plath*, edited by Anita Helle, The U of Michigan P, 2007, pp. 17–38.
Brandes, Rand. "Ted Hughes: *Crow*." *A Companion to Twentieth-Century Poetry*, edited by Neil Roberts, Blackwell Publishing, 2003, pp. 513–23.

Britzolakis, Christina. "*Ariel* and Other Poems." *The Cambridge Companion to Sylvia Plath*, edited by Jo Gill, Cambridge UP, 2006, pp. 107–23.

———. "Conversation amongst the Ruins: Plath and de Chirico." *Eye Rhymes: Sylvia Plath's Art of the Visual*. Edited by Kathleen Connors and Sally Bayley, Oxford UP, 2007, pp. 167–82.

———. *Sylvia Plath and the Theatre of Mourning*. Clarendon Press, 1999.

Bronfen, Elizabeth. *Sylvia Plath*. 2nd ed. Northcote House Publishers, Ltd., 2004.

Brooker, Peter, and Simon Perril. "Modernist Poetry and Its Precursors." *A Companion to Twentieth-Century Poetry*, edited by Neil Roberts, Blackwell Publishing, 2003, pp. 21–36.

Bundtzen, Lynda K. *The Other Ariel*. Sutton Publishing, Ltd, 2005.

———. "Poetic Arson and Sylvia Plath's 'Burning the Letters.'" *The Unraveling Archive: Essays on Sylvia Plath*, edited by Anita Helle, The U of Michigan P, 2007, pp. 236–53.

———. "Traumatic Repetition in *Capriccio*." *Ted Hughes: From Cambridge to Collected*, edited by Mark Wormald, Neil Roberts, and Terry Gifford, Palgrave Macmillan, 2013, pp. 130–44.

Butscher, Edward. *Sylvia Plath: Method and Madness*. The Seabury Press, 1976.

Campbell, Matthew. "Poetry and War." *A Companion to Twentieth-Century Poetry*, edited by Neil Roberts, Blackwell Publishing, 2003, pp. 64–75.

Castell, James. "The Nature of Ted Hughes's Similes." *Ted Hughes, Nature, and Culture*, edited by Neil Roberts, Mark Wormald, and Terry Gifford, Palgrave Macmillan, 2018, pp. 87–106.

Churchwell, Sarah. "Secrets and Lies: Privacy, Publication, and Ted Hughes's *Birthday Letters*." *Contemporary Literature* vol. 42, no. 1, Spring 2001, pp. 102–48.

———. "'Your Sentence Was Mine Too': Reading Sylvia Plath in Ted Hughes's *Birthday Letters*." *Literary Couplings: Writing Couples, Collaborators, and the Construction of Authorship*, edited by Marjorie Stone and Judith Thompson, U of Wisconsin P, 2006, pp. 260–87.

Clark, Heather. *The Grief of Influence: Sylvia Plath and Ted Hughes*. Oxford UP, 2011.

———. "Tracking the Thought-Fox: Sylvia Plath's Revision of Ted Hughes." *Journal of Modern Literature* vol. 28, no. 2, Winter 2005, pp. 100–12.

"Confessional Poetry." *The Oxford Dictionary of Literary Terms*. Oxford UP, 2015. Online.

Connors, Kathleen. "Living Color: The Interactive Arts of Sylvia Plath." *Eye Rhymes: Sylvia Plath's Art of the Visual*, edited by Kathleen Connors and Sally Bayley, Oxford UP, 2007, pp. 4–144.

Culler, Jonathan. "Apostrophe." *Diacritics* vol. 7, no. 4, Winter 1977, pp. 59–69.

Cwynar, Les C. "Elm." *The Gale Encyclopedia of Science*. 5th ed., vol. 3. Edited by K. Lee Lerner and Brenda Wilmoth Lerner, Gale, 2014, pp. 1567–68.

D'Aulaire, Ingri, and Edgar Parin. *D'Aulaires' Book of Greek Myths*. Bantam Doubleday Dell, 1962.

———. *D'Aulaires' Book of Norse Myths*. The New York Review of Books, 1967.

Davis, Angela Y. *Blues Legacies and Black Feminism: Gertrude "Ma" Rainey, Bessie Smith, and Billie Holiday*. Vintage Books, 1999.

Drangsholt, Janne Stigen. "Imagination Alters Everything: Ted Hughes and Place." *Ted Hughes, Nature, and Culture*, edited by Neil Roberts, Mark Wormald, and Terry Gifford, Palgrave Macmillan, 2018, pp. 125–39.

Eliot, T. S. "The Love Song of J. Alfred Prufrock." *The Waste Land and Other Writings*, edited by Mary Karr, Random House/Modern Library, 2002, pp. 3–7.

———. *The Waste Land*. Norton Critical Edition, edited by Michael North, W. W. Norton & Company, Inc., 2001, pp. 3–20.

"Elm Tree." *Encyclopedia of Occultism and Parapsychology*. 5th ed., vol. 1. Edited by J. Gordon Melton, Gale, 2001, p. 494.

Ely, Steve. *Ted Hughes's South Yorkshire: Made in Mexborough*. Palgrave Macmillan, 2015.

Faas, Ekbert. *Ted Hughes: The Unaccommodated Universe*. Black Sparrow P, 1980.

Faulkner, Sandra L. "Concern with Craft: Using *Ars Poetica* as Criteria for Reading Research Poetry." *Qualitative Inquiry* vol. 13, no. 2, March 2007, pp. 218–34.

Feinstein, Elaine. *Ted Hughes: The Life of a Poet*. W. W. Norton, 2001.

Fenton, James. "A Family Romance." *The New York Review of Books*, vol. 45, no. 4, March 5, 1998. Proxy.buffalostate.edu:2253/articles/1998/03/05/a-family-romance/. Accessed 16 Jan. 2018.

Ford, Karen Jackson. *Gender and the Poetics of Excess: Moments of Brocade*. UP of Mississippi, 1997.

Fraistat, Neil. "Introduction: The Place of the Book and the Book as Place." *Poems in Their Place: The Intertextuality and Order of Poetic Collections*, edited by Neil Fraistat, The U of North Carolina P, 1986, pp. 3–17.

Gifford, Terry. "Ted Hughes's 'Greening' and the Environmental Humanities." *Ted Hughes, Nature, and Culture*, edited by Neil Roberts, Mark Wormald, and Terry Gifford, Palgrave Macmillan, 2018, pp. 3–20.

Gifford, Terry, and Neil Roberts. *Ted Hughes: A Critical Study*. Faber and Faber, 1981.

Gilbert, Roger. "Contemporary American Poetry." *A Companion to Twentieth-Century Poetry*, edited by Neil Roberts, Blackwell Publishing, 2003, pp. 559–70.

Giles, Paul. "Double Exposure: Sylvia Plath and the Aesthetics of Transnationalism." *Symbiosis* vol. 5, no. 2, October 2001, pp. 103–20.

Gill, Jo. "'Exaggerated American': Ted Hughes's *Birthday Letters*." *Journal of Transatlantic Studies* vol. 2, no. 2, 2004, pp. 163–84.

———. "Ted Hughes and Sylvia Plath." *The Cambridge Companion to Ted Hughes*, edited by Terry Gifford, Cambridge UP, 2011, pp. 53–66.

Gjurgjan, Ljiljana. "The Metaphoric and the Patriarchal in Women's Writing." *Studia Romanica et Anglica Zagrabiensia* no. 42, 1976, pp. 135–44.

Goodby, John. "Ted Hughes's Apocalyptic Origins." *Ted Hughes, Nature, and Culture*, edited by Neil Roberts, Mark Wormald, and Terry Gifford, Palgrave Macmillan, 2018, pp. 177–94.

Goodspeed-Chadwick, Julie. *Reclaiming Assia Wevill: Sylvia Plath, Ted Hughes, and the Literary Imagination*. Louisiana State UP, 2019.

Graves, Robert. *The White Goddess: A Historical Grammar of Poetic Myth*. 1948. Faber and Faber, 1966.
Groszewski, Gillian. "'I fear a man of frugal speech': Ted Hughes and Emily Dickinson." *Ted Hughes: From Cambridge to Collected*, edited by Mark Wormald, Neil Roberts, and Terry Gifford, Palgrave Macmillan, 2013, pp. 160–76.
Hall, Caroline King Barnard. *Sylvia Plath, Revised*. Twayne Publishers, 1998.
Hammer, Langdon. "Plath at War." *Eye Rhymes: Sylvia Plath's Art of the Visual*, edited by Kathleen Connors and Sally Bayley, Oxford UP, 2007, pp. 145–57.
Hart, Henry. "Seamus Heaney and Ted Hughes: A Complex Friendship." *Ted Hughes: From Cambridge to Collected*, edited by Mark Wormald, Neil Roberts, and Terry Gifford. Palgrave Macmillan, 2013, pp. 145–59.
Hayman, Ronald. *The Death and Life of Sylvia Plath*. 1991. Sutton Publishing, 2003.
Heinz, Drue. "Ted Hughes: The Art of Poetry LXXI." *The Paris Review* vol. 37, no. 134, Spring 1995, pp. 54–94.
Homer. *The Iliad*. Trans. W. C. Green. Longmans and Co., 1884.
Hughes, Frieda. "Foreword." *Ariel: The Restored Edition*, by Sylvia Plath, Harper Perennial, 2004, pp. xi-xxi.
Hughes, Ted. "Bayonet Charge." Ted Hughes Papers, MSS 644 – Box 59, Folder 1, 99–01-04. Stuart A. Rose Manuscripts, Archives, and Rare Books Library, Emory University.
———. *Collected Poems,* edited by Paul Keegan. Farrar, Straus, & Giroux, 2005.
———. "Full Moon and Little Frieda." Ted Hughes Papers, MSS 644 – Box 59, folder 66. Stuart A. Rose Manuscripts, Archives, and Rare Books Library, Emory University.
———. "Hawk Roosting." Ted Hughes Papers, MSS 644 – Box 59, Folder 9. Stuart A. Rose Manuscripts, Archives, and Rare Books Library, Emory University.
———. "Introduction." *The Collected Poems*, by Sylvia Plath. Harper & Row, Publishers, 1981, pp. 13–17.
———. "Introduction." *Johnny Panic and the Bible of Dreams: Short Stories, Prose, and Diary Excerpts*, by Sylvia Plath. Harper Perennial Modern Classics, 2018, pp. 1–9.
———. *Letters*. Edited by Christopher Reid. Farrar, Straus, & Giroux, 2008.
———. "Lines to a Newborn Baby." Ted Hughes Papers, MSS 644 – Box 82, folder 18. Stuart A. Rose Manuscripts, Archives, and Rare Books Library, Emory University.
———. "My Uncle's Wound." Ted Hughes Papers, MSS 644 – Box 83, folder 20. Stuart A. Rose Manuscripts, Archives, and Rare Books Library, Emory University.
———. "Notes on the Chronological Order of Sylvia Plath's Poems." *The Art of Sylvia Plath*, edited by Charles Newman, Indiana UP, 1970, pp. 187–95.
———. "Notes on Poems 1956-1963." *The Collected Poems*, by Sylvia Plath. Harper & Row, Publishers, 1981, pp. 275–96.
———. "On Westminster Bridge." Ted Hughes Papers, MS 644 – Box 83, folder 43. Stuart A. Rose Manuscripts, Archives, and Rare Books Library, Emory University.
———. *Poetry in the Making: An Anthology of Poems and Programmes from Listening and Writing*. Faber and Faber Ltd., 1967.

―――. "Song of a Rat." Ted Hughes Papers, MSS 644 – Box 60, folder 13. Stuart A. Rose Manuscripts, Archives, and Rare Books Library, Emory University.

―――. *Winter Pollen: Occasional Prose*. Edited by William Scammell, Picador, 1995.

Jameson, Fredric. *Postmodernism, or, The Cultural Logic of Late Capitalism*. 1991. Duke UP, 2005.

Johnson, Barbara E. "Allegory and Psychoanalysis." *Journal of African American History* vol. 88, no.1, Winter 2003, pp. 66–70.

―――. "Apostrophe, Animation, and Abortion." *Diacritics* vol. 16, no.1, Spring 1986, pp. 28–47.

Keller, Lynn. "The Twentieth-Century Long Poem." *The Columbia History of American Poetry*, edited by Jay Parini and Brett C. Millier, Columbia UP, 1993, pp. 534–63.

Kendall, Tim. "From the Bottom of the Pool: Sylvia Plath's Last Poems." *English* vol. 49, Spring 2000, pp. 23–38.

―――. *Sylvia Plath: A Critical Study*. Faber and Faber, 2001.

Keniston, Ann. "The Holocaust Again: Sylvia Plath, Belatedness, and the Limits of Lyric Figure." *The Unraveling Archive: Essays on Sylvia Plath*, edited by Anita Helle, U of Michigan P, 2007, pp. 139–58.

Kirk, Connie Ann. *Sylvia Plath: A Biography*. Prometheus Books, 2009.

Kirsch, Adam. *The Wounded Surgeon: Confession and Transformation in Six American Poets*. Revised ed. W. W. Norton, 2013.

Knickerbocker, Scott. "'Bodied Forth in Words': Sylvia Plath's Ecopoetics." *College Literature* vol. 36, no. 3, Summer 2009, pp. 1–27.

Kroll, Judith. *Chapters in a Mythology: The Poetry of Sylvia Plath*. Harper & Row, 1976.

Lowell, Robert. "Foreword." *Ariel*, by Sylvia Plath. Harper Colophon, 1965, pp. vii-ix.

―――. *Life Studies* and *For the Union Dead*. Farrar, Straus, and Giroux, 1964.

Malcolm, Janet. *The Silent Woman: Sylvia Plath and Ted Hughes*. Reprint ed. Vintage, 1995.

McClatchy, J. D. "Short Circuits and Folding Mirrors." *Sylvia Plath*, edited by Harold Bloom, Chelsea House Publishers, 1989, pp. 79–93.

McHale, Brian. *The Obligation toward the Difficult Whole: Postmodernist Long Poems*. The U of Alabama P, 2004.

―――. *Postmodernist Fiction*. Methuen, Inc., 1987.

―――. "Telling Stories Again: On the Replenishment of Narrative in the Postmodernist Long Poem." *The Yearbook of English Studies* vol. 30, 2000, pp. 250–62.

Melhem, D. H. "Cultural Change, Heroic Response: Gwendolyn Brooks and the New Black Poetry." *Perspectives of Black Popular Culture*, edited by Harry B. Shaw, Bowling Green State U Popular P, 1990, pp. 71–84.

Middlebrook, Diane. "Creative Partnership: Sources for 'The Rabbit Catcher.'" *The Unraveling Archive: Essays on Sylvia Plath*, edited by Anita Helle, The U of Michigan P, 2007, pp. 254–68.

———. *Her Husband: Hughes and Plath—A Marriage*. Viking, 2003.

———. "Plath, Hughes, and Three Caryatids." *Eye Rhymes: Sylvia Plath's Art of the Visual*, edited by Kathleen Connors and Sally Bayley, Oxford UP, 2007, pp. 158–66.

———. "The Poetry of Sylvia Plath and Ted Hughes: Call and Response." *The Cambridge Companion to Sylvia Plath*, edited by Jo Gill, Cambridge UP, 2006, pp. 156–71.

Miner, Earl. "Some Issues for Study of Integrated Collections." *Poems in Their Place: The Intertextuality and Order of Poetic Collections*, edited by Neil Fraistat, The U of North Carolina P, 1986, pp. 18–43.

Mitchell, Paul. "Reading (and) the Late Poems of Sylvia Plath." *The Modern Language Review* vol. 100, no. 1, January 2005, pp. 37–50.

Narbeshuber, Lisa. *Confessing Cultures: Politics and the Self in the Poetry of Sylvia Plath*. ELS Editions, 2009.

Nelson, Deborah. *Pursuing Privacy in Cold War America*. Columbia UP, 2002.

O'Connor, Danny. "Why Look at Animals?" *Ted Hughes, Nature, and Culture*, edited by Neil Roberts, Mark Wormald, and Terry Gifford, Palgrave Macmillan, 2018, pp. 53–67.

Peel, Robin. *Writing Back: Sylvia Plath and Cold War Politics*. Fairleigh Dickinson UP, 2002.

Perloff, Marjorie. "The Two *Ariel*s: The (Re)Making of the Sylvia Plath Canon." *Poems in Their Place: The Intertextuality and Order of Poetic Collections*, edited by Neil Fraistat, The U of North Carolina P, 1986, pp. 308–33.

Plath, Sylvia. *Ariel*. Harper Colophon Books, 1965.

———. *Ariel: The Restored Edition*. Harper Perennial Modern Classics, 2004.

———. *The Collected Poems*. Edited by Ted Hughes. Harper Perennial Modern Classics, 2008.

———. *Johnny Panic and the Bible of Dreams: Short Stories, Prose, and Diary Excerpts*. 1979. Harper Perennial Modern Classics, 2018.

———. *The Letters, Volume I: 1940-1956*. Edited by Peter K. Steinberg and Karen V. Kukil. Harper Collins, 2017.

———. *The Letters, Volume II: 1956-1963*. Edited by Peter K. Steinberg and Karen V. Kukil. Faber & Faber, 2018.

———. *The Unabridged Journals*. Edited by Karen V. Kukil. Anchor Books, 2000.

"Poetic Snares: Ted Loves Sylvia: Ted Hughes's Book of Poems, *Birthday Letters*." *Globe and Mail*, 14 Feb. 1998, p. D16. http://link.galegroup.com/apps/doc/A30132193/OVIC?u=nysl_we_bsc&xid=3ac878d2. Accessed 16 Jan. 2018.

Pollitt, Katha. "Peering into the Bell Jar: Ted Hughes Gives His Version of Life with Sylvia Plath in 88 Poems." *The New York Times*, 1 Mar. 1998, p. BR4+.

Pound, Ezra. *The Cantos*. New Directions, 1998.

Regan, Stephen. "The Movement." *A Companion to Twentieth-Century Poetry*. Edited by Neil Roberts, Blackwell Publishing, 2003, pp. 209–19.

Reddick, Yvonne. *Ted Hughes: Environmentalist and Ecopoet*. Palgrave Macmillan, 2017.

Reed, B.M. "Poetics, Western." *The Princeton Encyclopedia of Poetry and Poetics.* Edited by Roland Green et al, Princeton UP, 2012. https://proxy.buffalostate.edu:2443/login?url=https://search.credoreference.com/content/entry/prpoetry/poetics_western/0?institutionId=2571. Accessed 09 Jun. 2020.

Rich, Adrienne. "Motherhood in Bondage." *On Lies, Secrets, and Silence: Selected Prose, 1966-1978*, W. W. Norton & Company, 1979, pp. 195–97.

Roberts, Neil. "Ted Hughes and Cambridge." *Ted Hughes: From Cambridge to Collected*, edited by Mark Wormald, Neil Roberts, and Terry Gifford, Palgrave MacMillan, 2013, pp. 17–32.

———. *Ted Hughes: A Literary Life.* Palgrave Macmillan, 2009.

Robinson, Katherine. "'The Remains of Something': Ted Hughes and *The Mabinogion.*" *Ted Hughes, Nature, and Culture*, edited by Neil Roberts, Mark Wormald, and Terry Gifford, Palgrave Macmillan, 2018, pp. 161–76.

Rollyson, Carl. *American Isis: The Life and Art of Sylvia Plath.* St. Martin's Press, 2013.

Rose, Jacqueline. *The Haunting of Sylvia Plath.* Harvard UP, 1993.

Rosenthal, M. L. "Poetry as Confession." *Our Life in Poetry: Selected Essays and Reviews*, by M. L. Rosenthal, Persea Books, 1991, pp. 109–13.

Rowland, Antony. *Holocaust Poetry: Awkward Poetics in the Work of Sylvia Plath, Geoffrey Hill, Tony Harrison, and Ted Hughes.* Edinburgh UP, 2005.

Sagar, Keith. *The Art of Ted Hughes.* 2nd ed. Cambridge UP, 1978.

Scigaj, Leonard M. *The Poetry of Ted Hughes: Form and Imagination.* U of Iowa P, 1986.

Sergeant, David. "Ted Hughes' Inner Music." *Ted Hughes: From Cambridge to Collected*, edited by Mark Wormald, Neil Roberts, and Terry Gifford, Palgrave Macmillan, 2013, pp. 48–63.

Seymour, Miranda. *Robert Graves: Life on the Edge.* Henry Holt & Co., 1995.

Sexton, Anne. "Sylvia's Death." *Poetry* vol. 103, no. 4, January 1964, pp. 224–26. https://www.poetryfoundation.org/poetrymagazine/browse?volume=103&issue=4&page=10. Accessed 19 June 2020.

Silliman, Ron. *The New Sentence.* Roof Books/The Segue Foundation, 1989.

Smyth, Daragh. *A Guide to Irish Mythology.* Irish Academic Press, 1996.

Stevenson, Anne. *Bitter Fame: A Life of Sylvia Plath.* Houghton Mifflin, 1989.

Tennyson, Alfred, Lord. "The Lady of Shalott." *The Major Works*, edited by Adam Roberts, Oxford University Press, 2009, pp. 22–25.

Theocritus. *Idylls 1-4.* In *The Greek Bucolic Poets.* Trans. J. M. Edmonds. Loeb Classical Library Vol. 28, Harvard UP, 1912.

Twiddy, Iain. *Pastoral Elegy in Contemporary British and Irish Poetry.* Continuum, 2012.

Upton, Lee. "'I / Have a self to recover': The Restored *Ariel.*" *Literary Review* vol. 48, no. 4, Summer 2005, pp. 260–64.

Uroff, Margaret Dickie. *Sylvia Plath and Ted Hughes.* U of Illinois P, 1979.

Van Dyne, Susan. *Revising Life: Sylvia Plath's* Ariel *Poems.* U of North Carolina P, 1993.

Vice, Sue. "Sylvia Plath: *Ariel.*" *A Companion to Twentieth-Century Poetry*, edited by Neil Roberts, Blackwell Publishing, 2003, pp. 500–12.

Viner, Katherine. "Ted Hughes, 1930-1998: Beneath the passion, a man plagued by demons: The doomed marriage: This year Hughes finally broke his silence over Sylvia Plath." *Guardian*, 30 Oct. 1998, p. 4.

Wagner, Erica. *Ariel's Gift: Ted Hughes, Sylvia Plath, and the Story of* Birthday Letters. W. W. Norton, 2002.

Wagner-Martin, Linda. *Sylvia Plath: A Biography*. Simon and Schuster, 1987.

———. *Sylvia Plath: A Literary Life*. 2nd ed. Palgrave Macmillan, 2003.

Webb, Laura. "Mythology, Mortality and Memorialization: Animal and Human Endurance in Hughes' Poetry." *Ted Hughes: From Cambridge to Collected*, edited by Mark Wormald, Neil Roberts, and Terry Gifford, Palgrave Macmillan, 2013, pp. 33–47.

Whitehead, Anne. "Refiguring Orpheus: The Possession of the Past in Ted Hughes' *Birthday Letters*." *Textual Practice* vol. 13, no. 2, 1999, pp. 227–41.

Williams, William Carlos. *Paterson*. New Directions, 1995.

Wilson, Andrew. *Mad Girl's Love Song: Sylvia Plath and Life Before Ted*. Scribner, 2013.

Wootten, William. *The Alvarez Generation: Thom Gunn, Geoffrey Hill, Ted Hughes, Sylvia Plath, and Peter Porter*. Liverpool UP, 2015.

Yeats, William Butler. *The Collected Poems*. The Macmillan Company, 1969.

Index of Names and Subjects

Adorno, Theodor, 6
African American poetry, 95
Alexander, Paul, 12–13
Alvarez, A., 10–11, 12, 19, 20, 79, 152
Amis, Kingsley, 9
Armitage, Simon, 152
Arnold, Alison, 59
Ashbery, John, 6
Athenaeus, 148–49
Auden, W. H., 3, 6
Axelrod, Steven Gould, 3, 14, 52, 56, 83, 84n4, 84n7, 85n11, 159

Badia, Janet, 17
Baraka, Amiri, 87–89, 98, 121
Barber, Jill, 152
Baskin, Leonard, 104, 122n3, 137, 154
Bassnett, Susan, 95
Bate, Jonathan, 15, 32, 46, 49–50n6, 105, 106, 114, 152, 154, 163–64n6
BBC, 32, 46, 151–53
Beat poetry, 95
Bentley, Paul, 8, 16, 90, 135
Beowulf, 108–9
Berryman, John, 87, 89, 95, 98, 121
Beuscher, Ruth Barnhouse, 50n9
Bishop, Elizabeth, 52
Black Mountain poetry, 95
Boscolo, Cristina, 122n5

Boyanowsky, Ehor, 152
Bradstreet, Anne, 64
Bragg, Melvyn, 152–53
Brain, Tracy, 2, 5, 17, 18, 23, 34, 40, 47–48, 49n1, 55, 72–73, 84, 122n2, 136, 150, 154, 158, 163n1
Brandes, Rand, 104, 110
Britzolakis, Christina, 4, 5, 6, 16–17, 64, 68, 94, 95–96, 102, 163n1
Bronfen, Elizabeth, 59
Brooker, Peter, 7
Brooks, Gwendolyn, 68
Bundtzen, Lynda, 32, 34, 91, 92, 93, 102, 124, 127, 133, 163n3
Butscher, Edward, 11

Campbell, Matthew, 6
Carey, Fr. Michael, 167
Castell, James, 39, 119
Chicano poetry, 95
Christianity, 159
Churchwell, Sarah, 73, 85n11, 121, 125, 134–35, 138, 141–42, 151
civil rights, 44
Clark, Heather, 4, 5, 7, 18, 20–21, 22, 23, 25, 34, 35, 72–73, 84n7, 85n10, 90, 97, 100, 102, 104, 121, 122n4, 135, 136, 147, 156
Confessional poetry, 4–5, 14, 95

Connors, Kathleen, 55, 60, 84n6
Court Green, 70
Crane, Hart, 95
Crockett, Wilbury, 60, 84n6
Csokits, János, 168
Cullen, Countee, 60
Culler, Jonathan, 68
Cwynar, Les C., 2

D'Aulaire, Edgar Parin, 122n5
D'Aulaire, Ingri, 122n5
Davie, Donald, 9
Davis, Angela, 88
Dejanira, 108–9
del Verrocchio, Andrea, 51
Derr, Mary Bailey, 124
Dickinson, Emily, 52, 85n11, 91, 167
Dorn, Edward, 95
Dostoevsky, Fyodor, 159
Drangsholt, Janne Stigen, 110

Eliot, T. S., 6, 40, 44, 56, 60, 95, 115, 118, 167
elm trees, 2, 148–49
Ely, Steve, 7–8, 9, 16, 33, 40
Evans, Matthew, 151–53

Faas, Ekbert, 42, 46, 98
Faber & Faber, 150
Fainlight, Ruth, 113, 152, 163n2
Faulkner, Sandra, 25
Feinstein, Elaine, 15, 152
feminism, 45
feminist poetry, 95
Fenton, James, 134
Fisher, Alfred Young, 53, 55–56, 84n1, 95
Fisher, John, 7, 28n1
Ford, Karen Jackson, 14
Fraistat, Neil, 92, 136
Freud, Sigmund, 20
Friedan, Betty, 6

Gifford, Terry, 8, 23, 38, 41, 90, 104, 111, 114

Gilbert, Roger, 6
Giles, Paul, 5
Gill, Jo, 17, 72–73, 136
Giza, Egypt, 159
Gjurgjan, Ljiljana, 120
Goodby, John, 9
Goodspeed-Chadwick, Julie, 18, 21
Graves, Robert, 2, 7, 10, 24, 28n1, 106, 114–15, 160
Gray, Thomas, 60
Groszewski, Gillian, 85n11, 91
The Group, 9, 29n2
Gunn, Thom, 5, 9

Haigh-Wood, Vivienne, 40
Hall, Caroline King Barnard, 91, 99
Hammer, Langdon, 60
Hart, Henry, 154
Hayman, Ronald, 3, 11, 12
Heaney, Seamus, 135
Hedden, Brenda, 164n6
Heinz, Drue, 4, 39, 91, 94, 104
Hejinian, Lyn, 95
Hercules, 108
H. D., 44, 90, 95
Hill, Geoffrey, 9
Hobsbaum, Philip, 9, 29n2, 49n6
Holocaust, 21, 95
Hopkins, Gerard Manley, 7, 42, 167
Houghton Library, Harvard, 70
Hughes, Carol Orchard, 164n6
Hughes, Frieda, 62, 70, 91, 92, 96, 140–41, 152
Hughes, Nicholas, 62
Hughes, Olwyn, 12, 43, 45
Hughes, Ted, 3, 4, 6–11, 12, 13, 15–16, 18–22, 24–26, 27–28, 31–50, 72–73, 87–91, 123–64, 165–69
  animal imagery, 7–8, 24, 26, 38–43, 45–46, 48, 49, 87, 97, 105, 118–19, 147, 163n5, 166, 169
  ars poetica, 10, 24–25, 35, 37–38, 41, 46–47, 48–49, 104, 115, 116–17, 118, 123, 129, 136–37, 143, 144–45, 146–47, 149,

150, 153, 155, 159, 160, 163,
    165–67, 168–69
astrology, 13, 133, 160, 161
class themes, 8–9
Cold War, 47
Crow, 21, 24, 87, 89–91, 98, 104,
    120–21, 122n1
drafts, 22–23, 25, 31–32, 38–39, 43,
    45–46, 135–53, 161–63, 165–66
ecological concerns, 7–9, 45–46,
    105–6, 121, 147, 169
elegy, 8, 147, 163n5
World War II, 42–43
Huws, Daniel, 152

Iliad, The, 149

Johnson, Barbara, 63, 66, 68, 71, 80
Joseph, Rosemary, 49n6
Joyce, James, 55
Jung, Carl, 16

Keller, Lynn, 95
Kendall, Tim, 1, 2, 34, 74, 75, 83, 91,
    92, 94, 102, 103, 120, 122n6
Keniston, Ann, 23
Kerr, David, 151, 153
Kirk, Connie Ann, 13
Kirsch, Adam, 4–5, 56
Knickerbocker, Scott, 5, 62–63
Kroll, Judith, 13

Laing, R. D., 100
language poetry, 36, 95
Larkin, Philip, 9
Lawrence, D. H., 33, 72
Leavis, F. R., 9
lesbian poetry, 95
Levertov, Denise, 6
long poems, 94–96
Longley, Michael, 147
Lowell, Robert, 3, 4, 7, 14, 56,
    61, 62, 95

MacBeth, George, 46

Mackey, Nathaniel, 95
Mackle, Joanna, 150
MacLeish, Archibald, 84n3
Malcolm, Janet, 18–19, 73
McClatchy, J. D., 94
McCullough, Ruth, 152
McCurdy, Philip, 60
McGrath, Thomas, 6
McHale, Brian, 24, 94, 95
Melhem, D. H., 88
Mermaid Festival, London, 70
Merwin, W. S., 94
Middlebrook, Diane, 7, 10, 18, 19–20,
    21, 25, 32, 47, 60, 71, 72, 78–79,
    84n7, 121, 123, 129, 133, 140, 158,
    159, 163n4
Miner, Earl, 92–93
Mitchell, Paul, 103
modernism, 3–4, 6–7, 16
Moore, Marcia, 59, 84n4
Moore, Marianne, 52, 59, 84n4
Morgan, Robin, 6, 152
Moss, Howard, 149
Movement poetry, 9
Muldoon, Paul, 147
Myers, Lucas, 140
mythology, classical, 7, 44, 111, 142,
    148–49, 155–56, 159
mythology, Irish, 111
mythology, Yoruba, 111

Napoleon, 132
Narbeshuber, Lisa, 17, 23
Native American poetry, 95
Nelson, Deborah, 14–15
neo-formalism, 5
Neruda, Pablo, 94
New Criticism, 3–4, 6–7, 94
Newnham College, Cambridge, 51, 139
New York School, 6, 95
Norton, Dick, 59
Norton, Perry, 59, 84n5

O'Connor, Danny, 8
Odyssey, The, 44, 90, 108–9, 117–18

O'Hara, Frank, 6
Olson, Charles, 95
Owen, Wilfred, 42, 47

Peel, Robin, 15, 61, 84, 95
Perloff, Marjorie, 85n9, 91, 92, 94, 102, 163n1
Perril, Simon, 7
Peters, Sandra, 59
Plath, Aurelia, 12, 32, 53, 56, 84n2, 124
Plath, Otto, 130, 132, 133, 161
Plath, Sylvia, 3–6, 10–15, 18–22, 23–24, 25–28, 31–38, 51–85, 91–104, 134–50, 162, 165–69
   allegory, 63, 70–71
   anti-war themes, 6, 95
   apostrophe, 68, 80
   ars poetica, 5, 10, 24–25, 37–38, 79, 81–82, 83, 90, 99–100, 101, 102, 103–4, 116, 119–20, 123–24, 127, 130–31, 133–34, 165–67, 168–69
   Boston, 59
   Cambridge, 59, 124
   Cold War, 14, 15, 95
   doubleness, 14
   drafts, 22–23, 25, 49n2, 51–60, 63–84, 165–66
   feminism, 6, 14, 17
   improvisation, 60
   the lyric, 23–24
   nationalism, 5
   Romanticism, 15
   Smith College, 3, 55, 59–60
   Wellesley, 59
   women readers, 17
Plath, Warren, 3, 32
Pollitt, Katha, 134
Porter, Peter, 9
postmodernism, 24, 94, 95
Pound, Ezra, 43, 44, 50n7, 60, 95, 167
projectivist verse, 95
Prouty, Olive, 59

Reddick, Yvonne, 7, 8, 16, 33, 39, 42, 72–73, 90, 98, 104, 105–6, 120, 147

Reed, B. M., 25
Regan, Stephen, 9
Rich, Adrienne, 6, 66–67
Roberts, Neil, 15–16, 23, 33, 38, 41, 42–43, 45, 90, 104, 111, 114
Robinson, Katherine, 90
Roethke, Theodore, 3, 56, 60, 129
Rollyson, Carl, 13
Romantic poetry, 5, 9
Rome, 43
Romulus and Remus, 43
Rose, Jacqueline, 10, 12, 13–14, 19, 32, 72–73, 74, 91
Rosenthal, M. L., 4
Rossetti, Christina, 47, 65
Rowland, Antony, 18, 21

Sagar, Keith, 15–16, 87, 90
Sappho, 101
Sassoon, Richard, 51–52, 54, 55
Sassoon, Siegfried, 42
Scigaj, Leonard, 6, 16
Sergeant, David, 139
Sexton, Anne, 4, 14, 47, 61–62
Seymour, Miranda, 114
Shakespeare, William, 85n11, 120, 156–57
Sigmund, Elizabeth, 152
Silliman, Ron, 36
Sillitoe, Alan, 113
Smyth, Daragh, 122n5
Snodgrass, W. D., 14, 95
Starbuck, George, 4
Stern, Marcia Brown, 59
Stevenson, Anne, 4, 12, 19, 124, 133
Stothard, Peter, 150–51
Sweeney, John Lincoln, 70

Teasdale, Sara, 3
Ted Hughes: Stronger Than Death, 152
Tennyson, Lord Alfred, 65–66
Theocritus, 149
Thwaite, Anthony, 32
Twiddy, Iain, 147, 155, 161

Uroff, Margaret Dickie, 18, 19, 20, 21, 23, 43, 50n10, 56, 84n3, 84n7, 97, 107, 127

Van Dyne, Susan, 4, 34, 49n3, 49n4, 64–65, 69, 84, 91, 92
Vice, Sue, 95, 102
Viner, Katherine, 134

Wagner, Erica, 93, 125, 127, 133, 163n1
Wagner-Martin, Linda, 3, 70, 85n12, 92, 120
Watling, Vicky, 152
Webb, Laura, 33, 97, 113, 147, 163n5
Wevill, Assia, 21, 34, 49n4, 80, 85n9, 104, 136, 156, 162, 163n3, 164n6

Wevill, David, 156
Wevill, Shura, 21, 104, 136
Whitehead, Anne, 134, 158–59
Williams, Mississippi Joe, 88
Williams, William Carlos, 43, 50n8, 60, 95
Wilson, Andrew, 11–12, 60, 84n6
Woolf, Virginia, 29n3
Wootten, William, 9, 24, 29n2, 79, 135
Wormald, Mark, 16
Wyatt, Thomas, 167

Yeats, W. B., 3, 6, 56, 87–88, 89, 98, 121, 163n2

Index of Works

TED HUGHES

"The Afterbirth," 28, 42, 142, 144–45, 146, 149
"Autobiography of Thomas Nashe," 38

"The Badlands," 149
"Bayonet Charge," 42–43
"The Bee God," 27, 83, 85n11, 129–33, 146, 148, 161
"Being Christlike," 28, 145–47
Birthday Letters, 1, 7, 10, 17, 20, 25, 27–28, 59, 72, 87, 121, 125, 129, 134–54, 158, 161–62, 163n3, 165, 166, 168
"Bones," 122n4

"Cadenza," 50n10
The Calm, 49n3
Capriccio, 163n3
"Caryatids," 136
Cave Birds, 122n1, 150
"The Chipmunk," 149
"Context," 168
"Cradle Piece," 49n1
"Crowcolour," 122n4
"Crowego," 108–9

Crow: From the Life and Songs of the Crow, 98
"Crow Goes Hunting," 107–8
"Crow Hill," 33
"A Crow Hymn," 105
"Crow Improvises," 105–6
"Crowquill," 105, 108
Crow sequence, 25, 27, 92–93, 94, 96–98, 99, 104–14, 116, 118, 122n3, 123, 125, 137, 144
"Crow's Feast," 105
"Crow's Nerve Fails," 108
"Crow and the Sea," 110, 111–12
"Crow's Song About England," 113
"Crow and Stone," 110–11
Crow Wakes, 98

Difficulties of a Bridegroom, 71
"A Disaster," 109
"Dog Days on the Black Sea," 117
"The Dogs Are Eating Your Mother," 136, 154–55
"The Dove Breeder," 38
"A Dream," 85n11, 161
"A Dream of Horses," 105
"Dreamers," 163n3

"The Earthenware Head," 27, 72, 124–26, 127

"Everyman's Odyssey," 43–45
"Existential Song," 107

"A Fable," 49n1
"Famous Poet," 39, 41
"Fate Playing," 149
"Fever," 28, 143–44, 146
A Few Crows, 98
"A Flayed Crow in the Hall of Judgment," 122n1
Flowers and Insects, 150
Four Crow Poems, 98
"To F. R. at Six Months," 32
"Fulbright Scholars," 136
"Full Moon and Little Frieda," 31, 85n10

Gaudete, 147, 150
"Glimpse," 109–10

"The Hare." *See* "The Afterbirth"
"The Hawk in the Rain," 38
The Hawk in the Rain, 9, 26, 32, 33, 38–43, 45, 72, 120, 123, 150, 166, 168
"Hawk Roosting," 45–46, 50n10
"Her Husband," 115–16
"Historian," 48
"The Horses," 38
"The Howling of Wolves," 32
"Howls and Whispers," 156–58
Howls and Whispers, 7, 10, 15, 26, 28, 121, 153–63, 165

Introduction to *The Collected Poems of Sylvia Plath*, 91
Introduction to *Johnny Panic and the Bible of Dreams*, 167

"The Jaguar," 38, 105, 119, 162

"Law in the Country of the Cats," 41–42
"Lines to a Newborn Baby," 32
"The Literary Life," 59
"Lovesong," 105–7
"A Lucky Folly," 112–13

Lupercal, 20, 26, 33, 38, 43–49, 123, 150

"Macaw and Little Miss," 38
"The Minotaur," 155–56
"The Minotaur 2," 155–56, 157
"A Modest Proposal," 39–41
Moortown Diary, 147, 150
"Myth and Education," 168
"My Uncle's Wound," 32

"Nicholas Ferrer," 47
"Notes on Poems," 2, 92, 116

"The Offers," 15, 158–60
"On Westminster Bridge," 32
Ovid, 153

"Parlour Piece," 38
"The Perfect Forms," 48
"Pike," 49n5
"A Pink Wool Knitted Dress," 28, 136, 138–39, 146, 148
Poems: Ruth Fainlight, Ted Hughes, Alan Sillitoe, 98
"Poltergeist," 49n1
A Primer of Birds, 150
"Publishing Sylvia Plath," 82

"The Rabbit Catcher," 42, 72–73, 142
Recklings, 104
"Religion," 154–55
Remains of Elmet, 147, 150
"Remission," 128–29
River, 150
"Roarers in a Ring," 33

St. Botolph's Review, 7, 54
"Sam," 149
Season Songs, 150
"Second Glance at a Jaguar," 118–19
"Secretary," 39–40
"The Shot," 27, 72, 127–28
"Skylarks," 97
"Song of a Rat," 32

"Soup," 162
"Sunstroke," 33
"Superstitions," 160–61, 163

"The Table," 1–3, 147–49, 169
"Things Present," 43–44
"This Game of Chess," 114–15, 116
"The Thought-Fox," 7, 26, 32, 33–34, 35, 36–37, 38, 39, 40–41, 49, 105, 107, 119, 142, 145, 149, 162
"Three Legends," 97–98, 110
"Toll of Air Raids," 49n1
"Trophies," 149
"Two Legends," 110
"Two Wise Generals," 38
"T.V. On," 120

"Unknown Soldier," 49n1

"Vampire," 38
"Visit," 28, 139–42

"Wilfred Owen's Photographs," 47
"Wind," 162
Winter Pollen, 33, 42, 82, 98, 168
"Witches," 47–48
"Wodwo," 118–19
Wodwo, 23, 32, 104, 115, 119, 120, 150
Wolfwatching, 147, 150
"A Woman Unconscious," 47
"Words and Experience," 168
"The Wound," 122n2

"You Hated Spain," 143, 149
"Your Paris," 149

SYLVIA PLATH

"All the Dead Dears," 32, 123
"Amnesiac," 49n3, 117–18
"The Applicant," 49n3, 100, 112, 122n2, 139, 144
"April Aubade," 59

"Ariel," 110, 122n4
Ariel, 11, 20, 25, 27, 29n4, 57, 61, 63, 71, 72, 74, 79, 82, 90, 91–96, 97, 98–104, 105, 107, 108, 117, 118, 119–20, 121, 123, 129, 132, 134, 135, 142, 168
"The Arrival of the Bee Box," 103, 129–30

"A Ballad," 59
"Balloons," 103
"Barren Woman," 100, 108
"The Bed Book," 32
"The Beekeeper's Daughter," 48
"The Bee Meeting," 103, 108, 129–30
The Bell Jar, 19, 32, 54, 59
"Berck-Plage," 102
"Bitter Strawberries," 13
"Black Rook in Rainy Weather," 32, 123
"The Bronze Boy," 26, 52–54, 57
"Burning the Letters," 26, 32, 34–37, 142

"Candles," 59
Circus in Three Rings, 59, 84n1
Cold War, 14, 15, 95
"The Colossus," 37, 48, 100
The Colossus, 20, 91, 168
"A Comparison," 167
"Context," 167
"Contusion," 103
"The Courage of Shutting-Up," 102, 104
"The Couriers," 102
Crossing the Water, 91
"Cut," 143, 144

"Daddy," 49n3, 63, 118, 132, 145, 148
"The Dead," 55–56, 84n2
"The Disquieting Muses," 100
"Doom of Exiles," 59, 84n2
"Doomsday," 57, 123

"Eavesdropper," 49n3
"Edge," 103
"Electra on Azalea Path," 48

"Elm," 1–3, 6, 147–49, 169
"Epitaph in Three Parts," 60
"Event," 156

feminism, 6, 14, 17
"Fever 103°," 108, 118, 143–44, 161
"Fog," 59
"Full Fathom Five," 59

"Goatsucker," 48
"Go Get the Goodly Squab," 59
"The Grackles," 59

"Half-Moon." See "Thalidomide"
"The Hanging Man," 103
"Have You Forgotten?," 59

"Incident," 60
"In Passing," 59, 60
"In Plaster," 63, 100, 128, 129

"The Jailer," 49n3
Johnny Panic and the Bible of Dreams, 26, 54, 57, 167

"Kindness," 62, 71–72, 77, 80, 103, 160

"The Lady and the Earthenware Head," 27, 124, 126–27, 130
"Lady Lazarus," 6, 27, 100, 101–2, 112, 127–28, 145, 148
"Lesbos," 49n3, 101
"Little Fugue," 103
"Lonely Song," 59
"Lyonnesse," 37, 38, 49n3

"Magi," 101, 108, 112, 116
"Medusa," 49n3, 144
"Metaphors," 32
"Mr. and Mrs. Ted Hughes's Writing Table," 3
"Moonrise," 55
"The Moon and the Yew Tree," 55
"Morning Song," 32, 61, 93, 96, 97, 99, 102, 103, 112, 128

"The Munich Mannequins," 103

"Nick and the Candlestick," 102

"ode on a bitten plum," 56–57
"The Other," 101, 108
"The Other Two," 3

"Paralytic," 103
"Poem for a Birthday," 60, 129
"Poems, Potatoes," 64–65, 129
"Poppies in July," 103, 142–43
"Poppies in October," 102, 108
"A Prospect of Cornucopia," 32
"Purdah," 117–18
"Pursuit," 123–24

"The Rabbit Catcher," 26, 36, 72–73, 74, 75–79, 98–99, 102–3, 106, 107, 114, 142

"A Secret," 49n3, 77
"Sheep in Fog," 102–3
"Sickroom Tulips." See "Tulips"
"The Smoky Blue Piano," 32
"Snakecharmer," 59
"Snares," 73–75
"Song of a Superfluous Spring," 59
"Sonnet: To a Dissembling Spring," 56
"Spinning Song," 59
"Stillborn," 64–65
"Stings," 103, 129, 131–32
"Stone Boy with Dolphin," 32, 54, 57, 123
"Stopped Dead," 101–2, 104, 139
"The Swarm," 77, 103, 129, 131–33

"Thalidomide," 62–67, 99–100, 112, 129
"This Earth Our Hospital," 32
"'Three Caryatids without a Portico,' by Hugo Robus. A Study in Sculptural Dimensions," 163n4
"Three Women," 36
"Totem," 103

"Tulips," 31, 32, 34–35, 49n2, 62, 67–70, 107–8, 128–29
"Twilight," 58
"Two Women Reading," 55

The Unabridged Journals, 3, 29n3, 51, 84–85n8, 124

"Widow," 32
"Wintering," 82, 93, 103, 129, 133

Winter Trees, 11, 91
"The Wishing Box," 49n5
"Words," 26, 80, 82–83, 85n11, 85n12, 93, 103, 133
"Words heard, by accident, over the phone," 26, 77, 80–82, 145

"Years," 103

Permissions

Excerpts from "A Disaster," "A Lucky Folly," "A Pink Wool Knitted Dress," "A Woman Unconscious," "Bayonet Charge," "Being Christlike," "Crow and Stone," "Crow and the Sea," "Crow Goes Hunting," "Crow Improvises," "Crow's Nerve Fails," "Crow's Song About England," "Crowego," "Dog Days on the Black Sea," "Everyman's Odyssey," "Existential Song," "Fever," "Glimpse," "Hawk Roosting," "Howls & Whispers," "Lovesong," "Religion," "Second Glance at a Jaguar," "Secretary," "Skylarks," "Superstitions," "TV On," "The Afterbirth," "The Bee God," "The Dogs Are Eating Your Mother," "The Earthenware Head," "The Minotaur," "The Minotaur 2," "The Offers," "The Table," "The Thought-Fox," "Things Present," "Two Legends," "Witches," "Wodwo," "A Modest Proposal," "Crowquill," "Famous Poet," "Her Husband," "Historian," "Law in the Country of the Cats," "Remission," "The Perfect Forms," "The Shot," "This Game of Chess," "Three," "Legends," and "Visit" from COLLECTED POEMS by Ted Hughes. Copyright © 2003 by The Estate of Ted Hughes. Reprinted by permission of Farrar, Straus and Giroux. All Rights Reserved.

Excerpts from Dream Song #1 "Huffy Henry" and Dream Song #4 "Filling her compact & delicious body" from THE DREAM SONGS by John Berryman. Copyright © 1969 by John Berryman, renewed 1997 by Kate Donahue Berryman. Reprinted by permission of Farrar, Straus and Giroux. All Rights Reserved.

Excerpts from "Pursuit," "The Other Two," "The Lady and the Earthenware Head," "Poems, Potatoes," "Stillborn," "Magi," "Morning Song," "Barren Women," "Tulips," "Three Women," "Elm," "The Rabbit Catcher," "Event," "The Other," "Poppies in July," "Burning the Letters," "The Courage of Shutting-Up," "The Bee Meeting," "The Arrival of the Bee Box," "Stings," "The Swarm," "Wintering," "Daddy," "Stopped Dead," "Fever 103," "Amnesiac," "Lyonnesse," "Cut," "Ariel," "Poppies in October," "Purdah," "Lady Lazarus," "Thalidomide," "Sheep in Fog," "Kindness," "Words," from

The Collected Poems, Sylvia Plath. Copyright © 1960, 1965, 1971, 1981 by the Estate of Sylvia Plath. Used by permission of HarperCollins Publishers.

Excerpts from Ted Hughes's Birthday Letters manuscripts at the British Library, from Farrar, Straus, and Giroux.

Excerpts from Sylvia Plath's manuscripts, from the Lilly Library, Indiana University.

Excerpts from the Ted Hughes Papers at the Manuscripts, Archives, and Rare Books Library, Emory University, from Farrar, Straus, and Giroux.

Excerpts from the Sylvia Plath collection at the Mortimer Rare Book Room, Smith College, from Farrar, Straus, and Giroux.

Excerpts from Amiri Baraka's The LeRoi Jones/Amiri Baraka Reader (1995), from Hachette Book Group.

Excerpts from W. B. Yeats's "Crazy Jane and the Bishop" (five lines) and "Crazy Jane Talks to the Bishop" (two lines), originally published in The Collected Poems, The Macmillan Company, 1969. Reprinted by permission of United Agents on behalf of W. B. Yeats.

About the Author

Jennifer Ryan-Bryant is professor of English at SUNY—Buffalo State, where she teaches courses in American poetry, the American novel, African American studies, and women's and gender studies. She is the author of *Post-Jazz Poetics: A Social History* (Palgrave Macmillan, 2010). Her articles have appeared in *Women and Performance, College Literature, Modern Fiction Studies, MELUS, African American Review, Radical Teacher*, and *The Journal of Popular Culture*, among others. She is currently at work on a book titled *The Human in This Place: American Literatures of Lynching*.

www.ingramcontent.com/pod-product-compliance
Lightning Source LLC
Chambersburg PA
CBHW020744020526
44115CB00030B/912